IMPACTS OF AFFIRMATIVE ACTION

Impacts of
Affirmative Action

Policies and Consequences in California

edited by

Paul Ong

ALTAMIRA
P R E S S

A Division of Sage Publications, Inc.
Walnut Creek • London • New Delhi

For information, contact:

AltaMira Press
A Division of Sage Publications, Inc.
1630 North Main Street, Suite 367
Walnut Creek, CA 94596
explore@altamira.sagepub.com
http://www.altamirapress.com

SAGE Publications Ltd.
6 Bonhill Street
London EC2A 4PU
United Kingdom

SAGE Publications India Pvt. Ltd.
M-32 Market
Greater Kailash 1
New Delhi 110 048
India

Library of Congress Cataloging-in-Publication Data

Impacts of affirmative action : policies and consequences in California /
  edited by Paul Ong.
    p. cm.
Includes bibliographical references and index.
ISBN 0-7619-9055-0
ISBN 0-7619-9056-9
1. Affirmative action programs—California. 2. Affirmative action programs—
Law and legislation—California. I. Ong, Paul M.
HHHF5549.5.A34 I575 1999
331.13'3'09794—dc21
                                99-6108
                                CIP

00 01 02 03 04 05 06 07 08 09 7 6 5 4 3 2 1

Interior Design and Production by Rachel Fudge
Editorial Management by Jennifer R. Collier
Cover Design by Joanna Ebenstein

Contents

Acknowledgments

This volume was made possible by the support of numerous individuals and organizations. The California Policy Research Center of the University of California funded much of the research. UCLA's Lewis Center for Regional Policy Studies, which was established by a generous gift from Ralph and Goldy Lewis, provided crucial support to manage and complete the project. We are indebted to the U.S. Bureau of the Census, the U.S. Department of Labor, the University of California Office of the President, UCLA's Social Science Data Archives, and the Consortium for International Earth Science Information Network for access to data. The following individuals provided valuable assistance and advice: William Bates, Cynthia Deutermann, Carla Ferri, William Harris, Paul Helms, Joseph Kennedy, Judy Kowarsky, James Litrownick, Richard Robinson, Rhonda V. Sharpe, Paula Sirola, William Spriggs, and Mark Westlye. Several people provided assistance in editing and preparing the manuscript: Al Averbach, Jennifer Collier, Rachel Fudge, Rose Lee, Elena Soohoo Ong, and Andrea Tinsley. Most of all, we are eternally grateful to our families and friends for their love and support.

Chapter 1

An Overview of Affirmative Action

Paul Ong

Introduction

In recent years, the discussion over affirmative action has escalated, becoming heated and often filled with polemic.[1] Nowhere is the debate more intense than in California, the first state to pass an initiative banning "preferential treatment" of individuals based on race or gender in governmental programs. Because opposing positions are grounded in conflicting visions and core values, it is impossible to avoid totally the emotions invoked by the debate. The contributors to this volume, however, undertook this research project with the belief that the discussion would be better informed if it was grounded in an analysis of the effects, impacts, and outcomes of California's affirmative action programs over the last quarter-century.[2] Only then can the political discourse in the Golden State and elsewhere move beyond rhetoric to a substantive debate on the strategies to address discrimination-based inequality. A central question for many decision makers, and one we cannot yet answer, is, "What will be the impact of ending affirmative action in the state?" At best, any answers would involve much speculation. We can, however, build a firmer foundation for considering the question if we have an understanding of the recent effects of affirmative action policies on employment, business opportunities, and admission to colleges and universities. To date, there have been no comprehensive evaluations of affirmative action policies at the national level, much less at the state level, because of the complexity of measuring the impact of these policies. What do exist are studies of very specific issues, such as the impact of affirmative action requirements in public contracts on the racial and gender composition of a firm's labor force. The component studies in this book are modeled on such research.

Affirmative action can be analyzed through many frameworks: by level of government, race and gender, functional sectors (employment, business, and education), or legislated and mandated programs. The strategy adopted for this research project was dictated by pragmatic concerns: The authors opted for a limited-scale approach that would provide a reasonable framework from which to analyze the impact of affirmative action. Given the project's limited scale, we focused our research on public-sector practices. We did so because the government is central to the efforts to address discrimination and equal opportunity and is the focal point of the current debate. Governmental policies affect public-sector employment, private-sector employment through contract requirements, business development through procurement, and human-capital development through admissions to institutions of higher education. The government is in the position to initiate and implement research and collect data on model policies. Information about public-sector employment activities is public record, and as such, the data is more readily accessible than information about private-sector activities, for which disclosure can sometimes be voluntary and hence incomplete.

This book does not purport to be comprehensive. Beyond the limitations already noted, there was neither the time nor the resources to produce an all-encompassing report. When possible, this project relies on adapting national studies to the specific conditions in California. This approach allows us to use methods and analytic frameworks that have already been peer reviewed or widely accepted within the economics profession.[3] *What is unique about this study is the use of California-specific data.* As a result, all of the findings are directly related to outcomes within this state, a state that has been a focal point of, if not a fulcrum for, the affirmative action debate nationwide. Unfortunately, we have not been able to address key issues such as set-aside contracting at the state level, hiring practices of state and local governments, or outcomes for public utilities, which are regulated by the state. Despite these limitations, the book does provide new insights into the employment, business, and educational effects of affirmative action. This has been made possible in part by unprecedented access to data that are not normally available to researchers. In particular, the research team is fortunate to have had the opportunity to work with the U.S. Bureau of the Census and the Department of Labor.

Framing the Policy Issue

Before previewing the book's chapters, it is important to contextualize affirmative action. The policy and its associated programs constitute a middle act in a historical play spanning its tumultuous origins to its current precarious existence. Affirmative action is rooted in a larger social movement to combat racism, a movement that eventually came to overlap with one to combat sexism. Most relevant to this book are the events surrounding and following World War II, which led to what some have called the Second Reconstruction based on executive orders and legislation. The goals of the civil rights movement were noble: to end racial discrimination and to promote greater integration of minorities into this nation's political and economic life. By all indications there was much to accomplish, because blacks and other minorities were very much at the margins. In 1959, median income for nonwhites was only about one-half of that for whites. There was glaring disparity in educational attainment. In 1960, 38 percent of nonwhite adults had no more than six years of schooling, compared to only 13 percent of white adults; and only 8 percent of nonwhite adults had at least one year of college, compared to 17 percent of whites. In 1950 and 1960, residential segregation was so extensive that approximately 9 out of 10 nonwhites would have had to relocate into a predominantly white neighborhood to achieve integration. The available evidence shows that nonwhites, and blacks in particular, were systematically denied the right to vote in elections. In some states, white voter-registration rates were two to four times higher than black registration rates. The civil rights movement was an effort by blacks and their allies to attack the racism producing these morally indefensible inequalities.

The civil rights movement—that is, the grassroots social movement and the accompanying advocacy groups—had a profound effect on government policy. What started as an effort to build a more effective military force through racial integration spread into other arenas. Beginning in 1941, the federal government sought to eliminate discriminatory hiring practices, first in defense industries, then among all federal contractors, and finally in all federal employment. The ruling in the 1954 *Brown v. Board of Education* case ended state-supported segregation in public schools. Over the next decade, the fight for racial equality encompassed demands for full political participation and greater economic opportunity. In 1961, the Kennedy administration used its executive power to require federal contractors to end any discriminatory employment practices and to establish the Equal Employment Opportunity Commission (EEOC). Under the Johnson administration, the Civil Rights Act of 1964 prohibited discrimination by privately owned facilities open to the public, by federally funded programs, and by both private and public employers. The 1965

Voting Rights Act added force to the drive to protect the rights of minorities to participate in elections. To promote equal business opportunities, these governmental agencies also adopted set-aside programs to direct more contracts to minority- and women-owned businesses.

It is plausible to conceptualize these historical events as an inevitable chain of progressively greater gains, but the reality was far more complex. The civil rights victories were more a product of an elite response to pressure politics and social unrest than to broad public opinion. Most Americans found the racial disparities produced by discrimination and prejudice troubling and unacceptable, but at the same time they were reluctant to accept the demands of the pro–civil rights protestors and advocacy groups.[4] By the early 1960s, a majority opposed school and housing segregation, and this opposition to racist practices extended to efforts to deny minorities the right to vote. For many, this stance was made easier by the fact that blatant, state-supported discrimination was seen as a Southern problem. There is no question that the conditions in this region were far worse than in other parts of the nation, with racism taking the form of Jim Crowism (i.e., a set of racially motivated legal restrictions and oppressive practices). Unlike other states, most Southern states still had laws that prohibited interracial marriages, required segregated public facilities, and hindered black voter registration.[5] Moreover, Southern prejudice had a very visible and ugly face because mass media broadcast and printed graphic scenes of violent actions by local officials to disperse peaceful demonstrations for civil rights. Clearly, the demonstrators held the moral high ground, in part by framing their fight as one consistent with the noble (although not always practiced) idea of the right of all Americans to freedom and equal opportunity to participate in our society. Despite this distaste for Southern racism, an overwhelming majority of the public did not fully support the civil rights movement. Throughout the 1960s, about two-thirds of those asked in various surveys felt that the civil rights movement was "moving too fast." Support became even more problematic in the second half of the decade, when the issue of racism moved out of the South in the form of urban riots.

Given public opinion, it is not surprising that the major civil rights laws did not come from a public plebiscite. Instead, they emerged out of presidential action, which was often moderated by other concerns and priorities, and was frequently conceded as a compromise or a necessity to maintain social order.[6] While the presidents during the Second Reconstruction of the 1960s shared the public's disdain for blatant racism and its support for the lofty goals of greater rights for blacks, their agendas were shaped by pragmatic concerns and electoral politics. Despite his often-inspiring public pronouncements, President Kennedy was slow to move on civil rights issues. While he had promised a civil rights initiative during his campaign, Kennedy moved cautiously, using his discretionary powers within limits and delaying the introduction of legislation out of concerns about his narrow victory and congressional resistance. During his tenure in Congress, Lyndon Johnson had a mixed record, first siding with segregationists, and then later, as Senate Majority Leader, accepting the necessity of addressing civil rights issues. As Vice President, he moved further in pressing for new legislation and, as President, he embraced a Great Society agenda, which was both a pragmatic stance in the wake of the nation's mourning over Kennedy's assassination and a way to claim a place in history. President Nixon is perhaps the most enigmatic of the 1960s presidents, for he was initially instrumental in expanding affirmative action but later became a fierce opponent of other elements of the civil rights agenda. His contradictory actions have been explained as a calculated political agenda to weaken his enemies and strengthen support for himself.

A key force that shaped the civil rights agenda was a broad social movement for equality. Like the laws and executive orders, the movement itself changed in nature over time. In the 1950s, the most visible parts of the movement focused on efforts to integrate schools and public facilities in the South, including the much-celebrated boycotts of public transportation and restaurant sit-ins. Voter-registration drives, bolstered by students participating in the freedom rides, escalated the conflict, with repressive violence directed at blacks and their white supporters. These efforts forced the issue of racial injustice onto the national stage, forcing the civil rights agenda forward in Congress and in the White House. Ironically, at the very time when the movement had its greatest legislative victories, in 1964 and 1965, the model of black protest transformed. Urban unrest outside the South emerged not as planned protest but as spontaneous mass riots, devastating scores of cities between 1964 and 1968.[7] The 1965 Watts riot in Los Angeles was one of the most destructive and most publicized. The civil unrest was rooted in a growing impatience on the part of urban blacks over slow progress, persistent and pervasive poverty, and the lack of economic opportunity. Paradoxically, the unrest occurred during a period of unprecedented economic progress for blacks. As Figure 1 shows, black average income as a percent of white average income rose dramatically over the decade. Part of the answer to this seeming paradox is that the expectations of blacks were rising faster than actual progress, which fueled a sense of frustration. The other part of the answer is that the gains were very unevenly distributed, with better-educated blacks receiving a disproportionate share of the new opportunities.[8]

Black protest changed not only in form but also in purpose. The demands shifted from political rights and integration to economic rights. There was a concomitant transition in leadership, from established civil rights organizations that relied on nonviolent demonstration and worked within the Democratic Party, toward more militant organizations that espoused the necessity of violence and rejected the notion of working within the system. Black nationalism and group rights—rather than integration and color-blindness—became the ideology that captured the attention of the public, for good and bad. This shift spurred other minority activists, and some women, to mobilize by appealing to group solidarity.

The transformation of the social movement contributed to a restructuring of affirmative action, a strategy that evolved out of the effort to combat racial and gender inequality but was very much influenced by pragmatic and political considerations. Starting in the 1950s and pursued more aggressively in the 1960s, the dominant strategy centered around the federal government's efforts to end blatant forms of racial discrimination in employment. Even when the term "affirmative action" was first introduced in 1961, the operative principle was the protection of the rights of individuals and providing equal opportunity. Kennedy's Executive Order 10952 included a clause directing federal contractors to "take affirmative action," but the envisioned remedy was strictly antidiscrimination in nature—"to ensure that applicants are employed, and employees are treated during their employment, without regard to race, creed, color or national origin." This was still, at its core, an antidiscrimination order, albeit one that placed a burden on employers to more consciously eliminate discriminatory practices. Johnson's 1965 Executive Order 11246 expanded the notion, establishing the Office of Federal Contract Compliance Programs (OFCCP) within the Department of Labor, and thereby requiring federal contractors to analyze the demographic composition of their workforce and, where needed, to develop plans to overcome disparities. This approach transformed the policy from equal opportunity to equal results, a change that the President acknowledged in his 1965 speech at Howard University, when he stated: "This is the next and more profound stage of the battle for civil rights. We seek not just freedom but opportunity—not just legal equity but human ability—not just equality as a right and a theory, but equality as a fact and as a result."

Despite a subsequent change in the political party controlling the White House, the policy of affirmative action continued to evolve toward a more aggressive stance and to cover an increasing number of eligible disadvantaged populations. The 1970 revised Philadelphia Plan developed under Nixon's administration required federal contractors to establish timetables and goals to address underrepresentation of minorities and women. Increasingly, underutilization was interpreted as having a workforce that did not mirror the racial and sex composition of the larger labor force. In practice, parity became the measurable objective. The application of this form of affirmative action was not limited to federal contracting but became increasingly more common in other federal activities such as education and housing, in operations of state and local governments, and even in private firms that voluntarily adopted the approach. While affirmative action was not a quota-based program in strict technical terms, it had certainly emerged as a group-based program.

The evolution of affirmative action represented a major philosophical shift that has raised fundamental constitutional questions and conflicts over what ought to be the core value guiding civil rights. Throughout the 1950s and the early 1960s, the dominant theme was to eliminate race as a factor in the way government—and ultimately society—functions. Some have labeled this as a drive to produce a color-blind nation. For others, preventing acts of individual discrimination was not sufficient to eliminate racial inequality. Affirmative action was conceived on the belief that government has an obligation to remedy the legacies of past discrimination against groups of people. The state could not be neutral or color-blind in the short run if it was to act as a counterforce against persistent prejudices and institutionalized discrimination over the long term. This policy approach redefined the way groups are socially constructed in this country. Race and gender were no longer the criteria for continued subjugation of disadvantaged populations; they became the criteria for identifying groups eligible for special consideration in hiring, contracting, and education.[9] Equally important, affirmative action provided an incentive for minorities to strengthen group formation and identity, although this incentive pales relative to the obstacles facing the disadvantaged. While identity politics mobilized minority groups, it also generated a backlash among white males.[10] Affirmative action also transformed politics within the civil rights movement. Many Jewish supporters felt that affirmative action was too similar to a quota system that had been used against them, and this lead some to actively oppose the policy.[11]

Those opposed to affirmative action turned to the courts to challenge its constitutional legality. They argued that the affirmative action violates the Fourteenth Amendment, which provides for "due process of law" before "any State deprives any person of life, liberty, or property" and guarantees all persons "equal protection of the laws." Moreover, Title VII of the Civil Rights Act of 1964 proscribes "discrimination based on race, color, religion, sex, or national origin." Strict quotas might constitute "reverse discrimination" against white males, but there are legitimate and defensible grounds for government to redress the legacy of past discrimination. Starting in 1970, affirmative action in employment, contracting, and education came under challenge in the courts. The central issue before the courts was how far the state could go to proactively ensure equal opportunity. Early rulings supported the use of group-based programs, but since then the courts have become increasingly less willing to support affirmative action programs. The court's standards have now shifted from an "intermediate" to a "strict" level of court scrutiny, a change that applies to employment, contracting, and admission to colleges and universities. The implications of this shift are significant. "Intermediate scrutiny" requires the government to demonstrate that affirmative action is rationally related to an important government interest. "Strict scrutiny," on the other hand, requires government to demonstrate a compelling government interest for the program and to narrowly tailor the program to accomplish that end. In the case of affirmative action, there is the additional burden of showing that past governmental action contributed to inequality. The progressively greater restrictions on affirmative action are due in part to an ideological realignment of the Supreme Court. In 1969, Nixon appointed conservative judge Warren Burger to replace the more liberal Earl Warren as Chief Justice. Moreover, Republican presidents appointed all nine additions to the Supreme Court from 1970 to 1991. Despite its conservative leanings, the U.S. Supreme Court has left the door open for programs to remedy past discrimination, but has struck down group-based approaches with an overly broad scope and in the absence of a history of discriminatory conduct.

The attack on affirmative action had a second front, the use of presidential powers to weaken the administration of programs. As discussed earlier, various presidents used their discretionary powers in the form of executive orders to establish civil rights policies, programs, and agencies. This power, however, is double-edged: A change in the White House could also bring about a reversal in the use of executive discretion. This was clearly the case when Ronald Reagan replaced Jimmy Carter, ushering in a neoconservative era that extended into George Bush's administration.[12] The Reagan administration adhered to a philosophy of downsizing government, decentralizing power, and relying on supply-side economics. The administration opposed redistributive social and tax policies to address economic inequality, and pushed to cut income transfer programs to the poor and to increase the tax burden on the poor while decreasing the rates on the rich. These actions were justified on the grounds that supply-side policies would promote economic growth benefiting everyone, including the disadvantaged. The application of this neoclassical philosophy had a profound impact on civil rights programs. Reagan (or his key staff) appointed individuals opposed to affirmative action in strategic positions, including the Civil Rights Division in the Department of Justice and the Department of Education, the Commission on Civil Rights, and the Equal Employment Opportunity Commission. With key people in place, including some conservative minorities, the administration weakened the enforcement of affirmative action and antidiscrimination laws. Consistent with its effort to decentralize through the new Federalism, Housing and Urban Development (HUD) pushed the enforcement of housing antidiscrimination laws to the states, some of which did not fully embrace the task. In the employment area, a backlog developed at EEOC, which also minimized the use of class-action suits. A common denominator in these efforts was to move civil rights away from a group-based orientation inherent in affirmative action to a "color-blind" orientation. In other words, the government should not be in the business of using race or sex as criteria for any of its programs, even ones designed to remedy past discrimination. (In a break with past administrations, to implement this policy the Reagan administration became party to suits against affirmative action.)

Not every effort to turn back the clock on civil rights was a complete success. Entrenched bureaucratic and economic interests prevented the President from simply rescinding the executive order establishing affirmative action, and efforts by the Department of Education to eliminate scholarships for minorities also met a similar fate. While Reagan and Bush were unable to entirely wipe out the civil rights gains of the 1960s, there was a noticeable retrenchment under these two administrations. Equally important, these two presidents had a long-term impact by appointmenting conservative judges to the courts and by legitimizing and giving greater currency to the political attack on affirmative action based on the color-blind argument.

The third front of attack on affirmative action came through direct appeal to the voters. California was the first state in the nation to launch, and pass, a proposition that prohibits the state and its local jurisdictions from using race- or gender-based criteria in hiring, admissions, or contracting (Proposition 209, the 1996 "California Civil Rights Initiative").[13] Since that time, similar initiatives have appeared elsewhere, including the city of Houston and the state of Washington. This book returns to the details of this attack on affirmative action in the last chapter.

Affirmative Action in California

While it is clear that California has emerged at the center of the current debate over affirmative action, questions remain as to why this is the case. Has the state been able to eliminate or reduce racial and gender inequality to the point that affirmative action is less needed? Are laws and programs in California more onerous, thus increasing opposition to the policy? Is there something in the very nature of how the programs function that provides a clue? Or is the reaction in California a product of a unique political climate? The following chapters provide some answers to these questions.

The body of the book begins with two background chapters. In Chapter 2, "U.S. and California Affirmative Action Policies, Laws, and Programs,"

Ward Thomas and Mark Garrett document the development of federal and state policies and laws regulating employment and contracting practices of both public and private employers. More often than not, the state followed the agenda established at the national level, although it is worth noting that California's first antidiscrimination law was adopted in 1934, predating similar federal laws by almost a decade. In the years preceding enactment of the Civil Rights Law and Voting Rights Law, California already had antidiscrimination laws covering voting, education, employment, and public accommodation, and had overturned its law banning interracial marriage.[14] Paralleling, and at times responding to, federal initiatives, in subsequent years the state established affirmative action programs governing hiring and contracting. The state and many local public agencies (as well as private businesses with government contracts) adopted such race- and gender-conscious policies as targeted recruitment and employment goals to eliminate hiring disparities. To promote equal business opportunities, these governmental units also adopted set-aside programs to direct more contracts to minority- and women-owned businesses.

By the late 1970s and 1980s, these programs were themselves under fire from opponents as unlawfully discriminatory and were challenged in California's courts. As a result of Supreme Court rulings, cities or state agencies proposing voluntary affirmative action plans must conduct a disparity study to establish the extent of existing discrimination and to ensure that any remedial race-conscious hiring policies are narrowly tailored to achieve their purpose. (A disparity study measures the difference between the availability of minority- and women-owned businesses in a given market and their utilization.) They must also first consider adopting gender- or race-neutral alternatives to increase minority participation. These standards affect many affirmative action programs in California, such as those administered by the State Personnel Board and the Office of Small and Minority Business (OSMB).

In Chapter 3, "Race and Gender in California's Labor Market," I analyze changes in California's growing and diverse labor market and the differential effect of affirmative action policies on improving wages and employment levels of minority groups and women in the private sector. The focus on private-sector employment provides a useful baseline for the assessments of public-sector affirmative action policies in the succeeding studies. This work reveals a mixed picture of progress and setbacks in eliminating inequality among minority groups. Since the 1970s, the wages and earnings of the three most numerous minority groups (African Americans, Hispanics, and Asian Americans[15]) have diverged from one another. These differences are only partially explained by educational attainment, age composition, and employment levels. By contrast, gender inequalities among non-Hispanic whites are not related to educational attainment and age composition, but are affected by degree of labor-market attachment. As women have become more career-oriented, there has been a concomitant gain in their earnings.

While it is difficult to determine how much of these racial and gender differences are due to discriminatory employment practices, I found that there has been a dramatic increase in the number of gender- and race-based complaints filed with the state Fair Employment Practices Commission (FEPC). Data from the FEPC also reveal a two-decade trend of declining state support to address the growing number of discrimination complaints, a factor that may account for a decrease in the number of settlements reached. I conclude that a ban on affirmative action programs would only further limit remedies for racial and gender discrimination in the labor market.

The next five chapters present case studies designed to assess the impact of federal, state, and local affirmative action programs on employment and small businesses in California. The chapters cover the public-sector workforce and private employers with government contracts. The authors also provide some thoughts on the potential consequences of implementing Proposition 209.

In Chapter 4, "The Impact of Affirmative Action on Public-Sector Employment in California, 1970–1990," M. V. Lee Badgett focuses specifically on employment of women and people of color in California's public sector and the potential impact of eliminating affirmative action there. Because of the relatively direct links between public policy and the government's own employment practices, public-sector employment is likely to better reflect the impact of local and state affirmative action policies than does private-sector employment. Previous studies also would lead one to expect that the public sector would have a better record than the private sector in hiring and promoting women and people of color. National data and previous studies indicate that the public sector has generally demonstrated both earlier and greater success in attaining workforce diversity than has the private sector. Explanations range from differences in skill levels to worker perceptions that public employers treat women and minorities more fairly, to the impact of affirmative action policies. Federal-, state-, and local-government employers also tend to pay women and minorities higher wages. But although public employers appear to have more equitable hiring practices in this regard than private-sector employers, evidence remains that women and people of color are still at a disadvantage compared to white men in the public sector.

With regard specifically to California, Badgett estimates the impact of equal opportunity laws and programs by comparing the changes in public- and private-sector employment patterns in the state between 1970 and 1990. Her analysis shows an increase in the employment of women and people of color, especially Latinos and Asian Americans, over time in both the public and private sectors, reflecting the increasing diversity of the state's workforce. Controlling for labor-force composition, black workers and Latinas have made proportionately larger gains in public-sector employment, and both men and women of color have greater access to public managerial and professional jobs, suggesting some positive impact from affirmative action policies. She concludes that depending on the ability of the private labor market to absorb "displaced" public-sector workers, eliminating public-sector affirmative action programs would likely result in lower wages for women and people of color in general, and underemployment for some female and minority managers and professionals in particular.

In Chapter 5, "Federal-Contractor Status and Minority Employment: A Case Study of California, 1979–1994," William M. Rodgers III examines federal-contractor status as an explanation of racial and ethnic differences in employment patterns among California firms. This research replicates a national study that revealed that, with the exception of Hispanic women, there is a greater presence of nonwhite workers among federal contractors than among noncontractor firms. For California, the results suggest that while contractor status continues to contribute positively to improving the representation of California's nonwhite workers, a business establishment's county location, major industry, and occupational structure contribute more to explaining the variation in the workforce than does contractor status. While the white share of employment has fallen over the last decade, whites still have a larger share of employment in businesses that have federal contracts. Asian Americans and blacks have a slightly higher share of employment in firms with federal contracts; however, Hispanic men's employment shares are lower and have decreased over time. A major reason for the disproportionately high white share of the federal-contractor workforce can be attributed to their higher representation in defense, energy, and construction industries, which dominate the federal procurement process. A possible explanation for the negative impact of contract status on the proportion of Hispanic workers may be the recent increase in less skilled labor provided by immigrants and the higher likelihood of their employment in noncontractor establishments. This factor cautions against making broad generalizations based on superficial data from affirmative action programs. Rodgers concludes that federal-contractor programs have had their intended employment effect and that they may also help allocate workers across firms in an economically more efficient fashion than would be the case without such programs: By placing minorities and women in work environments that are potentially less discriminatory, they may eliminate economic losses associated with artificial racial and gender barriers.

In Chapter 6, "Proposition 209: Which Firms Stand to Lose and How Much?", Darrell L. Williams investigates which California firms are most likely to lose with the repeal of affirmative action policies by looking at the extent of sales to state and local governments by women- and minority-owned small businesses. Based on a sample of California small businesses taken from the Characteristics of Business Owners database of the U.S. Bureau of the Census, Williams creates a profile of minority- and women-owned business enterprises (MWBEs). The analysis of these firms' reliance on government procurement serves to highlight minority- and women-owned businesses that are at particular risk of being adversely affected by a significant reduction in state/local procurement opportunities. Although only a small percentage of MWBE firms specialize in selling to state and local governments (i.e., obtain more than 50 percent of their revenue from them), Williams concludes that Proposition 209 will have a disproportionately large impact on these firms because they rely more heavily on government sales than do more diversified MWBE firms. Minority- and women-owned businesses with state or local contracts are also larger and employ more people than do noncontractors. The largest and most successful minority-owned firms are thus more likely to be affected by changes in procurement policies because they tend to be more dependent on revenue from sales to government than are smaller firms. Williams cautions, however, that the full impact will depend on several factors, including the cost of finding alternative customers, the level of private-sector demand for these firms' products, and the cost of switching to producing other goods and services for which there would be a demand.

In Chapter 7, "Affirmative Action Programs for Minority- and Women-Owned Businesses," Tom Larson tests the hypothesis that a city with an MWBE set-aside program designed to address underrepresentation among women- and minority-owned businesses in publicly awarded contracts will increase its use of MWBEs. MWBE programs are based on the fact that not only are there large differences in self-employment rates among minority groups, women, and non-Hispanic white men, but that firms owned by African Americans and Hispanics tend to have much lower average sales and to employ fewer workers. This research is based on analysis of data from a number of California cities and counties that have conducted disparity studies. By comparing data across cities and counties in California, Larson assesses the effectiveness of different set-aside programs in producing significantly greater use of MWBEs.

In Los Angeles, which between 1973 and 1993 had an African American mayor committed to affirmative action, there was an initial increase in the utilization of all minority- and women-owned firms following implementation of an MWBE set-aside program, though these firms remained underutilized relative to their overall availability. Following certain program modifications to comply with the Supreme Court ruling in the landmark *City of Richmond v. J. A. Croson Co.* case, utilization rates for MWBEs in Los Angeles (with the exception of Asian-owned firms) began to decline, particularly for women-owned businesses. In examining disparity studies from other cities, Larson finds further evidence that affirmative action programs have had positive effects on MWBE participation in public contracting, while in the absence of such programs MWBEs are underutilized; that race-neutral programs are ineffective; and that the *Croson* decision has had a chilling effect, as many cities have dropped or modified their programs. On the other hand, some cities, such as Oakland, have continued to maintain successful programs.

In Chapter 8, "Affirmative Action and Admission to the University of California," Cecilia A. Conrad examines the affirmative action policies that affected undergraduate and professional programs. Based simply on grades and test scores, a disproportionate number of California's African American and Hispanic high school graduates would not be very competitive with white and Asian students. However, under an admissions system that includes a broader range of criteria—including athletic and artistic talent, unusual leadership ability, socioeconomic disadvantage, or membership in an underrepresented minority group—many more underrepresented applicants qualify for admission. Without race-based affirmative action, the numbers of African American, Hispanic, and Native American students would be considerably smaller, particularly at the most competitive campuses, Berkeley and UCLA. The available evidence indicates that the gains to minority students who are beneficiaries of affirmative action probably outweigh the losses imposed on students whose probability of admission is reduced. Moreover, racial diversity of the student body may enhance the educational experience of all students. Affirmative action also increased the enrollment of underrepresented students in law and medical schools in the UC system. One of the benefits of the resulting racial diversity is the facilitation of the teaching of differences in culture and social practices that influence the effectiveness of health care and legal services. Affirmative action can also have a spillover benefit by increasing the supply of practitioners serving disadvantaged communities. Eliminating race as a criterion in UC admissions is likely to significantly reduce the number of underrepresented students and concomitantly reduce the direct and indirect economic benefits to those groups. Alternative admissions criteria, such as an increased emphasis on socioeconomic disadvantage, are unlikely to replicate the racial diversity achieved with affirmative action.

In the concluding chapter, I examine California's 1996 Proposition 209 and its implications. This state was the first where opponents of affirmative action used the initiative process to appeal directly to the voting public. California was fertile ground for such a campaign because of a confluence of political, social, and economic conditions. By the mid-1990s, the initiative process had become a well-established form of special-interest, big-finance politics, and Governor Wilson had turned to wedge issues such as affirmative action to rebuild his popularity for reelection and for an unsuccessful run for the GOP presidential nomination. During this period, California was undergoing an immigration-driven demographic recomposition that created a backlash from an increasing number of whites who felt uneasy and displaced by the cultural changes. Finally, the state was experiencing a deep and prolonged recession, with the underlying structural changes displacing a significant number of white males. The affirmative action opponents took advantage of this climate of economic and social anxiety to push Proposition 209, which was passed by 54 percent of the voters. The election result sent a shock wave throughout the nation, triggering similaring campaigns in other locations.

While Proposition 209 represents another victory for those opposing affirmative action, the debate is far from over. This nation still faces the vexing problem of how to come to terms with intergroup inequality, and how to balance that obligation with other fundamental principles. Affirmative action is at the heart of this dilemma. Collectively, the chapters demonstrate that affirmative action is not just a single policy or program, but rather a complex set of laws, executive orders, policies, and programs. While the federal government has often taken the lead in antidiscrimination efforts, state governments have also played key roles. Despite these efforts, discrimination is still a serious problem. Assessing the impact of employment and contracting programs in general is difficult because of their multiple objectives and because they have been applied to both state and local government hiring practices, as well as to private entities with government contracts. The same is true for college and university admissions, where the federal government not only imposes some requirements but also acts as a policy role model. One major conclusion that can be drawn from these analyses, however, is that affirmative action has increased employment, business, and educational opportunities for minorities and women.

No one knows what will happen over the next few years. Will the implementation of Proposition 209 mean that these opportunities will disappear? While it is tempting to say that Proposition 209 would eliminate the gains made over the past several decades, societal attitudes and private employment practices may mitigate those effects. In the absence of strict enforcement of nondiscrimination policies, however, it is very likely that further progress in eliminating employment, busines, and educational disparities will be slow.

Notes

1. See, for example, Steven M. Cahn, ed., *The Affirmative Action Debate* (New York: Routledge, 1995); George E. Curry and Cornel West, eds., *The Affirmative Action Debate* (Reading, MA: Addison Wesley Publishing Co., 1996); Nicolaus Mills, ed., *Debating Affirmative Action: Race, Gender, Ethnicity, and the Politics of Inclusion* (New York: Dell Publishing, 1994); Carol M. Swain, *Race Versus Class: The New Affirmative Action Debate* (Lanham, MD: University Press of America, 1996).

2. Much of the material for this book is based on reports commissioned by the California Policy Seminar to examine the past impact of federal, state, and local affirmative action programs on hiring, contracting, and admission to colleges and universities.

3. To estimate the potential effects of affirmative action in California, the case studies in this book analyze intergroup variations (e.g., differences between men and women or differences between workers in covered sectors and exempt sectors) or temporal variations (e.g., before and after the implementation of a specific program). Even the best methods, however, suffer from the fact that affirmative action programs are not implemented as controlled experiments; thus, it is very difficult to isolate their effects. For discussions on the problems and potentials of using statistical methods to analyze a "social experiment," see Burtless, "The Case for Randomized Field Trials in Economic and Policy Research," *The Journal of Economic Perspectives* 9 (2): 63–84 (1995), and Heckman and Smith, "Assessing the Case for Social Experiments," *The Journal of Economic Perspectives* 9 (2): 85–110 (1995). For issues specifically related to analyzing affirmative action programs, see Leonard, "Wage Disparities and Affirmative Action in the 1980s," *American Economic Review* 86 (2): 285–289 (1996).

4. The statistics cited in this section come from two sources: Tom Smith, "Intergroup Relations in Contemporary America: An Overview of Survey Research," in Wayne Winborn and Renae Cohen, eds., *Intergroup Relations in the United States: Research Perspectives* (Bloomsburg, PA: Haddon Craftsmen, Inc., for the National Conference for Community and Justice, 1998), pp. 69–155; and Seymour Martin Lipset and William Schneider, "The *Bakke* Case: How Would It Be Decided at the Bar of Public Opinion?" *Public Opinion* 2: 38–44 (April 1978).

5. See Richard Barnett and Joseph Garai, *Where the States Stand on Civil Rights* (New York: Sterling Publishing Co., 1962).

6. This section is based on Hugh Davis Graham, *The Civil Rights Era: Origins and Development of National Policy, 1960–1972* (New York: Oxford University Press, 1990); James W. Riddlesperger Jr. and Donald W. Jackson, *Presidential Leadership and Civil Rights Policy* (Westport, CT: Greenwood Press, 1995); John David Skretny, *The Ironies of Affirmative Action: Politics, Culture, and Justice in America* (Chicago: The University of Chicago Press, 1996); and Mark Stern, *Calculating Visions: Kennedy, Johnson, and Civil Rights* (New Brunswick, NJ: Rutgers University Press, 1992).

7. United States Kerner Commission, *Report of the Advisory Committee on Civil Disorders* (New York: Bantam Books, 1968).

8. William J. Wilson, *The Truly Disadvantaged* (Chicago: University of Chicago Press, 1987).

9. For a discussion on the social construction of race see: Michael Omi and Howard Winant, *Racial Formation in the United States: From the 1960s to the 1980s* (New York: Routledge & Kegan Paul, 1986). A socially constructed definition does not necessarily preclude the use of phenotypes, but the point here is that racial categories are embedded in our formal and informal institutions. Some racial groups are ethnic groups or are composed of a set of ethnic groups. For example, Hispanics, or Latinos, are often considered an ethnic group because they are either of Latin American origin or Spanish-speaking heritage. On the other hand, Hispanic is also an ascriptive category—an identity imposed on an individual by the dominant population and reinforced by institutional practices. Reducing groups to simple racial categories has serious limitations because it ignores intragroup cultural and economic variations.

10. George Lipsitz, *The Possessive Investment in Whiteness: How White People Profit from Identity Politics* (Philadelphia: Temple University Press, 1998).

11. Murray Friedman and Peter Binzen, *What Went Wrong? The Creation and Collapse of the Black-Jewish Alliance* (New York: The Free Press, 1995).

12. See Norman C. Amaker, "The Reagan Civil Rights Legacy," in Eric J. Schmetz, Natalie Datlof, and Alexej Ugrinsky, eds., *Ronald Reagan's America, Volume I* (Westport, CT: Greenwood Press, 1997); Robert R. Detlefsen, "Affirmative Action and Business Deregulation: On the Reagan Administration's Failure to Revise Executive Order No. 11246," and Charles M. Lamb and Jim Twombly, "Decentralizing Fair Housing Enforcement During the Reagan Presidency," in Riddlesperger and Jackson, *Presidential Leadership and Civil Rights Policy*; Peter Gottschalk, "Retrenchment in Antipoverty Programs in the United States: Lessons for the Future," and R. Kent Weaver, "Social Policy in the Reagan Era," in B. B. Kymlicka and Jean V. Matthews, eds., *The Reagan Revolution?* (Chicago: The Dorsey Press, 1988); and Raymond Wolters, *Right Turn: William Bradford Reynolds, the Reagan Administration, and Black Civil Rights* (New Brunswick, NJ: Transaction Publishers, 1996).

13. In the language of Proposition 209, the prohibition is against discrimination or preferential treatment on the basis of race, sex, color, ethnicity, or national origin. For brevity, many of the contributors to this book refer simply to race and gender.

14. Barnett and Garai, *Where the States Stand on Civil Rights,* pp. 23–25.

15. Here and in the following papers, the term "Asian American" (and "Asian" in some cases, such as in some tables) refers to both the U.S.-born and to immigrants, and among the latter to both noncitizens and naturalized citizens. All the race/ethnic data in the other studies—whether black, white, or Latino—also cover noncitizen immigrants.

Chapter 2

U.S. and California Affirmative Action Policies, Laws, and Programs

Ward Thomas and Mark Garrett

The development of antidiscrimination laws in the United States has been a dynamic issue and must be placed in the historical context of discrimination against certain groups. African Americans have a long history of racial discrimination in the United States, including the institution of slavery in the 18th and 19th centuries. Women and members of many other racial, religious, and nationality groups have also suffered from discrimination. For much of this century, racial and ethnic minorities and women have confronted legal and social barriers to employment and business opportunities and have sometimes experienced complete exclusion.

The conflict between American ideals of liberty, equality, and justice and pervasive societal discrimination has been called the "American dilemma."[1] Some people have advocated antidiscrimination laws as a potential solution to this dilemma. The adoption of antidiscrimination laws by federal and state governments has been linked to the ability of supporters of civil rights to mobilize social protest against discrimination. Major equal employment opportunity and affirmative action legislation has been passed following major antidiscrimination and civil rights marches in Washington, D.C., and elsewhere around the country.[2]

Historically, federal and state governments have attempted to ameliorate discrimination in employment and business in four fundamental ways: (1) by regulating the employment practices of governmental institutions; (2) by regulating the employment practices of private businesses that contract with government through the procurement process; (3) by regulating the employment practices of private employers; and (4) by modifying government contracting and procurement through set-aside contracts for minority- and women-owned businesses. Affirmative action programs, designed to increase the number of minority and women hires in both the public and private sectors, grew in importance during the 1960s and 1970s.

After decades of governmental efforts to rectify the underrepresentation of minorities and women in employment and business, affirmative action programs have been significantly curbed, however, in recent years. During the Reagan and Bush administrations, affirmative action programs came under increasing attack as race-based quota systems that discriminated against white males. In 1989, and again in 1995, the United States Supreme Court tightened the standard for reviewing the constitutionality of affirmative action programs that apply to race and ethnicity. In 1995, President Clinton ordered a review of federal affirmative action programs; the efficacy of these programs was a central issue in the 1996 presidential race. Efforts to reverse affirmative action programs have also taken place at the state level. In November 1996, California voters approved a ballot initiative, Proposition 209, designed to end affirmative action programs within the state and local governments. In Chapter 1 of this book, Paul Ong analyzes why this political and legal shift toward restricting the scope of affirmative action took place.

This chapter examines the history of antidiscrimination and affirmative action law and policies at the federal level and in California. These include presidential initiatives, congressional actions, and judicial rulings. The first section examines federal equal employment opportunity legislation and judicial rulings. Federal government efforts to combat racial discrimination through equal employment opportunity laws began in the early 1940s. The antidiscrimination effort at this time was narrowly conceived and enforcement efforts were weak.[3] However, congressional proponents of equal employment opportunity policies continued to introduce legislation, culminating in the passage of the Civil Rights Act of 1964. The Civil Rights Act of 1964 stands today as the country's major equal employment opportunity law.

The second section examines affirmative action regulations in employment adopted by the federal government since the 1960s. Affirmative action is premised on the belief that government has a responsibility to remedy the effects of past discrimination and current discrimination as well as to prevent future discrimination or exclusion.[4] Executive Order 11246, signed by President Johnson in 1965, remains the primary federal affirmative action law. Major Supreme Court rulings that have affected affirmative action programs are also reviewed.

The third section examines federal set-aside contracting programs. Since the 1950s, the federal government has used antidiscrimination programs in its procurement process. Specifically, the government has provided set-aside contracts for minority-owned businesses (MBEs), women-owned businesses (WBEs), and more broadly, "socially and economically disadvantaged" businesses.[5] These set-aside programs have been the focus of recent Supreme Court cases that have restricted the scope of affirmative action.

After World War II, there was a strong movement among the states to enact antidiscrimination legislation. The fourth section reviews this effort in California and provides an overview of equal employment and affirmative action laws and policies that have been implemented in the state since that time. The fifth section examines set-aside contracting in California. Affirmative action laws in employment and contracting at the state level have been significantly affected by recent Supreme Court rulings.

This chapter also includes four appendices that contain a chronological summary of the major national and California antidiscrimination laws. Additional information on federal antidiscrimination laws and the civil rights movement may be found in several sources.[6] Detailed information on antidiscrimination policies in California may be found in the annual reports of the California Department of Fair Employment and Housing, the annual reports prepared by the Public Employment and Affirmative Action Division of the California State Personnel Board, and the annual reports prepared by the Office of Small and Minority Business, State of California. "The Status of Affirmative Action in California," a 1995 report prepared by the California Senate Office of Research, and the 1995 California Legislative Black Caucus's Annual Black Family Hearing are also informative.[7]

Federal Equal Employment Opportunity Laws

In July of 1941, Philip Randolph, president of the Sleeping Car Porters Union, threatened to disrupt the defense effort by leading a mass demonstration of blacks in Washington, D.C., to protest employment discrimination. To head off the demonstration and avoid the appearance of a divided country during wartime, President Roosevelt issued Executive Order 8802, which mandated that "there shall be no discrimination in the employment of workers in defense industries or government because of race, creed, color, or national origin."[8] Roosevelt subsequently broadened the coverage to include all organizations, unions, or industries working under a federal contract. The president's actions were followed by a series of executive orders issued by the Truman and Eisenhower administrations prohibiting discriminatory employment practices by federal departments and agencies and private businesses contracting with the federal government.[9] These were significant because they ended a "tradition of federal unconcerned-ness about racial discrimination" in employment.[10]

The government's antidiscrimination policy at this time was narrowly conceived; it only proscribed blatant acts of individual discrimination in hiring and employment.[11] The enforcement provisions of the executive orders of the 1940s and 1950s, moreover, "lacked any real teeth."[12] The legal status and authority of these orders were ambiguous, and there were no clear sanctions against those who did not comply.[13] After World War II, gains that had been made by women and blacks receded as returning GIs reclaimed their jobs.

During the 1960s the antidiscrimination effort evolved to embrace the broader concept of equal employment opportunity. "Equal employment opportunity" is a concept that maintains that the personnel activities of businesses be conducted in such a manner as to ensure fair and equitable treatment of all persons who participate in or seek entrance to its work-force, and to ensure that all artificial non-job-related barriers to employ-ment are eliminated.

Before 1964, the federal government's efforts to prohibit employment discrimination had been limited to regulating the employment practices of federal government agencies and private businesses contracting with the federal government. The private labor market had not been subject to such regulations. There had been, however, dozens of legislative propos-als to prohibit employment discrimination in the private labor market introduced in Congress since 1942.[14] From 1942 to 1963, legislation pro-hibiting employment discrimination in the private sector was the focus of intense scrutiny in more than 21 congressional hearings, arguments cov-ering thousands of pages of the Congressional Record, and countless pub-lic and scholarly debates.[15] It was not until Congress passed the Civil Rights Act of 1964 that a law prohibiting employment discrimination in the private labor market was enacted.

The Civil Rights Act of 1964 represents today's central equal employ-ment opportunity law. Title VII of the act, as amended by the Equal Employ-ment Opportunity Act of 1972, prohibits discrimination by employers, employment agencies, and labor organizations on the basis of race, color, religion, sex, or national origin. In addition to covering most federal, state, and local governmental employers and educational institutions, the law also applies to all federally assisted programs and to most private employers with 15 or more employees, labor unions with 15 or more members, and employment agencies. Title VII governs all aspects of employment, includ-ing recruitment, hiring, promotion, discharge, classification, training, com-pensation, and other terms, privileges, and conditions of employment.[16]

Title VII created the Equal Employment Opportunity Commission (EEOC) to enforce its provisions. Individuals who believe they have been subjected to employment discrimination may file complaints with the EEOC. After referral to appropriate state or local agencies, the EEOC may file a formal charge against the offending party if the agency finds that organization has violated the provisions of Title VII. If the EEOC determines that a violation of Title VII has occurred, it must first attempt to resolve the matter through conciliation. Where conciliation efforts fail to resolve allegations of unlawful discrimination, the EEOC is empowered to bring a civil action against the offending private party. If the party is a state or local governmental unit or political subdivision, the EEOC must refer the matter to the Department of Justice for enforcement.

Today's major federal equal employment opportunity and affirmative action laws and policies were initiated in the 1960s and interpreted and clarified by the United States Supreme Court in the 1970s. The first significant Supreme Court ruling came in 1971 in *Griggs v. Duke Power Co.*, where the Court held that the Title VII ban on discrimination in employment hiring covered non-race-based practices causing a "disparate impact" on minorities in addition to intentional disparate treatment based on race. Disparate impact refers to employment practices that more frequently exclude legally protected classes—minorities and women—than white men. The Court also ruled that employers must show that any employment tests are job-related.[17]

Employer recruitment practices were key issues in several subsequent Supreme Court cases. In *McDonnell Douglas v. Green* (1973), the Court held that a prima facie case is established under Title VII by showing that a qualified applicant belonged to a racial minority and was rejected, while the position remained open to others with the same qualifications.[18] The burden then shifts to the employer to articulate some legitimate nondiscriminatory business reason for rejecting the applicant. The applicant then has the opportunity to demonstrate that the reasons given are merely a pretext. In *Albermarle Paper Co. v. Moody* (1975), the Court increased the technical standards that must be met by employers in conducting validation studies of their hiring tests.[19]

Griggs and related cases held that Congress has the power to prohibit public and private conduct having a discriminatory *effect*, provided there is no legitimate business justification for the practice.[20] Many lower courts applied the *Griggs* rule to cases of discrimination arising directly under the Constitution. In *Washington v. Davis* (1976), however, the Supreme Court refused to extend the *Griggs* rule to a case brought under the Fifth Amendment challenging the use of a verbal ability test by the Metropolitan Police Department in Washington, D.C. The Court ruled that the test was proper, despite the appearance of adverse impact, and that the plaintiff, who was alleging a constitutional violation in this case, would have to provide proof of "intentional discrimination."[21]

These cases, dealing with situations of employment discrimination against minorities and women, formed the backdrop for the Court's subsequent analyses of the validity of affirmative action programs. As the 1970s ended, government and private efforts to increase the representation of minorities and women in the workplace were attacked in court as "reverse" discrimination against nonminorities and men. Opponents of affirmative action argued that Title VII and the Fourteenth Amendment banned any hiring preferences based on race. While the Court did not forbid affirmative action programs outright, it did restrict their scope, mainly to prevent the use of racial quota systems. The following section will review these legal issues.

Affirmative Action Programs

By the 1960s, the federal government began to adopt the position that merely providing equal employment opportunity was not enough. The additional step of "affirmative action," a term coined by President Kennedy in 1961, was needed to effectively remedy racial discrimination in employment. President Johnson characterized this sentiment in a 1965 speech:

> You do not take a person who had been hobbled by chains, liberate him, bring him up to the starting gate of a race and then say, "You are free to compete with all the others," and still justly believe you have been completely fair. . . . It is not enough to open the gates of opportunity. All of our Citizens must have the ability to walk through those gates. . . . Men and women of all races are born with the same range of abilities. But ability is not just the product of birth. Ability is stretched or stunted by the family you live with, . . . the neighborhood . . . the school . . . and the poverty or richness of your surroundings. It is the product of a hundred unseen forces playing upon the infant, the child and the man.[22]

The affirmative action concept is premised on the belief that government has a responsibility to remedy the effects of both past and current discrimination, as well as to prevent future discrimination or exclusion. For government agencies and private businesses, affirmative action involves developing a planned, results-oriented management program that critically analyzes all personnel procedures and practices to ensure equal employment opportunity. It also includes statistically evaluating the outcomes of personnel procedures (e.g., recruitment, selection, promotion) to ensure that they do not have a disparate impact upon a minority group or women.

In response to the civil rights movement, President Kennedy issued Executive Order 10925 in 1961, creating the President's Committee on Equal Employment Opportunity; he gave the committee authority to debar noncomplying contractors or to terminate their contracts.[23] Executive Order 10925 also, for the first time, used the term "affirmative action" to refer to measures designed to remedy the effects of past discrimination.

One year after the Civil Rights Act of 1964 was passed by Congress, President Johnson signed Executive Order 11246. This order significantly broadened and strengthened Executive Order 10925 initiated by President Kennedy four years earlier.[24] Executive Order 11246 requires federal contractors with 50 or more employees and over $50,000 in federal contracts to "take affirmative action to ensure that applicants are employed, and that employees are treated during employment, without regard to their race, sex, creed, color, or national origin."[25] Executive Order 11246 created the Office of Contract Compliance to monitor its provisions. In 1979, enforcement agencies from different departments were consolidated into the Office of Federal Contracts and Compliance Programs (OFCCP).

Federal contractors are required to develop a written affirmative action program within 120 days of the beginning of a government contract. They must track any underrepresentation of minorities and women in their workforce and report their findings to the OFCCP. The OFCCP enforces Executive Order 11246 through compliance reviews and through complaint investigations. If violations are found, the OFCCP solicits, by means of conciliation and persuasion, the contractor's agreement to correct them within certain time frames. The OFCCP may impose sanctions, including contract termination or debarment.[26]

The most far-reaching expansion of affirmative action was implemented by President Nixon and Labor Secretary George Schultz in 1969. Federal contractors in Cleveland and Philadelphia were told to submit, under the pre-award policy, affirmative action plans assuring minority group representation in all trades and in all phases of work. They were required to establish goals and timetables in a "manning table," stating the number of minority employees to be hired. Federal officials informed contractors that although the choice of methods was their own, their affirmative action plans "must have the result of producing minority group representation." Some consider this so-called Philadelphia Plan the first truly enforceable affirmative action plan.[27]

In the 1960s and 1970s, many state and local public agencies, as well as private businesses, adopted such race-conscious policies as minority set-asides to eliminate the effects of discrimination or avoid Title VII liability. By the late 1970s and 1980s, these affirmative action programs themselves came under fire from opponents as unlawfully discriminating against non-minorities. With the inauguration of the Reagan administration in 1981, these affirmative action programs were attacked as unlawful discrimination. Opponents claimed they violated Title VII's ban on discrimination or, in the case of governmental programs, that they also violated constitutional equal protection guarantees that forbid purposeful discrimination based on suspect classifications such as race or ethnicity. The issue before the courts became how far federal, state, and private programs may go to assure equal opportunities before running afoul of these protections. These decisions reflect the justices' increasing concern about the impact of affirmative action programs on the principle of reward for individual merit and the constitutional rights of nonminorities to be free from discrimination.

The first major indication of a change in direction came in the 1978 Supreme Court ruling in *Regents of the University of California v. Bakke*, which is significant in that for the first time the Court narrowed the scope of acceptable affirmative action programs.[28] In this case, the University of California at Davis medical school had reserved 16 of the 100 places in each year's entering class for minority applicants in its admissions program. Alan Bakke, a white male who had been denied admission, contended that the program violated both Title VI[29] and the Equal Protection Clause of the Fourteenth Amendment. A divided Supreme Court ruled that the school's objective of increasing the number of minority doctors was "facially invalid" because "preferring members of any one group for no reason other than race or ethnic origin is discrimination for its own sake." Justice Powell, who authored the plurality opinion, relied on equal protection grounds and argued that all racial classifications created by state or local governments are unconstitutional unless they pass "strict scrutiny," that is, they are narrowly tailored to achieve a "compelling governmental purpose."[30] Four other justices decided only that the program violated Title VI, leaving the constitutional standard of review of affirmative action programs unclear. A majority of the Court also ruled, however, that minority status could be used as a flexible factor in the admissions process.

The next year, the Supreme Court upheld a private voluntary affirmative action program in *United Steelworkers of America, AFL-CIO-CLC v. Weber* (1979). The union of steel workers at Kaiser Aluminum and Chemical Corporation and the company initiated a voluntary affirmative action program in which 50 percent of the vacancies in a training program would be reserved for black workers. The Supreme Court ruled five to two that voluntary affirmative action plans by private employers giving preferential treatment to minorities to correct a racial imbalance in the workforce do not violate the Title VII ban on discrimination.[31] The case gave employers with traditionally segregated workforces the opportunity to adopt affirmative action plans to increase minority participation and thereby avoid potential liability under Title VII.

In *Firefighters Local Union No. 1794 v. Stotts* (1984), however, the Supreme Court ruled against the preferential protection of minorities in employment layoff decisions. In this Title VII case there had been no discrimination against the protected employees and the Court held that the lower court's order preventing the city from firing black employees as part of a fiscal recovery plan threatened the seniority rights of white employees.[32] Two years later, in *Wygant v. Jackson Board of Education* (1986), an affirmative action program was also rejected by the Supreme Court in a case involving the layoff of schoolteachers. In this case, the union and the school district had worked out a collective bargaining agreement that gave black teachers special protection from layoffs to alleviate the effects of past discrimination. In a plurality decision, the Supreme Court ruled that the affirmative actions taken by the board were unconstitutional on the grounds that they were not implemented as a result of either an existing past history of discrimination by the board or statistical proof of under-utilization of available minorities in the workforce.[33] With the *Wygant* decision, the Court moved closer to endorsing Justice Powell's strict scrutiny standard in constitutional cases.

Johnson v. Transportation Agency of Santa Clara County (1987) involved an allegation of reverse discrimination when a white man was passed over for promotion in favor of a female employee who had a lower interview score. The Supreme Court ruled that this promotion decision was nondiscriminatory under Title VII. The ruling clarified the conditions under which voluntary affirmative action programs may be legally defensible when no previous history of employment discrimination exists. The test under Title VII was whether the program corrected a "manifest imbalance" in the workforce. A defensible program must show an underutilization of qualified minorities or women, be temporary in duration, and take into account the rights of nonminorities.[34]

Antidiscrimination laws and policies developed over several decades in the United States. They were significantly broadened during the 1960s, incorporating the concept of affirmative action and providing effective enforcement mechanisms to ensure their compliance. Beginning in the early 1970s, the Supreme Court began to issue important interpretations of these antidiscrimination laws, particularly with respect to the concept of disparate impact in hiring, generally upholding congressional action. After the mid-1970s, however, the Supreme Court began to place limits upon the reach of affirmative action programs designed to counter societal discrimination, but has still permitted more leeway to private employers where the government is not involved, and in hiring and promotions, than in layoffs. More recent Supreme Court rulings, which will be presented below, have narrowed the scope of government affirmative action programs still further.

Federal Set-Aside Contracting

Federal set-aside procurement contracting began in 1953 with the passage of the Small Business Act.[35] The act was established specifically to assist small businesses. The Small Business Administration (SBA) interpreted its authority under Section 8(a) of the act broadly, though, to permit it to develop set-asides for minority contractors. The set-aside program for minority businesses was relatively small until the 1960s, when its use was actively encouraged by the executive branch. In an October 1967 memorandum to the heads of certain governmental agencies, including the SBA, President Johnson announced a pilot program to help industry provide jobs and training in areas of severe unemployment. The SBA was encouraged to award subcontracts on a noncompetitive basis to firms that agreed to locate in or near ghetto areas. The SBA, instead, focused its efforts on encouraging the development of successful firms owned by disadvantaged minority businesses. The Section 8(a) program grew rapidly, from $8.9 million in 1969 to $64.5 million in 1971, and continued to expand thereafter.[36]

The Nixon administration also assisted minority business enterprises (MBEs). Nixon issued Executive Order 11458 in 1969, creating the Office of Minority Business Enterprises (OMBE) within the Department of Commerce.[37] The administration developed this program based on the belief that "both morally and economically, we will not realize the full potential of our nation until neither race nor nationality is any longer an obstacle to full participation in the American marketplace."[38] The OMBE provided for the mobilization and coordination of state- and local-government business resources to assist MBEs. The OMBE was also given the authority to provide financial assistance to public and private organizations that would provide management and technical assistance.

In 1977, Congress passed the Public Works Employment Act of 1977 (PWEA), which for the first time statutorily authorized set-aside contracts for MBEs. The PWEA provided that 10 percent of the federal funds granted for local public works projects were to be used by the state or local grantee to procure services or supplies from businesses owned and controlled by members of minority groups. In 1978, Congress passed Public Law No. 95-507, which provided a statutory basis for the SBA's Section 8(a) program and authorized the SBA to enter into procurement contracts with federal agencies and to subcontract that work to small businesses that are owned by "socially and economically disadvantaged" individuals. Socially disadvantaged persons are those who have been subjected to racial or ethnic prejudice or cultural bias because of their group identity; economically disadvantaged persons are those whose ability to compete in the economy is impaired by lack of capital and credit.[39] Under regulations adopted by the SBA, persons from certain racial and ethnic groups—but not women—are presumed to be socially disadvantaged.[40]

Today the federal government provides assistance to MBEs primarily through Section 8(a). Eligible firms also have access to technical and managerial services. It should be noted that once a firm is certified and brought into the Section 8(a) program, there is both a "graduation" period of nine years[41] and a requirement that firms achieve an increasing mix of business from outside the Section 8(a) program and outside federal contracting.[42]

Federal departments, such as the Department of Defense and the Department of Transportation, administer their own set-aside contracting programs.[43] Programs operated by the Department of Defense are significant because they execute roughly two-thirds by dollar amount of all federal prime contracts. The Department of Transportation manages a significant effort to encourage business with minority- and women-owned firms though its grants to state and local entities.

Government set-aside programs that give preference to minorities have been challenged as violating the equal protection guarantee of the Fourteenth Amendment. The central issue has been what standard of review to use in evaluating the constitutionality of these programs. Federal set-aside procurement contracting for MBEs was challenged in the Supreme Court in *Fullilove v. Klutznick* (1980). The plaintiffs in this case, several associations of construction contractors and subcontractors, brought suit alleging that the minimum 10 percent set-aside provision in favor of MBEs contained in the PWEA violated the Equal Protection Clause of the Fourteenth Amendment.[44] The Supreme Court ruled that the MBE set-aside provision in the PWEA was constitutional. The Court declared that considerable deference should be accorded to race-conscious actions taken by Congress, especially when Congress has "abundant evidence" to conclude that minority businesses have been denied effective participation in public procurement contracting opportunities. The Court also ruled six to three that combating the present effects of past discrimination was a permissible congressional goal.[45] Although the Court upheld the program, the justices were divided on the proper standard of review. Three justices agreed that the statute satisfied a test somewhat akin to strict scrutiny.[46] Three other justices argued for applying only an intermediate scrutiny test rather than the more searching standard.

The issue was again raised when a municipal minority set-aside contracting program was challenged in the Supreme Court in *City of Richmond v. J. A. Croson Co.* (1989). The city of Richmond, Virginia, finding that the local population was 50 percent African American while less than 1 percent of the city's contracts were awarded to MBEs, adopted an affirmative action program requiring at least 30 percent of city construction contracts to be set aside for minority subcontractors. A white-owned firm,

Croson Company, challenged the policy. In a five-to-four decision, the Supreme Court declared the Richmond plan unconstitutional. For the first time, a majority of the Court agreed that state and local laws creating racial preferences must be subjected to strict scrutiny.[47] Here there was no showing that the city had engaged in any prior discriminatory conduct; for the majority of the justices, remedying the effects of "societal discrimination" alone did not rise to a compelling interest. Nor was the program narrowly tailored to achieve its objectives, since the plan adopted rigid quotas and benefited some minorities who had not suffered any discrimination. In addition, the city failed to consider other non-race-based remedies before adopting the set-aside program.

In *Metro Broadcasting Inc. v. FCC* (1990), the Supreme Court considered a congressionally mandated FCC program that sought to increase minority representation in broadcasting. The program was designed to consider minority ownership in proceedings for new licenses. It allowed broadcasters whose licenses had either been designated for a revocation hearing or whose renewal applications had been designated for a hearing to assign their licenses to an FCC-approved minority enterprise. The plaintiff in this case, Metro Broadcasting, filed suit against the FCC, alleging that the congressionally approved program violated the Fourteenth Amendment. In a five-to-four decision the Court ruled that the program was constitutional after subjecting it to the less exacting standard of review, intermediate scrutiny. According to the Court, intermediate scrutiny required merely that congressionally approved race-conscious measures be substantially related to the achievement of an important government objective. The Court distinguished the case from *City of Richmond v. J. A. Croson Co.* by interpreting that case as mandating the higher standard of review to be used when examining state and local affirmative action programs, not those created by Congress to which the Court owed "appropriate deference."[48] This approach made it easier to justify efforts by the federal government to achieve racial balance, compared to similar efforts by state and local governments.

The Supreme Court's decision in *Metro Broadcasting Inc. v. FCC* was, however, subsequently overruled in *Adarand v. Pena* (1995). There, a contractor, Adarand, challenged a federal program modeled on Section 8(a) that gave prime contractors dealing with federal agencies financial incentives to hire subcontractors controlled by racial minorities. The Court, in another five-to-four decision, ruled that federal laws granting a preference based on race or ethnicity are unconstitutional unless narrowly tailored to achieve a compelling governmental interest, thus abandoning the federal/state distinction originated in *Fullilove*. The Court has now held that all federal, state, and local government programs containing racial classifications are subject to a single standard of review, strict scrutiny.[49]

Significantly, though, the various opinions in *Adarand* appear to leave open the question of congressional authority under Section 5 of the Fourteenth Amendment to foster racial equality and whether the Court will accord those efforts greater deference compared to state and local actions. Also, the holding in *Fullilove* that increasing racial diversity may be a sufficiently compelling interest in some circumstances to sustain affirmative actions seems intact. Although the case was remanded to the lower court for further proceedings, it is important to note that the program in *Adarand* was much more narrowly tailored than that involved in *Fullilove*. It provided that minority status raised only a refutable presumption of program eligibility, rather than imposing rigid quotas, and it merely offered financial incentives but did not require that anyone be hired.

As a result of the Court's latest rulings, all public race-conscious hiring policies are now subject to strict judicial scrutiny and are justified only if they are narrowly tailored to achieve a compelling government interest. Remedying the general effects of societal discrimination is not enough to justify government actions that give preferences to minorities; the compelling interest standard requires evidence of specific acts of unlawful discrimination. Federal, state, or local agencies proposing new voluntary affirmative action plans or wishing to continue existing programs after *Croson* and *Adarand* must conduct a disparity study to document the presence of existing discrimination or establish a history of past discrimination against minority firms or employees, and they must show that the remedial program is limited in duration, confined to those minority groups that have been affected by the discrimination found to exist, and that it does not unduly burden nonminorities. Finally, the government must also first consider adopting gender- or race-neutral alternatives to increase minority participation before approving a set-aside program, and must also establish procedures to waive the set-aside requirements in the event there are no qualified minority contractors available.

These new standards affect many affirmative action programs in California. While some state and local affirmative action programs were eliminated in response to *Croson*, in other cases cities undertook disparity studies to establish the requisite basis for defending their plans in court. Such studies may also help to refine programs so that they are more likely to survive legal challenge.[50]

Equal Employment Laws in California

There was a strong movement among the states to enact antidiscrimination legislation after World War II. Most state initiatives were modeled on the practices of the federal wartime Fair Employment Practices Committee, which was disbanded in 1945. New York and New Jersey were the first states to enact fair employment legislation, in 1945.[51] Fair employment initiatives were introduced in the California State Legislature in the early 1940s, but failed to gain sufficient support. In 1946, a fair employment practices initiative became a proposition on the election ballot, but was readily defeated. Subsequent fair employment initiatives were introduced in the California State Legislature in 1947, 1949, 1951, and 1953, all of which were defeated. The prospects for fair employment legislation improved in 1954 with the formation of the California Committee for Fair Employment Practices, which enlisted the support of labor, civil rights, religious, and community groups. Fair employment practices bills were again defeated in 1955 and 1957. Finally, following a Democratic victory in the 1958 California general elections, the Fair Employment Practices Act of 1959 (FEPA) was enacted and signed into law on April 16, 1959, by Governor Edmund Brown.[52]

FEPA declared as public policy the need to protect the right and opportunity for all persons to seek, obtain, and hold employment without discrimination. Under FEPA, it is unlawful for an employer to "refuse to hire or promote a person, to discriminate in any terms or conditions of employment, or to discharge him from employment because of race, religious creed, color, national origin, or ancestry."[53]

In 1970, FEPA was amended to prohibit sex discrimination.[54] In signing Assembly Bill 22 in 1970, Governor Reagan said, "A nation that prides itself on providing equal opportunities to all certainly cannot afford to ignore or prevent the contributions to our society made by women."[55] Furthermore, FEPA states:

> The practice of denying employment opportunity and discrimination in the terms of employment for such reasons foments domestic strife and unrest, deprives the state of the fullest utilization of its capacities for development and advancement, and substantially and adversely affects the interests of employees, employers, and the public in general.[56]

Labor organizations and employment agencies are also covered by FEPA. The term "employer" includes any person regularly employing five or more employees, the state (or any of its political or civil subdivisions), cities, and counties. The FEPA established the Fair Employment Practices Commission (FEPC), a five-member group (now seven) appointed by the governor, to enforce the act, and an administrative agency, the Division of Fair Employment Practices, to carry out the policies and dictates of the commission.[57]

In 1981, the FEPA and the Rumford Fair Housing Act were combined to form the California Fair Employment and Housing Act.[58] While the substance of the FEPA with respect to prohibiting employment discrimination did not change, the name of the act changed to the Fair Employment and Housing Act (FEHA). The name of the commission also changed, to the Fair Employment and Housing Commission (FEHC). The scope of its authority was broadened to include housing discrimination. The Fair Employment and Housing Commission (hereafter "the commission") also became responsible for enforcing the Unruh Civil Rights Act and the Ralph Civil Rights Act. The following analysis will concern itself with the commission's authority solely as it relates to employment discrimination.[59]

The commission holds considerable authority to take action against employers or unions that discriminate. The commission can conduct a full investigation into an alleged act of employment discrimination and has the power to subpoena evidence. If the commission finds probable cause, it can pursue conciliation or it may issue a cease and desist order compelling parties to rectify a particular problem through such actions as hiring, reinstatement, upgrading of employees, payment of back wages, or restoration of union membership. Decisions made by the commission may be appealed to the Superior Court. However, the review is limited; the commission's orders must be sustained if the record contains substantial evidence supporting them, regardless of the weight of the evidence.[60]

In addition to individual complaint-oriented procedures, Section 1421 authorizes the commission to investigate practices of employment discrimination on a broader scale. The commission may, for example, take action against larger entities, such as entire firms, firms and unions controlling a given occupation, or major corporations within a certain industry. The commission can undertake Section 1421 investigations on its own, without an individual filing a complaint.[61] Remedial programs developed by the commission under this authority are believed to be more effective because they are designed to achieve a broader impact than do resolutions of individual complaints.

The commission is also empowered to "engage in affirmative actions with employers, employment agencies, and labor organizations in furtherance of the purposes [of the act]."[62] At the fifth anniversary observance of the FEPA in September 1964, Governor Brown praised employers who had undertaken cooperative work with the FEPC as "a new breed of employers who are not waiting for complaints or grievances to be lodged against them, . . . [but are] actively seeking ways in which to employ more minority personnel." Affirmative action plans promulgated by the commission typically included a means of preventing underrepresentation of minorities and women in recruiting, hiring, assignment, and upgrading.

Since 1973, the commission has held responsibility for investigation, approval, and certification of affirmative action programs on state-awarded public works contracts over $200,000.[63] Each affirmative action program includes 16 specific steps directed at increasing minority workforce utilization and identifies an equal employment opportunity officer. The contract compliance staff works cooperatively with the Office of Federal Contracts and Compliance Programs, the agency that monitors federal contractors. Federal and state duplication is thereby avoided.

We now shift the analysis from FEPA to antidiscrimination and affirmative action programs administered by the State Personnel Board (SPB) in the California State Civil Service System. The SPB is a constitutional agency established in 1934 to enforce civil service statutes. Its duty is to ensure that appointments and promotions in the state civil service system are based on merit and free of favoritism, patronage, and discrimination.

The SPB's formal involvement in affirmative action began in 1971 (12 years after the passage of FEPA) in response to Executive Order 74-2 issued by Governor Ronald Reagan. In this order, Governor Reagan explained:

Time and experience have shown that laws and edicts of nondiscrimination are not enough; justice demands that every citizen consciously adopt and accentuate a personal commitment to affirmative action which will make equal opportunity a reality. This is not only necessary in the internal affairs of state government, but also in its relations with the general public, including correction of any past inequities which may tend to deny equal opportunity to all.[64]

In 1974, Governor Reagan directed all agencies and departments within California to submit to the SPB written affirmative action plans. These affirmative action plans were required to include specific program activities for the implementation of the affirmative action program, including hiring goals and timetables designed to overcome any underutilization of minorities and women.

The SPB was given responsibility for overseeing the affirmative action programs developed by state agencies. This includes reviewing departmental plans and progress reports to determine whether they are appropriate and consistent with federal and state guidelines. The SPB is also required to provide leadership to the affirmative action effort and assistance to departments in the development of their programs, and to review and monitor affirmative action programs for compliance. Executive Order 74-2, issued in 1971 and fully carried out by 1974, was codified into statute in 1977.[65] There were few changes for the next two decades.[66]

On June 1, 1995, Governor Pete Wilson issued Executive Order 124-95, leaving the status of affirmative action in the California State Civil Service System in question.[67] The order directed state agencies, departments, boards, and commissions to eliminate all state preferential-treatment requirements that exceed federal or state statutory requirements, including, but not limited to, those concerning hirings and layoffs. It also directed state employment goals and timetables required by the Government Code to be based on an analysis that compares the percentage of minorities and women in the employer's workforce with the percentage in the "relevant" labor market rather than the "general" labor market. The general labor market is made up of all persons in the local-area labor market or the general population, whereas the relevant labor market consists of only those persons in the general labor market who possess the relevant qualifications for the particular job in question.[68]

The ultimate effect that Executive Order 124-95 will have on affirmative action programs in California remains to be seen. Ostensibly, an executive order can repeal existing executive orders, but it cannot repeal statutes. Therefore, it should not affect any of California's affirmative action laws, which can only be changed by legislation that is passed by the Senate and Assembly and signed by the governor.[69] The governor can, however, have an impact by determining how to implement the laws. One change, for example, is redefining what constitutes the "available" labor force. The State Personnel Board is now using more occupation-specific categories to determine whether the state is underutilizing minorities and women, while in the past the SPB used the minority and women's share of the total labor force in California as its benchmark. The governor can also affect affirmative action programs by determining how many resources are devoted to these programs. As demonstrated in the studies by Badgett and Rodgers in Chapters 4 and 5, respectively, changes in resources can have an impact on the outcomes associated with affirmative action programs, and this has been evident at the federal level.

California Set-Aside Contracting

The origin of government assistance for MBEs and WBEs in California can be traced back to President Nixon's Executive Order 11458 in 1969, which created the federal Office of Minority Business Enterprise (OMBE). The federal OMBE program was designed, in part, to foster the creation of similar programs at the state level. By 1972, 13 states, including California, had established a state OMBE, jointly subsidized by federal OMBE grants and state funds.[70] The California OMBE was established within the State

Office of Economic Opportunity. CAL-JOBs assumed the responsibility for the administration of the California OMBE under a grant extended by the federal OMBE in 1972.[71] CAL-JOBs had been established in 1968, when the California State Legislature enacted the California Job Development Corporation Law (AB 1046) to facilitate the flow of capital and business expertise into low-income areas to stimulate businesses.

The California OMBE and CAL-JOBs worked under a five-point program:[72]

1. Coordinate California minority business enterprise activities and utilize available resources to develop business opportunities for minority businesses.

2. Develop and coordinate education and training programs for minority businesses.

3. Identify and assist in providing capital for minority businesses.

4. Provide management and technical assistance and related services to minority businesses.

5. Assist minority businesses with procurement contracts.

In 1973, the California Legislature passed the Small Business Procurement and Contract Act (AB 1816), which established the Office of Small Business Procurement and Contracts within the Department of General Services. The intent of the act was to aid and assist small businesses "in order to preserve free competitive enterprise and to ensure that a fair proportion of the total purchases and contracts or subcontracts for property and services for the state be placed with small business enterprises."[73] A small business is defined by the act as a business that is independently owned and operated and "which is not dominant in its field of operation." In addition to the 5 percent set-aside for small businesses, the Small Business Procurement and Contract Act of 1973 authorized the Office of Small Business Procurement and Contracts to coordinate their efforts with the federal Small Business Administration, the Minority Business Development Agency, and the Office of Small Business Development of the Department of Economic and Business Development.

In the early 1980s, two important organizational changes took place.[74] First, in 1981 the Office of Small Business Procurement and Contracts and the California OMBE were consolidated into the Small and Minority Business Procurement Assistance Division within the Department of General Services. This replaced the Office of Small Business Procurement and Contracts. The two offices were consolidated to improve the effectiveness of their assistance to the minority, women's, and small-business communities, and to avoid duplicating their efforts to their respective constituencies. In 1983, with the passage of AB 2105, the Small and Minority Business Procurement Assistance Division was renamed the Office of Small and Minority Business (OSMB). There have been no further major organizational changes.

California legislation for contracting set-aside programs specifically for MBEs and WBEs lagged 10 years behind similar legislation at the federal level. Efforts to establish set-aside legislation in California began in the mid-1980s. In 1985, AB 720 attempted to set 40 percent set-aside goals for freeway construction contracts. In 1986, legislation assigned the task of certifying MBEs and WBEs to the California Department of Transportation (Caltrans), which took effect in 1987. In 1987, AB 1059 attempted to set 15 percent and 5 percent set-aside contracting goals for MBEs and WBEs, respectively, but this legislation was vetoed by the governor.[75]

It was not until the passage of AB 1933 in 1988 (effective January 1, 1989) that set-aside contracts for MBEs and WBEs were statutorily authorized (California Public Contract Code, 10115 et seq.). Assembly Bill 1933 was intended to increase MBE and WBE participation among prime contractors and subcontractors in state procurement by requiring all contracts awarded by state agencies to have statewide contracting participation goals of at least 15 percent for MBEs and 5 percent for WBEs. The goals apply to the overall dollar amount expended each year by each awarding agency. For each applicable contract, prime contractors must achieve the minimum MBE and WBE participation goals or demonstrate that they made a "good faith effort" to achieve the required participation level. The irony of AB 1933 is that it took effect in the same year that the U.S. Supreme Court ruled on *City of Richmond v. J. A. Croson Co.* As stated above, this ruling declared that state laws creating racial preferences must be subjected to strict scrutiny, putting the provisions of the California law into question. According to a recent report by the California Senate Office of Research,[76] a post-*Croson* study, which is now considered to be necessary to justify any governmental set-aside program for minorities, has not been prepared by the state of California.

Conclusion

The policy of affirmative action is now in a state of flux, filled with uncertainties. With recent Supreme Court rulings, particularly *Croson* and *Adarand,* this nation has significantly curbed affirmative action programs without totally eliminating them. In California, there have been reductions in funding for antidiscrimination efforts, and Governor Wilson's Executive Order 124-95 marked a significant reversal in affirmative action in the state. In light of federal laws and programs requiring affirmative action, the possible effects of the passage of Proposition 209 on affirmative action programs are uncertain.[77] The prohibition against affirmative action programs may exacerbate ambiguities in current affirmative action policy by requiring state government, its local subdivisions, and public colleges and universities to eliminate preferential treatment on the basis of race, sex, color, ethnicity, or national origin in employment, contracts, or admissions.

Despite legal ambiguities associated with state and federal relations over affirmative action, one pattern is clear: The political and judicial climate has changed dramatically, creating an environment that is less supportive of affirmative action as a strategy to eliminate race and gender inequalities in employment and business. Affirmative action was originally seen as a way to "level the playing field" to permit women and minorities to compete on an equal basis with established majority firms. It presumed that all women and minorities were disadvantaged by societal discrimination. Many people today, including some women and minorities, believe these programs are too broad. They are often criticized as giving preferential treatment to women and minorities, whether or not the individuals are in fact victims of discrimination. Some believe minorities and women are actually hurt by such programs because they stigmatize those they are intended to assist. Others see them as discriminating against more qualified white males who are not responsible for societal discrimination and may be equally disadvantaged economically. Still others believe that proclamations of a color-blind society merely serve to perpetuate deeply entrenched structural barriers to racial and gender equality.

While the future of affirmative action is not clear, it is possible that the focus may shift from sweeping efforts to combat racism and sexism to more carefully tailored programs designed to correct specific instances of inequality caused by social and economic disadvantage. As one example, after the passage of Proposition 209, which appeared to ban affirmative action programs in student enrollment in the University of California system, state legislators began considering legislation to provide that the top 10 percent of students in all California high schools would be guaranteed enrollment in the UC system. The intent was to counter the effect of disparities in state educational funding that primarily affect low-income and mostly minority school districts. The approach is ostensibly race-neutral—selection is based on merit—and some nonminorities would also benefit; proponents believed it would help address educational disparities that tend to fall more heavily on minorities.

At this point, it is still uncertain whether passage of Proposition 209 will eliminate all state affirmative action programs, as some of its supporters believe. One state court has already ruled that it only prohibits programs that contain illegal preferences such as rigid numerical quotas. The decision would allow state agencies to continue to take race and gender into account to equalize opportunities in employment, education and contracting. Supporters of the ballot initiative opposed to any preferences may appeal this decision, so it could be some time before there is a definitive ruling on its scope. In the meantime, the future of affirmative action will no doubt remain a contentious issue.

Appendix A

Federal Equal Employment Opportunity Orders and Laws

1941 President Roosevelt's Executive Order 8802 prohibited employment discrimination by federal contractors in defense industries and by the federal government because of race, creed, color, or national origin. Roosevelt also established the Fair Employment Practices Committee (FEPC) to oversee the implementation and enforcement of Executive Order 8802. The order was significant because it marked the first time since Reconstruction that the federal government intervened in the labor market in the federal-government sector.

1943 President Roosevelt's Executive Order 9346 extended Executive Order 8802 to include all organizations, unions, or industries working under a federal contract. It reorganized and strengthened the FEPC (which was terminated by Congress in 1945).

1948 President Truman's Executive Order 9980 created the Fair Employment Board within the Civil Service.

1951 President Truman's Executive Order 10308 created the Government Contract Compliance Committee.

1953 President Eisenhower's Executive Order 10479 created the Government Contract Committee.

1955 President Eisenhower's Executive Order 10590 prohibited discrimination in federal employment and removed the Government Employment Committee from the Civil Service Commission and placed it in direct line of authority to the president.

1961 President Kennedy's Executive Order 10925 prohibited discrimination in government and among federal-government contractors. It required federal contractors to take affirmative action to ensure that individuals were treated without regard to race, creed, color, or national origin. Executive Order 10925 for the first time required federal contractors to take affirmative action to ensure nondiscrimination in employment. It also established the President's Committee on Equal Employment Opportunity and gave the committee authority to debar noncomplying contractors or to terminate their contracts.

1964   Congress passed Title VII of the Civil Rights Act of 1964, today's central equal employment opportunity law. Title VII, as amended, prohibits discrimination by employers, employment agencies, and labor organizations on the basis of race, color, religion, sex, or national origin by most private employers with 15 or more employees, labor unions with 15 or more members, and employment agencies. It applies to discrimination in all aspects of employment, including recruitment, hiring, promotion, discharge, classification, training, compensation, and other terms, privileges, and conditions of employment. Title VII also created the Equal Employment Opportunity Commission (EEOC) and empowered it to conciliate disputes arising from individual complaints of discrimination.

1965   President Johnson issued Executive Order 11246, broadening and strengthening Executive Order 10925 issued by President Kennedy four years earlier. Executive Order 11246 confirmed the affirmative action obligation imposed by Executive Order 10925 and prohibited discrimination among federal contractors on the basis of race, religion, or national origin in government contracts and in federal employment. It defined affirmative action in employment as specific outcome-oriented hiring procedures in ensuring racial equality in the outcomes of all employment practices. The term affirmative action is henceforth used for the purpose of actively pursuing racial equality in employment opportunities. Executive Order 11246 also assigned federal contract programs to the Department of Labor and authorized the Secretary of Labor to create the Office of Federal Contract Compliance (OFCC).

1966   The EEOC's Guidelines on Testing embodied the disparate-impact theory of discrimination and require employers to validate tests for minorities under the differential validation rule.

1967   President Johnson's Executive Order 11375 amended Executive Order 11246 to prohibit employment discrimination by sex.

1969   The Nixon administration devised the Philadelphia Plan, which required quota hiring in the construction industry in Philadelphia and three other cities in the form of goals and timetables. A "manning table" stating the number of minority employees to be hired was the key feature of the required affirmative action plans. Federal officials informed contractors that the choice of methods was their own, but an affirmative action plan "must have the result of producing minority group representation."

1970   OFCC Order No. 4 extended the goals and timetables required under the Philadelphia Plan to nonconstruction contractors as part of written affirmative action plans that contractors were obligated to submit.

1970   EEOC Guidelines on Testing revised and extended the 1966 guidelines into a systematic policy imposing stringent validation requirements on employers who use tests that have a disparate impact.

1971   *Griggs v. Duke Power Co.*, 401 U.S. 424. The Supreme Court ruled against Duke Power Company on the grounds that a high school diploma and tests were not shown to be valid predictors of job performance. The ruling represented the first time that the Court required employers to validate tests they use for hiring and other employment purposes. The ruling also helped to redefine discrimination in employment hiring in terms of adverse or disparate impact.

1972　The Equal Employment Act of 1972 extended Title VII to private employers and unions with 15 or more employees or members, to public employers in state and local government, and to educational institutions. It also authorized the EEOC to enforce Title VII by bringing suit in federal district court and created the Equal Employment Opportunity Council in federal government to formulate uniform policy on employee selection procedures.

1973　*McDonnell Douglas v. Green*, 411 U.S. 792. The Supreme Court again recognized the disparate treatment concept of discrimination, in a case that determined the order and allocation of burdens of proof in an individual discrimination suit under Title VII.

1975　*Albermarle Paper Co. v. Moody*, 422 U.S. 405. The Supreme Court affirmed the disparate-impact theory of discrimination in this class action case, which involved back-pay awards. Although Albermarle Paper Co. carried out validation studies on its hiring requirements, they still resulted in adverse impact. The Supreme Court ruled against Albermarle Paper Co. on the grounds that its validation studies did not comply stringently enough with the 1970 EEOC Guidelines on Employee Selection Procedures. As a result, the Court tightened the technical standards of all validation studies in employment hiring.

1976　*Washington v. Davis*, 426 U.S. 279. This Supreme Court case involved the use of a verbal ability test by the Metropolitan Police Department in Washington, D.C., in its selection of police recruits. Although the test was validated, black applicants were hired at a significantly lower rate than white applicants, resulting in adverse impact. The Court ruled that the use of the verbal ability test was legitimate and rejected the disparate-impact theory of discrimination. In this Fourteenth Amendment constitutional case, the Court held that proof of intent to discriminate is required in bringing discrimination charges under the equal protection clause.

1978　Presidential Reorganization Plan No. 1 established the EEOC as the lead federal agency for achieving equal employment opportunity in the public as well as the private sector. The federal equal employment opportunity function was also transferred from the Civil Service Commission to the EEOC, and the administration of the Equal Pay Act and the Age Discrimination Act from the Department of Labor to the EEOC. Also, the OFCC was renamed the Office of Federal Contract Compliance Programs (OFCCP) and was reorganized and given more centralized authority over contract compliance.

1978　Uniform Guidelines on Employee Selection Procedures were issued by the EEOC on behalf of all federal agencies. The guidelines describe how tests should be used to make employment decisions that are consistent with federal equal employment opportunity laws. The following terms were defined: (1) "discrimination" is defined in terms of the presence of adverse impact; (2) "adverse impact" is present when the minority hiring rate is less than 80 percent of the nonminority hiring rate (this is known as the four-fifths rule); and (3) "unfairness" of a selection procedure takes place when it results in lower scores for minority members and such score differences are not reflected in the differences in job performance.

1978　*Regents of the University of California v. Bakke*, 438 U.S. 265. In this Supreme Court case, the medical school at the University of California at Davis had reserved 16 of the 100 places in each year's entering class for minority applicants in its admissions program. The Court ruled that this affirmative action program setting quotas for admission of minorities was in violation of Title VI of the Civil Rights Act of 1964. The Court ruled that: (1) for any preferential treatment of minorities to be considered legal, the employer would have to demonstrate that the organization has discriminated against minorities in its personnel policies in the past; (2) affirmative action or preferential treatment is allowed only on an individual basis and not on a quota basis; and (3) affirmative action or preferential treatment is allowed only when it is used as a remedy for past discrimination.

1979   *United Steelworkers of America, AFL-CIO-CLC v. Weber,* 443 U.S. 193. Kaiser Aluminum and Chemical Corporation and its union, the United Steelworkers of America, jointly initiated a voluntary affirmative action program in which 50 percent of the vacancies in a training program were to be reserved for black workers. This quota program was initiated because an analysis of workforce utilization showed that 39 percent of the local available workforce was black, while only 2 percent of the skilled workers were black. Weber was an unskilled white worker who was passed over in favor of a less senior black worker. The Supreme Court ruled against Weber. The Court ruled that employers can initiate voluntary affirmative action quota programs to rectify a racial imbalance in the workforce on a temporary basis and until a set goal is achieved.

1984   *Firefighters Local, Union No. 1794 v. Stotts,* 467 U.S. 561. In Memphis, the district court ordered that race should override seniority in the layoff plans adopted by the city and the firefighters union under a court-ordered affirmative action plan. The Court of Appeals also upheld the order. The Supreme Court, however, reversed both lower court rulings by arguing against the preferential protection of minorities in employment layoff decisions. The seniority rights of white employees were upheld against minority preferences.

1986   *Sheet Metal Workers, Local 28 v. EEOC,* 478 U.S. 421. This Supreme Court case arose after the EEOC found the Sheet Metal Workers Union had discriminated against minority candidates in the past and ordered it to implement a numerical hiring quota. The hiring quota involved a numerical goal of 29 percent of minority hiring by a specified time period. The Court upheld this order on the grounds that these quotas were for remedial purposes and intended as a temporary measure.

1986   *Wygant v. Jackson Board of Education,* 476 U.S. 267. In this Supreme Court case, more senior white teachers were laid off before less senior minority teachers by the Jackson Board of Education. The affirmative actions were implemented by the board with the intention to proactively address the issue of discrimination and to provide role models in education for minorities. The Court ruled that these actions were unconstitutional because they were not implemented as a result of either an existing past history of discrimination by the board or a statistical proof of underutilization of available minorities in the workforce.

1987   *Johnson v. Transportation Agency of Santa Clara County,* 480 U.S. 616. In this Supreme Court case, a white man was passed over for promotion by the Santa Clara Transportation Agency in favor of a female employee who had a lower interview score. The Court upheld this voluntary affirmative action plan against a reverse discrimination charge. In this ruling, the Court clarified the conditions for a nonremedial voluntary affirmative action program to be considered legal. These conditions include: (1) conducting a stringent workforce utilization analysis to prove an underutilization of qualified minority talents; (2) having a voluntary plan that is intended to be temporary in duration; and (3) taking into account the rights of nonminorities or the nonprotected members.

1987 The Civil Rights Restoration Act of 1987 overturned *Grove City College v. Bell* and allowed the federal government to cut off funding to an entire college that discriminates in one of its departments or programs.

1989 *Wards Cove Packing Co. v. Atonio*, 490 U.S. 642. The Supreme Court ruled in this Title VII case that the fact that an employment hiring practice results in adverse impact is not a sufficient proof of discrimination. Rather, the proof of discrimination has to be made in the context of the general workforce or labor market and the plaintiff, rather than the employer, carries the burden of proof.

1991 The Civil Rights Act of 1991, Pub.L. No. 102-166, 105 Stat. 1071, overturned a number of U.S. Supreme Court cases limiting the reach of civil rights statutes. Among its many provisions, it (1) specifies when compensatory and punitive damages are available; (2) specifies when jury trials are available; and (3) clarifies who carries the burden of proof in different kinds of employment discrimination actions.

Appendix B

Federal Orders and Laws Regarding Federal-Government Procurement Contracting by Minority- and Women-Owned Firms

1953 The Section 8(a) program is one of several government efforts to aid minority businesses. Enacted as part of the Small Business Act of 1953, Section 8 authorized the Small Business Administration (SBA) to contract with government procurement agencies to arrange for the performance of their subcontracts by small businesses. The SBA took the initiative of developing Section 8(a) into a minority-based set-aside in order to foster the development of "socially or economically disadvantaged businesses." The program continued to evolve as an administratively created affirmative action program until 1978, when Congress enacted Public Law 95-507, which provides a statutory basis for the Section 8(a) program.

1969 The Office of Minority Business Enterprise (OMBE) was created by Executive Order 11458, dated March 5, 1969, and expanded and strengthened by Executive Order 11625, dated October 13, 1971. These orders charged the Secretary of Commerce with: (1) coordinating the programs, operations, and plans of federal agencies that may affect minority business development; (2) providing for the mobilization and coordination of state and local governments and appropriate business resources to assist the minority business effort; and (3) rendering technical assistance through public and private organizations to minority business enterprises.

1977   The Public Works Employment Act of 1977 (PWEA) provided that, absent administrative waiver, 10 percent of the federal funds granted for local public works projects were to be used by the state or local grantee to procure services or supplies from businesses owned and controlled by members of statutorily defined minority groups. A minority business enterprise (MBE) was defined as a business that was at least 50 percent owned by such a minority group. Minorities were defined as "citizens of the United States who are Negroes, Spanish-speaking, Orientals, Indians, Eskimos, and Aleuts." The administrative waiver provided that contractors who could not find a qualified MBE were released from this requirement.

1978   Public Law No. 95-507 authorized the SBA to operate a preferential set-aside program under Section 8(a). Congress attempted to provide objective criteria for the SBA to use in determining whether an applicant should be entitled to program participation. One key change in the statute was that eligibility was defined to include both social and economic disadvantage, which means that one can no longer qualify for the program solely on racial or ethnic criteria. The law also established the Minority Small Business and Capital Ownership Development Program under Section 7(j) of the Small Business Act, to provide a full range of management and technical services to Section 8(a) firms.

1980   Affirmative action jurisprudence in the area of government contracting began with *Fullilove v. Klutznick*, 448 U.S. 448. *Fullilove* involved the MBE provisions of the PWEA. Plaintiffs—several associations of construction contractors and subcontractors—brought suit, alleging that the minimum 10 percent set-aside provision in favor of MBEs contained in the PWEA violated the equal protection clause of the Fourteenth Amendment. In a plurality opinion, the Supreme Court found the MBE provision to be constitutional. The Court held that a great deal of deference should be accorded to race-conscious actions taken by Congress, especially when Congress has "abundant evidence" from which it could conclude that minority businesses have been denied effective participation in public contracting opportunities by procurement practices that perpetuated the effects of prior discrimination. The Court also found that combating the present effects of past discrimination was a permissible congressional goal.

1989   *City of Richmond v. J. A. Croson Co.*, 448 U.S. 469. This nonfederal case involved a municipal set-aside program that was modeled after the federal program upheld in *Fullilove*. The city of Richmond had adopted an affirmative action policy requiring at least 30 percent of the city construction contracts to be set aside for minority subcontractors. This program was based on the finding that the local population was 50 percent African American, while less than 1 percent of the city's contracts were awarded to minority business enterprises. Richmond's plan also included an administrative waiver in the event that no MBEs were available.

   In a five-to-four decision, the U.S. Supreme Court found the Richmond plan to be unconstitutional. For the first time, a majority of the Court agreed that state and local laws creating racial preferences must be subjected to strict scrutiny. Strict scrutiny requires race-based classifications to be narrowly tailored to the achievement of a compelling government interest. Remedying the present effects of present or past discrimination is generally the only acceptable compelling government interest for programs in this area of affirmative action.

1990 *Metro Broadcasting, Inc. v. FCC,* 497 U.S. 547, involved a congressionally mandated FCC program that sought to increase minority representation by considering minority ownership in proceedings for new licenses and by allowing broadcasters whose licenses had either been designated for a revocation hearing or whose renewal applications had been designated for a hearing to assign the license to an FCC-approved minority enterprise.

The plaintiff in this case, Metro Broadcasting, had lost a license to a minority-owned business and filed suit against the FCC, alleging that the congressionally approved program was in violation of the Fourteenth Amendment. In a five-to-four decision the Court found the program to be constitutional after subjecting it to a less exacting standard of review, intermediate scrutiny. Intermediate scrutiny requires that congressional race-conscious measures be substantially related to the achievement of an important government objective.

1995 *Adarand Constructors, Inc. v. Pena,* 115 U.S. 2097. A contractor, Adarand, challenged a federal program that gave prime contractors dealing with federal agencies financial incentives to hire subcontractors controlled by socially and economically disadvantaged individuals. Members of racial minorities were presumed to be socially and economically disadvantaged under this program. The Supreme Court, in a five-to-four decision, ruled that federal laws that grant a preference based on race or ethnicity are unconstitutional unless they are narrowly tailored to achieve a compelling governmental interest. The Court sent the case back to the trial court to evaluate whether the program's presumption of disadvantage met this standard of strict scrutiny. The court's decision to apply the same standard to local, state, and federal programs overruled its 1990 decision in *Metro Broadcasting v. FCC.*

Appendix C

California Equal Employment Opportunity Laws

1959 The Fair Employment Practices Act (FEPA) was signed into law by Governor Edmund G. Brown on April 16, 1959. FEPA made it an unlawful employment practice for an employer to "refuse to hire or promote a person, to discriminate in any terms or conditions of employment, or to discharge him from employment because of race, religious creed, color, national origin, or ancestry." The act established a five-member Fair Employment Practices Commission (FEPC) to be appointed by the governor to carry out the policies of the act. The commission was given the power to investigate, hold hearings, and issue cease and desist orders. The act also prohibited discrimination in employment by labor organizations and employment agencies. The term "employer" includes any person regularly employing five or more persons or acting as an agent of an employer (directly or indirectly), the state or any political or civil subdivision thereof, and cities.

1970   The first substantive amendment to FEPA added sex as a prohibited basis for discrimination.

1971   The FEPC was directed by an Assembly resolution to adopt rules and regulations on employee selection procedures to implement the U.S. Supreme Court decision in *Griggs v. Duke Power Co.*

1971   The State Personnel Board's formal involvement in affirmative action began in 1971 when Governor Reagan issued Executive Order 74-2, redefining the Code of Fair Practices.

1973   The FEPC was given the responsibility for investigation, approval, and certification of equal employment opportunity programs on state-awarded public works contracts exceeding $200,000.

1974   Governor Reagan issued a memo (following Executive Order 74-2) to all agencies and departments requesting them to develop and submit to the State Personnel Board written affirmative action plans. Each plan was to include: (1) a departmental nondiscrimination/affirmative action statement; (2) hiring goals as appropriate to address workforce underrepresentation; and (3) specific program activities for the implementation of an affirmative action program and achievement of goals.

1977   Executive Order 74-2 was finally codified into statute. As written into the government code, current law requires each agency to establish an effective affirmative action program that includes goals and timetables designed to overcome any underutilization of women, minorities, and persons with disabilities. Each agency is required to designate an employee as an Affirmative Action Officer who is responsible for managing the department's program and providing advice and assistance to the department's director. In departments with more than 500 employees, the Affirmative Action Officer must be someone other than the Personnel Officer.

   The State Personnel Board is required to provide leadership and assistance to departments in developing their affirmative action programs, and to review and monitor affirmative action programs for compliance. Since 1978, the board has provided an annual report to the legislature and the governor on the status of the state's affirmative action program. The requirement for the report was waived by statute for several years because of budget constraints but has been reinstated.

1977   The FEPC was given the power to issue precedential decisions.

1980   In the governor's Reorganization Plan No. 1, the FEPC in the Department of Industrial Relations was abolished and replaced by the Department of Fair Employment and Housing and the Fair Employment and Housing Commission within the State and Consumer Services Agency. To codify this reorganization, the California Legislature adopted Assembly Bill 3165 (Fenton), which was signed by the governor on September 10, 1980. As a result, effective January 1, 1981, the Fair Employment Practices Act and the Rumford Fair Housing Act were combined to form the California Fair Employment and Housing Act, which has been codified in the California Government Code at Sections 12900–12996.

1995   Governor Wilson on June 1, 1995, signed Executive Order 124-95 ordering state agencies, departments, boards, and commissions to take the following actions: (1) eliminate all state preferential treatment requirements that exceed federal statutory or regulatory, or state statutory, requirements, including but not limited to those concerning hiring and layoffs and state contractors or grantees; (2) terminate any consultant contracts, disband any advisory committees, and abolish any performance-recognition awards, where those contracts, advisory committees, and recognition awards foster or encourage preferential treatment; (3) quantify and report to the governor within 75 days the cost to state taxpayers of implementing federal and state requirements that grant preferential treatment; (4) draft 1995–96 state employment goals and timetables required by the Government Code so as to be based on the employment pool possessing the necessary qualifications for the particular job classification at issue, rather than on general workforce parity.

Appendix D

California Orders and Laws Regarding State-Government Procurement Contracting by Minority- and Women-Owned Firms

1969 The federal Office of Minority Business Enterprise (OMBE) program was designed to encourage the establishment of an office of minority business enterprise akin to the federal OMBE in each of the states. Where established, such offices would stimulate and coordinate public and private resources at the state level. By 1972, there were 13 state OMBEs in operation, including in California, jointly subsidized by federal OMBE grants and state funds. Their goals included the development of minority business participation in state procurement needs, involvement of minority-owned construction firms in state-supported construction, development of subcontracting opportunities for minority entrepreneurs from prime contractors receiving state business, deposit of state funds in minority-owned banks, and the strengthening of minority business through use of resources inherent in state and local educational systems.

1972 CAL-JOBs originated in 1968 when the California Legislature enacted the California Job Development Corporation Law (Assembly Bill 1046) to help facilitate the flow of capital and business expertise into low-income areas to stimulate businesses. In 1972, the CAL-JOBs Board assumed from the State Office of Economic Opportunity the responsibility for administering the California Office of Minority Business Enterprise under a grant extended by the federal OMBE. The California Office of Minority Business Enterprise, in conjunction with CAL-JOBs, worked under a five-point program: (1) coordinate California minority enterprise activities and utilize available resources to develop business opportunities for minority businessmen; (2) develop and coordinate education and training programs for minority businessmen; (3) identify and assist in providing capital for minority businessmen; (4) provide management and technical assistance and related services to minority businessmen; (5) assist minority businessmen with procurement contracts.

1973 The CAL-JOBs and OMBE staff worked closely in the development of the Small Business Procurement and Contract Act, Assembly Bill 1816. This legislation established the Office of Small Business Procurement and Contracts within the Department of General Services. The intent of the act is to aid and assist small business "in order to preserve free competitive enterprise and to ensure that a fair proportion of the total purchases and contracts or subcontracts for property and services for the state be placed with small business enterprises." A small business was defined as a business that is independently owned and operated and "which is not dominant in its field of operation." The maximum number of employees and dollar volume defining a small business varies from industry to industry as determined by the director of General Services.

The Small Business Procurement and Contract Act authorized the director of General Services to establish goals for the extent of participation of small businesses in state procurement and in Office of Architecture and Construction contracts. Furthermore, the legislation provided for a 5 percent preference for small businesses "for the lowest responsible bidder meeting specifications."

1981   An administrative reorganization of two divisions, the Small Business Office and the California Office of Minority Business Enterprise, created the Small and Minority Business Procurement Assistance Division as an office of the State of California Department of General Services. The two offices were consolidated to improve the effectiveness of their closely related Procurement Assistance Division by providing greater resources to the small, minority, and women's business communities. The merger was also intended to avoid overlapping and/or duplication of efforts to their respective constituencies.

1983   The Small and Minority Business Procurement Assistance Division was renamed the Office of Small and Minority Business (OSMB) under AB 2105.

1985   Assembly Bill 720 was introduced to set a 40 percent set-aside goal for freeway construction contracts, but failed to pass.

1986   Assembly Bill 1059 attempted to set 15 percent and 5 percent set-aside targets for minority- and women-owned government contractors, respectively, but was vetoed by the governor.

1987   Assembly Bill 1464 specified that all agencies shall accept the certification of a socially and economically disadvantaged business concern by the Department of Transportation as valid status of that business when awarding contracts. The bill further stated that "no state agency shall require the business to comply with any other certification process for certifying socially and economically disadvantaged business concerns."

1989   Assembly Bill 1933 became effective on January 1, 1989. This bill required all contracts awarded by any state agency, department, officer, or other state-governmental entity to have statewide contracting participation goals of not less than 15 percent for minority-owend business enterprises and not less than 5 percent for women-owned business enterprises. The goals established apply to the overall dollar amount expended each year by the awarding department.

For each applicable contract, prime contractors must achieve the minimum minority, women, and disabled veteran business enterprise (M/W/DVBE) participation goals or demonstrate that they made a "good faith effort" to achieve participation. If a prime contractor submits a bid with less than minimum participation, that contractor must make and document that it made a good faith effort to obtain participation.

Notes

1. Gunnar Myrdal, *An American Dilemma: The Negro Problem and Modern Democracy* (New York: Harper and Row, 1944).

2. Paul Burstein, *Discrimination, Jobs, and Politics: The Struggle for Equal Employment Opportunity in the United States Since the New Deal* (Chicago: University of Chicago Press, 1985); Frances F. Piven and Richard A. Cloward, *Regulating the Poor: The Functions of Public Welfare* (New York: Vintage Books, 1971).

3. Jonathan S. Leonard, "The Effectiveness of Equal Employment Law and Affirmative Action Regulation," *Research in Labor Economics* 8 (B): 319–350 (1986).

4. Ibid.

5. George Stephanopoulos and Christopher Edley Jr., "Affirmative Action Review: Report to the President" (Washington, DC: Office of the President, 1995).

6. Herman Belz, *Equality: A Quarter-Century of Affirmative Action, Transformed* (New Brunswick, NJ: The Social Philosophy and Policy Center, 1991); Burstein, *Discrimination, Jobs, and Politics*; Christopher Edley, *Not All Black and White: Affirmative Action, Race, and American Values* (New York: Hill and Wang, 1996); Hugh Davis Graham, *The Civil Rights Era: Origins and Development of National Policy: 1960–1972* (New York: Oxford University Press, 1990); Stephanopoulos and Edley, "Affirmative Action Review."

7. California Legislative Black Caucus, "Annual Black Family Hearing" (October 1995); California Senate Office of Research, "The Status of Affirmative Action in California" (Sacramento, 1995).

8. Burstein, *Discrimination, Jobs, and Politics*, p. 8.

9. Belz, *Equality*.

10. Myrdal, *An American Dilemma*, p. 416

11. Burstein, *Discrimination, Jobs, and Politics*.

12. Leonard, "Effectiveness of Equal Employment Law," p. 321.

13. Burstein, *Discrimination, Jobs, and Politics*.

14. Ibid.

15. Ibid, p. 9.

16. United States Commission on Civil Rights, "Promises and Perceptions: Federal Efforts to Eliminate Employment Discrimination Through Affirmative Action" (Washington, DC, 1981).

17. Michael K. Braswell, Gary A. Moore, and Bill Shaw, "Disparate Impact Theory in the Aftermath of *Wards Cove Packing Co. v. Atonio*: Burdens of Proof, Statistical Evidence, and Affirmative Action," *Albany Law Review* 54 (1): 1–34 (1989).

18. M. Singer, *Diversity-Based Hiring* (Newcastle-upon-Tyne: Athenaeum, 1993).

19. Ibid.

20. In *Wards Cove Packing Co. v. Atonio* (1989), the Supreme Court rejected a disparate-impact discrimination charge under Title VII. The Court ruled that although an employment hiring practice results in some adverse impact, it is not a sufficient proof of discrimination. The proof of discrimination has to be made in the context of the general workforce or labor market, and the plaintiff, rather than the employer, carries the burden of proof. The ruling represented a departure from the Court's 1971 ruling on adverse impact in *Griggs v. Duke Power Co.* and

removed some of the legal incentive employers had to voluntarily adopt affirmative action (Braswell, Moore, and Shaw, "Disparate Impact Theory"). Congress responded in the Civil Rights Act of 1991 by largely restoring the legal test to that in effect prior to the decision in *Wards Cove*.

21. Singer, *Diversity-Based Hiring*; David Jung and Cyrus Wadia, "Affirmative Action and the Courts," Legal Issue Summary (Sacramento: California Research Bureau, California State Library, 1996).

22. Stephanopoulos and Edley, "Affirmative Action Review," p. 115.

23. Belz, *Equality*.

24. Leonard, "Effectiveness of Equal Employment Law."

25. Ibid, p. 322.

26. United States Commission on Civil Rights, "Promises and Perceptions."

27. Belz, *Equality*.

28. Glen D. Nager, "Affirmative Action After the Civil Rights Act of 1991: The Effects of a 'Neutral' Statute," *Notre Dame Law Review* 68 (5): 1057–1077 (1993).

29. Title VI of the Civil Rights Act prohibits discrimination in any state or private program receiving federal funds, 42 U.S.C. 200d.

30. Nager, "Affirmative Action After the Civil Rights Act," p. 1065.

31. Singer, *Diversity-Based Hiring*; Jung and Wadia, "Affirmative Action and the Courts."

32. Singer, *Diversity-Based Hiring*.

33. Alan Freeman, "Antidiscrimination Law: The View from 1989," *Tulane Law Review* 64 (6): 1407–1441 (1990).

34. Singer, *Diversity-Based Hiring*.

35. Daniel R. Levinson, "A Study of Preferential Treatment: The Evolution of Minority Business Enterprise Assistance Programs," *The George Washington Law Review* 49 (1): 61–99 (1980).

36. Dominic L. Ozanne, "Minority Construction Contractors," *Harvard Civil Rights–Civil Liberties Law Review* 12 (3): 693–724 (1977).

37. Levinson, "A Study of Preferential Treatment."

38. United States Department of Commerce, "Progress of the Minority Business Enterprise Program" (Washington, DC, 1972), p. 1.

39. Levinson, "A Study of Preferential Treatment."

40. 13 CFR § 124.105(b)(1).

41. 13 CFR § 124.110(a).

42. Stephanopoulos and Edley, "Affirmative Action Review."

43. Ibid.

44. Lucy Katz, "Public Affirmative Action and the Fourteenth Amendment: The Fragmentation of Theory after *Richmond v. J. A. Croson Co.* and *Metro Broadcasting, Inc. v. Federal Communications Commission*," *Thurgood Marshall Law Review* 17 (2): 317–358 (1992).

45. Katz, "Public Affirmative Action"; Mitchell F. Rice, "State and Local Government Set-Aside Programs, Disparity Studies, and Minority Business Development in the Post-*Croson* Era," *Journal of Urban Affairs* 15 (6): 529–553 (1993).

46. Only Justice Powell endorsed applying the strict scrutiny test used in *Bakke*.

47. Rice, "State and Local Government Set-Aside Programs."

48. Katz, "Public Affirmative Action"; Rice, "State and Local Government Set-Aside Programs."

49. Edley, *Not All Black and White.*

50. Jung and Wadia, "Affirmative Action and the Courts."

51. Richard Couser, "The California FEPC: Stepchild of the State Agencies," *Stanford Law Review* 18: 187–212 (1965).

52. Marjorie Gelb and JoAnne Frankfurt, "California's Fair Employment and Housing Act: A Viable State Remedy for Employment Discrimination," *The Hastings Law Journal* 34: 1055–1105 (1982–83). By this time 16 states had passed similar fair employment practice initiatives. Also, the Unruh Civil Rights Act, prohibiting discrimination in business establishments, was passed in California in 1959.

53. State of California, Fair Employment Practices Commission, "FEPC Report: September 18, 1959" (Sacramento, 1960), p. 10.

54. Couser, "The California FEPC."

55. State of California, Fair Employment Practices Commission, "FEPC Report: July 1, 1968" (Sacramento, 1969).

56. State of California, "FEPC Report" (1960), p. 9.

57. Couser, "The California FEPC."

58. In 1964, the Department of Industrial Relations was originally given the responsibility for enforcing the Rumford Fair Housing Act. The FEHA also established the Department of Fair Employment and Housing as independent from the Department of Industrial Relations and placed the department under the State and Consumer Services Agency.

59. State of California, Fair Employment and Housing Department, "Report to the Legislature on the Operations of the Department of Fair Employment and Housing" (Sacramento, 1981).

60. Michael C. Tobriner, "California FEPC," *The Hastings Law Journal* 16 (3): 333–349 (1965). It should be noted that the commission and the EEOC work in coordination with one other. The EEOC, for example, must notify the commission first when an alleged discriminatory act is brought to its attention. The commission then has 60 days to undertake some action. The commission does not have to exercise its jurisdiction and often does not do so because of an insufficient staff to deal with a heavy case load. Since the jurisdiction of the EEOC and the commission overlap, complainants may have two attempts at remedial efforts.

61. John Gherini, "California's Approach to Racial Discrimination in Employment: The Complaint Process vs. Voluntary Affirmative Action," *University of San Francisco Law Review* 5 (2): 404–432 (1971).

62. State of California, Fair Employment Practices Commission, "FEPC Report: July 1, 1964" (Sacramento, 1965).

63. Gelb and Frankfurt, "California's Fair Employment and Housing Act."

64. State of California, "Public Contract Code Classification" (Sacramento, 1995), p. 112.

65. Ibid.

66. Ted Edward, telephone interview by Ward Thomas (August 1, 1996).

67. California Legislative Black Caucus, "Annual Black Family Hearing."

68. California Legislative Black Caucus, "Annual Black Family Hearing"; California Senate Office of Research, "The Status of Affirmative Action in California."

69. Ibid.

70. United States Department of Commerce, "Progress of the Minority Business Enterprise Program."

71. State of California, Department of Finance, "The California Job Creation Program Board (CAL-JOBs)" (Sacramento, 1975).

72. Ibid.

73. California Government Code, § 14835. State of California, Office of Small and Minority Business, "Annual Report" (Sacramento, 1983).

74. State of California, Office of Small and Minority Business, "Annual Report" (Sacramento, 1983).

75. State of California, Office of Small and Minority Business, "Annual Report" (Sacramento, 1988).

76. California Senate Office of Research, "The Status of Affirmative Action in California."

77. Erwin Chemerinsky, "Preliminary Report on the Impact of the Proposed California Civil Rights Initiative" (Los Angeles: University of Southern California Law Center, 1996); Kate Sproul, "The Constitutionality of the Proposed California Civil Rights Initiative" (Sacramento: California Senate Office of Research, 1995); California Legislative Black Caucus, "Annual Black Family Hearing."

Chapter 3

Race and Gender in California's Labor Market

Paul Ong

This chapter provides a historical overview of California's labor market. As documented in the first section ("Growth and Diversity"), this state's labor force has not only expanded rapidly over the last half-century, it has also become more heterogeneous, with increasing numbers of minorities and women seeking employment. Greater diversity in itself does not necessarily justify the need for affirmative action; however, the persistence of racial and gender inequality does. In order to provide important contextual information for subsequent chapters, which focus on specific affirmative action programs, this chapter will examine the historical trend of group disparities in wages and earnings since 1960. This research relies heavily on census data, particularly the decennial microsamples. For practical and empirical reasons, the analysis has limitations, but can nonetheless provide an overview of the trend.

In examining group differences, the first section of this chapter focuses on two separate but illustrative comparisons: (1) racial disparities among white, African American, Hispanic, and Asian American men,[1] and (2) gender disparities between white men and white women. The first comparison is used to eliminate the confounding effects of gender on racial outcomes, and the second comparison is used to eliminate the confounding effects of race on gender-based outcomes. Clearly, it would be preferable to examine racial differences among females and gender differences among minorities; however, limited time and resources preclude the pursuit of a more comprehensive analysis. Despite the limitations, these comparisons provide important insights into the persistent nature and magnitude of racial and gender inequality in California.

The second section of this chapter ("Racial Disparities Among Men") reports the findings on racial disparities among male workers in the private (for-profit) sector. The analysis reveals a mixed picture of progress and setbacks in eliminating wage and earnings inequality. Minorities made considerable gains during the 1960s, though their progress slowed noticeably during the subsequent decade. They gained little if any ground during the 1980s. Systematic differences in educational attainment, age composition, and employment levels contribute to intergroup differences in wages and earnings, but racial inequality cannot be traced to these factors alone. In other words, there is a sizable residual racial effect.

The third section ("The Gender Gap") examines the gender gap among non-Hispanic whites. The analysis shows that progress has been made in closing the gap, with much of the gains made during the 1980s. Unlike the case with racial disparity, educational attainment and age composition are not key factors in explaining gender inequality. Instead, the key factors are the level of labor-market attachment and occupational segregation. As women have become more career-oriented, there has been a concomitant gain in their earnings; but there is still a substantial difference in women's and men's earnings that is due in part to persistent gender segregation.

While the empirical analyses document the extent of racial and gender inequality, the data do not reveal what proportion of the disparity is due to discrimination in the labor market. The findings show that factors such as education and years of experience cannot account for all of the inequality, but there is much debate among social scientists and policy analysts about the meaning of the unexplained gap in racial and gender wages and earnings. The proponents of affirmative action tend to argue that these residuals constitute reasonable evidence that discrimination exists; the problem is socioeconomic in nature, and therefore requires governmental action. By contrast, opponents of affirmative action tend to argue that the unexplained residuals are due to unobserved personal characteristics; therefore the problem lies with the individual, not the system.

To assess this question of the extent of discrimination, the fourth section ("Combating the Role of Discrimination") examines data from California's Fair Employment Practices Commission (FEPC).[2] There has been a general increase since the 1960s in the number of race- and gender-based complaints, with the numbers accelerating in the 1990s. Yet despite this growth in complaints, the number of settlements has actually declined since the early 1980s. An analysis of the trends in funding reveals that the state of California has become less willing to support the FEPC, which in turn has weakened the state's ability to enforce antidiscrimination laws.

Growth and Diversity

Over the last half-century, the number of employed civilians in California has increased dramatically, from 2.5 million in 1940 to over 14 million in 1995.[3] The build-up of the military industry during World War II attracted millions to the Golden State, and the labor force continued to grow in subsequent decades. Between 1960 and 1995, the number of civilian workers increased by 143 percent, a considerably higher rate than the 90 percent for the nation as a whole.[4] California's private sector has provided the vast majority of the jobs for its growing populace. In 1960, 75 percent of all employed civilians worked in the private sector. There was a slight decline in the figure to 72 percent in 1970, but the percentage has increased gradually since that year. By 1995, once again 75 percent worked in the private sector. Self-employment has accounted for approximately one-tenth of the employed civilian labor force, although there have been some variations over time.[5] Finally, employment in state and local government (not including schools, colleges, and universities) accounted for 6 to 7 percent of the employed civilian labor force, with the figure declining slightly over time.[6]

Although the distribution by employment class (private, self-employed, or public) has not fluctuated much, the ethnic distribution of the employed labor force (including both males and females) has undergone a dramatic recomposition, which paralleled a recomposition of the population. The correlation between changes in the total population and the total labor force can be seen in Figure 1. Figure 2 traces the changes in the employment share for the three major minority groups.[7] African Americans increased their share of the employed civilian labor force from about 2 percent in 1940 to 6.4 percent in 1980. The most dramatic increase occurred during the 1940s, when large numbers migrated to California in response to the industrial build-up during World War II. Their share declined moderately in the following years to slightly less than 6 percent in 1995. The Asian American share remained fairly stable from 1940 to 1970, in the 2 to 3 percent range, but increased dramatically thereafter. By 1990, Asian Americans comprised 9.5 percent of California's employed labor force. The 1995 statistics indicate a decline to 8.4 percent, but that decline may be an artifact of the data source.[8] Hispanics showed the most dramatic increase among the minority groups, climbing from approximately 4 percent in 1940 to 22 percent in 1990. This growth in the Hispanic labor force over the last two decades has been driven largely by immigration. (California has been the dominant receiving state for Hispanic as well as Asian immigration.) The 1995 statistics indicate continued growth, although the figure may be artificially biased upward because of the nature of the data source.[9] While the white share of the employed civilian labor force has declined, it is important to note that the decline has not been absolute. The

Figure 1: Racial/Ethnic Distribution of California's Population and Labor Force for People Between the Ages of 24 and 64 (1950 and 1995)

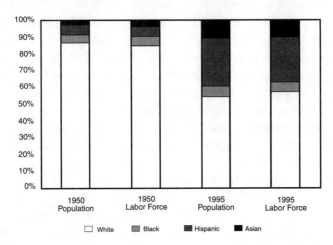

Source: Ong et al., "Socio-Economic Trends in California (Sacramento: California Employment Development Department, 1986); "Current Population Survey" (U.S. Department of Commerce, Bureau of the Census).

number of working whites increased every decade, from 4.9 million in 1960 to 8.6 million in 1995. The relative and absolute figures reveal that the ethnic recomposition is due not to any replacement of whites by minorities but to differences in growth rates. The number of minority workers in general increased much more rapidly than the number of white workers, thus accounting for the changes in the labor force.

Along with ethnic recomposition, there has also been a shift in the distribution of the labor force by sex, as shown in Figure 2. In 1940, approximately one-fourth of all workers were female (25.5 percent); by 1995, nearly one in two was female (44.7 percent). This mirrors the changes at the national level, where the respective figures increased from 24.7 percent in 1940 to 46.1 percent in 1995.[10] One unique aspect of California's working women is that a relatively large percentage are minorities. In 1940, 1 in 12 employed women was African American, Hispanic, or Asian American; by 1995, 1 in 5 was a minority. Again, it should be noted that this shift was accomplished not by an absolute decline in the number of white women, but by a more rapid increase in the number of minority women relative to white women.

One unfortunate characteristic of California's diverse workforce is economic inequality along race and gender lines.[11] These disparities are not unique to California. Numerous national studies have documented both the racial and gender gap in wages and earnings, although some of these studies find that progress has been made over the last half-century.[12]

Figure 2: Minorities and Women as a Proportion of the Employed Labor Force in California (1940–1995)

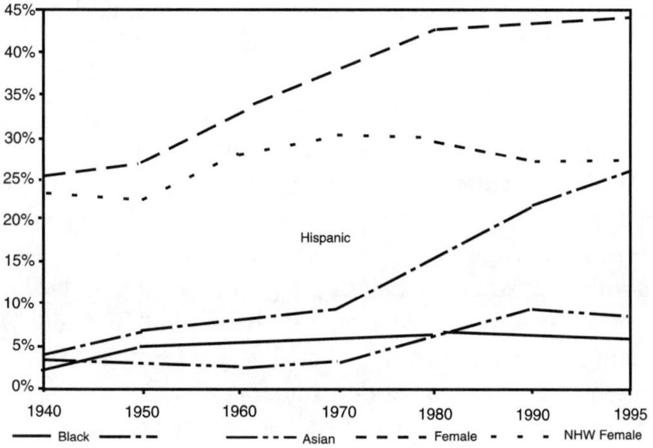

*NHW = Non-Hispanic Whites

Source: Ong et al., "Socio-Economic Trends in California"; 1990 Public Use Microsamples (PUMS); "Current Population Survey." (1995).

The following two sections examine these inequalities among Californians. The analysis is limited to adults of prime working age (24 to 64) employed in the for-profit, private sector who were born in the U.S.[13] The private sector is the focus because it is the dominant segment of the economy. (Issues related to self-employment and public-sector employment are covered in other chapters.) In order to eliminate any confounding effects of immigrant status on earnings and wages, only U.S.-born workers are included. This approach is used in order to isolate the effects of race and gender. As stated earlier, the analysis of racial disparity is based on examining minority and white men, and the analysis of gender disparity is based on examining white men and white women. The sample is restricted to those with at least $1,000 (in 1989 dollars) in earnings, and the analysis focuses on total annual earnings, although estimated hourly wages are also examined.[14] Because experience and educational attainment have strong effects on earnings and wages, multivariate techniques are used to control for these factors.[15]

Racial Disparities Among Men

This analysis examines the unadjusted hourly wage (Table 1, top panel) because it is a standardized measure of compensation for a fixed unit of labor service. Moreover, the hourly wage is tied to the contribution of labor to the production of goods and services.[16] For all four reporting years (1959, 1969, 1979, and 1989),[17] minority men received less than white men (not shown), but there was considerable variation in the magnitude of the racial disparity. This can be seen in Table 1, which depicts the minority-to-white wage ratio based on geometric means.[18] There was noticeable progress in the 1970s for African Americans, with a moderate retrenchment in the 1980s.[19] The pattern for Hispanics is one of essentially no change throughout the first two decades, followed by noticeable erosion in wages in the 1980s. Asian Americans, on the other hand, experienced continuous progress, with approximately half of the gain occurring in the 1960s.

The second panel of Table 1 reports the minority-to-white wage ratio after adjusting for education and potential years of experience. These ratios can be interpreted as the wage of a minority worker relative to that of a white worker with similar years of schooling and experience. For African Americans and Latinos, the adjusted wage ratios are higher than the unadjusted ones reported in the first panel. Differences in schooling and experience account for a quarter to one-half of the racial disparities, with some variation across time and group (see Table 2). The adjusted ratios show that African Americans made moderate gains in the 1970s. In other words, over

Table 1: Minority-to-White Earnings Ratios for Men in California (1959–1989)

Race/Ethnicity	1959	1969	1979	1989
Unadjusted Hourly Wages				
Black	73%	73%	78%	76%
Latino	80%	80%	81%	76%
Asian American	84%	90%	94%	96%
Adjusted Hourly Wages				
Black	80%	81%	83%	83%
Latino	90%	92%	92%	91%
Asian American	85%	89%	94%	96%
Unadjusted Annual Earnings				
Black	60%	65%	69%	67%
Latino	74%	77%	76%	71%
Asian American	80%	88%	93%	94%
Adjusted Annual Earnings				
Black	68%	73%	75%	74%
Latino	86%	90%	89%	88%
Asian American	80%	86%	93%	94%

Source: PUMS data for 1960, 1970, 1980, and 1990 (U.S. Department of Commerce, Bureau of the Census, Census of Population and Housing).

half of the gain in the unadjusted wage ratio was driven by a gain in educational attainment. Unfortunately, there were no noticeable gains in the economic status of African Americans in the 1980s. This is surprising since the differences in educational attainment and age were smaller in 1989 than in 1979. However, there was an overall increase in the returns to education; thus, smaller differences in schooling were magnified in 1989 compared to 1979. For Hispanics, the adjusted ratios are considerably higher than the unadjusted ratios, revealing that lower levels of educational attainment were a major contributor to Hispanic-white disparity. The adjusted ratios show moderate progress between 1959 and 1979, followed by a moderate decline. For Asian Americans, there is little difference between the adjusted and unadjusted ratios, thus leaving unchanged the secular trend toward parity with whites. Nevertheless, greater educational attainment by Asian Americans has not completely eliminated racial disparity.

While hourly wage is an important measure of the compensation per unit of labor service, annual earnings are also important because they determine an individual's (and family's) standard of living. In fact, for the vast majority of Americans, total income from paid work is a key determinant of socioeconomic status and well-being. While wage disparity matters, when most people discuss economic inequality they refer to income, or earnings.

Table 2: Mean Values of Earnings-Related Variables for Employed Men in California by Race (1959–1989)

Year/Variables	White	Black	Hispanic	Asian
1959				
Age	40.3	39.7	36.0	36.3
Education (yrs.)	11.4	9.2	8.9	11.9
Annual Hours	2,096	1,837	1,973	1,997
1969				
Age	41.4	39.7	38.6	39.0
Education (yrs.)	12.3	10.7	10.0	12.9
Annual Hours	2,110	1,907	2,041	2,053
1979				
Age	39.6	38.0	37.5	39.1
Education (yrs.)	13.6	12.5	11.3	13.9
Annual Hours	2,085	1,923	1,984	2,057
1989				
Age	38.4	37.3	36.4	37.0
Education (yrs.)	13.8	13.0	12.1	14.2
Annual Hours	2,136	1,929	2,002	2,087

Source: Author's compilation from PUMS data for 1960, 1970, 1980, and 1990.

Earnings are a function of both wage level and hours worked; consequently, a difference in number of hours worked can accentuate or attenuate the disparities observed in wages. Data in Table 2 show that minorities tend to work fewer hours per year than whites do. African Americans work approximately one-tenth less relative to whites; Hispanics average a little more work time than African Americans; and Asian Americans come the closest to whites in hours worked. The number of hours worked is smaller because of higher rates of unemployment and shorter work weeks among minorities.

The third panel in Table 1 reports the unadjusted minority-to-white ratio for annual earnings. The data show a consistent racial hierarchy among minorities: African Americans at the bottom, Hispanics in the middle, and Asian Americans at the top. The data also show progress in the 1960s for all three groups, with gains of 3 to 8 percentage points. African Americans and Asian Americans continued to make progress in the 1970s, while Hispanics did not. The 1980s was a period of retrenchment for both African Americans and Hispanics, while Asian Americans approached parity with whites. Adjusting annual earnings for education and experience increases the ratios for African Americans and Latinos (because these two factors contributed to the observed disparities), but the minority-white gap does not disappear.

The Gender Gap

Analyzing the gender gap—the difference between the earnings and wages of white men and women—is a difficult task because gender differences in labor-market outcomes are generated by a complex set of economic and social factors. One important factor is a gender difference in labor-market attachment. In the United States, the prevailing (and historical) norm is that adult males are expected to work, a norm that has translated into higher male labor-force participation rates.[20] As a result of strong and persistent differences in gender roles within the household, women are less attached to the labor market on average, and this is observed as a lower female labor-force participation rate. The labor-force participation rate is particularly low among women with young children, because it is a life stage in which many mothers are expected to be the primary childcare provider. Even among households with older children, continued household obligations can limit the number of hours women can commit to paid employment.

The prevailing gender division of household duties also affects employer behavior. Many employers and female workers are reluctant to invest in training because the future value of the training is reduced by periodic movement in and out of the labor market.[21] Consequently, wage increases and career promotions occur less frequently. Moreover, it is not just women with disrupted careers who are affected: Gender-based stereotypes hurt even those women who are highly committed to a career and have a strong attachment to the labor market. With imperfect information and little foresight, employers rely on group characteristics to evaluate individuals and decide which individuals should receive training. Their biased behavior, in turn, creates disincentives for some women to remain attached to the labor market. From a strictly economic perspective, this behavior is rational—but incurs significant societal costs.

The other major factor generating the gender gap is occupational segregation. There is a long history of gender division within job categories. Despite recent progress, many occupations continue to be either predominantly male or predominantly female.[22] This has had profound economic consequences,[23] as female-dominated occupations tend to have lower wages, even after accounting for differences in human capital. Overcrowding in these labor niches also plays a role in depressing wages, while fewer opportunities for training and promotion exacerbate the problem over time.

In summary, limited upward mobility in women's occupations is part and parcel of the gender division between paid employment and unpaid household work discussed earlier. Moreover, because females are stereotyped as being marginally attached to the labor market, employers have few economic incentives to provide training and promotional opportunities for them. Employers act on this prejudice by steering women applicants into female niches. These employer decisions operate at the group level rather than the individual level—a form of statistical discrimination that affects both the hiring and the internal personnel practices. Women who are permanently attached to the labor market are also subjected to the same lack of opportunities and low wages if they are trapped in a predominantly female occupation. Because occupational segregation produces gender inequity in the world of work, the differences in potential lifetime earnings reinforce the economic biases in the existing gender division between paid employment and unpaid domestic labor.

While these patterns exist, gender-based norms and behavior are not necessarily static. For example, during World War II an extreme shortage of male labor forced this nation to hire massive numbers of women to work in the military industry as well as other sectors of the economy, thereby giving many women the opportunity to develop employment experience and an employment history. Since that time, a greater number of women have pursued careers in male-dominated professions, such as medicine, law, and business, though the gains in job desegregation have been modest. Over the past 50 years there has also been a transformation in the public's expectations regarding work, such that working for pay has become the norm for both men and women.

Public attitudes regarding welfare have also been affected by these normative expectations. For example, when the Aid to Families with Dependent Children program was established in 1935, the expected norm was that mothers would remain at home to raise their children. Today, the public expectation is that women can work for wages. This expectation is now embodied in the 1996 Personal Responsibility and Work Opportunities Act, where mothers are expected to find paid employment as soon as possible.

An analysis of employment outcomes for white women and white men reveals progress, but also lingering problems. (See Table 3.) The analysis finds that average educational attainment levels for men and women are similar for all four decades, with women having about half a year less schooling than men. Average age of employed women decreased over time. This shift in ranking by age is likely due to the growing numbers of working mothers with young children, changes in the timing of having children, and changing numbers of children per family. A clear sign of secular changes in the labor-market attachment of women can be seen in the proportion of women working full-time and full-year (FT/FY), which is defined as working at least 35 hours per week and 50 weeks per year. In 1959, 22 percentage points separated the sexes; three decades later, the difference narrowed to 13 percentage points.[24]

Table 4 reports the average earnings and wages of white women relative to those of white men. The first row contains the estimated ratios for the observed annual earnings, which shows an increase of 14 percentage points from 1959 to 1989, with two-thirds of the gain occurring in the 1980s. Adjusting for education and experience (second row) does not substantially change the gender gap in earnings. A comparison of hourly wages (third row) also shows a considerable difference between male and female workers. In 1989, for example, we can see that, after controlling for education and potential years of experience, women earned only 72 percent of the hourly wage of men. Once again, the adjusted wage ratios show that women made noticeable economic gains during the 1980s.

The bottom panel of Table 4 reports the gender ratios for the earnings of FT/FY white workers. As expected, given the lower total hours of work for women as a group (reflected in the top panel), the estimated percentages for unadjusted and adjusted earnings among the FT/FY workers are higher than those for all workers. Interestingly, the ratios based on hourly wages among FT/FY workers are very similar to those for all workers, which indicates that the gender gap in wages is not due to differences in the percentage of female versus male workers who are employed full-time for the full year.

Additional analysis of the 1989 earnings data indicates that the gender difference in hourly wages was smaller among FT/FY workers below the age of 45, the generation most affected by the changing norms of the 1970s

Table 3: Mean Values of Earnings-Related Variables for White Workers in California by Gender (1959–1989)

Gender/Variables	1959	1969	1979	1989
Men				
Age	40.3	41.4	39.6	38.4
Education (yrs.)	11.4	12.6	13.6	13.0
FT/FY*	73%	73%	77%	76%
Annual Hours	2,096	2,110	2,085	2,136
Women				
Age	41.7	42.2	38.9	38.
Education (yrs.)	11.3	12.1	13.0	13.4
FT/FY*	51%	52%	58%	63%
Annual Hours	1,636	1,668	1,730	1,840

*Percent employed full-time for the full year (35 or more hours per week, 50 or more weeks per year).

Source: Author's compilation from PUMS data for 1960, 1970, 1980, and 1990.

and 1980s. Using an expanded framework that includes not only years of schooling and experience but also marital status, number of children in the family, and gender-specific returns to potential years of labor-market experience, we find a female-to-male wage ratio of 85 percent among those between the ages of 24 and 34, and 90 percent among those between the ages of 35 and 44. This would indicate that the gender gap is closing among those most attached to the labor market, the likely beneficiaries of the historical transformation in attitudes and expectations. However, there remains a gender gap that is not limited to the differences in wages. This analysis indicates that women continue to pay a price for raising their children. For each child added to the family, the wage gap increases by approximately 8 percentage points; this suggests that FT/FY working mothers sacrifice more lucrative jobs in order to raise their children and provide their childcare.

Continuing occupational segregation also contributes to the gender gap, though this is not to deny that there has been progress in integrating some job categories.[25] A majority of non-Hispanic white women (56 percent) in 1970 were in an occupation where females comprised at least 75 percent of the workforce; but two decades later, only a minority (39 percent) were in an occupation where females comprised at least 75 percent of the workforce. Despite this progress, many job categories continue to be gender-niched. In 1990, at least 90 percent of secretaries, childcare providers, receptionists, and registered nurses were females.[26] At the other extreme, 90 percent of carpenters, auto mechanics, construction laborers, painters, truck drivers, and civil engineers were males. Clearly, occupational segregation by gender remains a major problem.

Table 4: Female-to-Male Average-Earnings Ratios for Employed White Workers in California (1959–1989)

Worker Categories	1959	1969	1979	1989
All Workers ($1,000 or More in Earnings)				
Unadjusted Earnings	44%	43%	48%	58%
Adjusted Earnings	43%	44%	50%	61%
Adjusted Hourly Earnings	62%	61%	63%	72%
Full-Time/Full-Year*				
Unadjusted Earnings	58%	60%	64%	66%
Adjusted Earnings	57%	56%	61%	70%
Adjusted Hourly Earnings	62%	61%	64%	74%

*35 or more hours per week, 50 or more weeks per year.

Source: Author's estimates based on PUMS data for 1960, 1970, 1980, and 1990.

Combating the Role of Discrimination

The previous two sections documented the magnitudes of and trends in racial and gender disparity in the private sector. It is difficult to determine precisely what proportion of the observed inequality is due to discrimination in the labor market.[27] Economic theories do not provide an unambiguous answer because economists are divided on this subject. Many believe that discrimination either does not exist or is of minor importance because competitive market forces eliminate practices based purely on racial and gender prejudices.[28] In the absence of perfect competitive conditions, there is still room for white male workers to demand and win favorable treatment and for employers to use biased information to screen applicants.[29]

Even if one accepts that racism and sexism affect labor-market outcomes, there remains the question of how these prejudices and institutional practices operate. The foregoing empirical analysis reveals that factors outside the labor market (such as age composition, educational attainment, and variation in labor-market attachment) contribute to group differences. Controlling for these factors reduces the size of the unexplained portion of the racial and gender gap. There are likely to be other factors that can further reduce this residual. For example, when differences in the quality of education and performance on standardized tests, which vary systematically across groups, are included in the analysis, more of the disparity can be explained.[30] Similarly, including the sex composition of occupations reduces the size of the unexplained gender gap.[31]

Using more variables to reduce the size of the unexplained residuals, however, is not the same as saying that racism and sexism do not exist. Such analysis only points to other possible sources of inequality. This certainly is the case for education.[32] Minorities, particularly African Americans and Hispanics, receive not only fewer years of schooling but also a poorer education than whites because the educational system throughout this country has remained segregated and unequal, despite limited progress since *Brown v. The Board of Education*.[33]

Changes in macroeconomic conditions can also contribute to maintaining or increasing inequality. Recent structural shifts in demand, for example, have hurt African American progress.[34] Increased product competition from low-wage countries and the inflow of a significant number of low-skilled immigrants have put greater wage pressure on those with limited skills and formal education.[35] There has also been a decline in the effectiveness of unionism.[36] As a consequence of these and other structural changes, economic inequality has increased, for the U.S., California, and metropolitan areas such as Los Angeles.[37] Because minorities are disproportionately concentrated in the most adversely impacted sectors, they have experienced a larger share of the increased downward market pressures on employment and wages.[38] However, the inequality associated with macroeconomic changes should not be viewed as being generated solely by exogenous forces: Past and current race-based employment practices have concentrated minorities in these economically vulnerable sectors.[39]

While we cannot determine precisely how much of the racial and gender inequality is due to discriminatory employment practices, there is little doubt that such practices do exist.[40] There is certainly evidence of continued discrimination in this country. For example, audit studies, which send in equally qualified whites and minorities to apply for the same jobs, show that employers are less likely to interview and hire minority applicants.[41] Firms are also likely to have recruitment practices that avoid minority areas, particularly those in the inner city.[42] In Los Angeles, field interviews reveal that many employers hold negative stereotypes of minorities, and of blacks in particular.[43] Another source of evidence comes from the investigations undertaken by California's FEPC and its associated administrative agency, the Department of Fair Employment and Housing (DFEH). These agencies investigate charges of race-based and gender-based discriminatory employment practices and seek settlements for valid claims. The numerous examples summarized in the earlier FEPC annual reports illustrate both individual acts of discrimination and biased institutional practices. The question, then, is not one of whether discriminatory practices exist, but of the prevalence of discriminatory practices, and how the prevalence changed over time.

The individual complaints filed with the FEPC/DFEH and the number of settlements provide a partial answer to this question. Ideally, these data provide us with a measure of the extent of discrimination; however, the statistics should be viewed with some caution. The number of reported events for any given year is influenced by factors such as the willingness and ability of individuals to pursue claims, the receptiveness and resources of the FEPC/DFEH, and the broader social and political climate. These either encourage individuals to file or discourage them from filing; they also affect the likelihood of the commission acting on these claims. Despite the limitations, the data show that a large number of minorities and women believe that they have been discriminated against. The trend since 1960, when the data were first available, exhibits a general secular rise, with periods when the numbers were either stagnant or declining. Figure 3 plots the number of new claims filed because of alleged discrimination based on race/ancestry or gender.[44]

For those filing discrimination charges based on race or ancestry, the numbers increased throughout most of the first two decades, reaching 3,588 claims in 1980–81.[45] The numbers declined in the early 1980s to a nadir of 2,318 in 1985–86. Two factors probably contributed to the decrease. There may be a substitution effect because women of color could file a claim based on either race or sex discrimination in this period. (In the prior period, all complaints by women of color has been filed as a claim based on race.) During this period the number of complaints based on gender discrimination increased rapidly, and at the same time funding for the FEPC/DFEH did not increase. (The latter point is discussed below.) Regardless of the problems, the decline was transitional. In the late 1980s, the number of race- and ancestry-based charges started to increase, and then accelerated to a historical high of 6,467 in 1995–96.

The FEPC/DFEH started receiving complaints based on gender-based discriminatory practices in 1970–71, when the state's law was amended to allow for such actions.[46] By 1983–84, the number of gender-based complaints surpassed that of race-based complaints (2,859 and 2,657, respectively), and by the late 1980s gender-based complaints outnumbered race-based complaints. In 1995–96, the number stood at 8,014.

The number of settlements is another indication of the relative prevalence of discriminatory employment acts. A settlement occurs when the FEPC/DFEH finds that a claim has validity and when both parties are willing to enter into an agreement to rectify a wrong through actions such as hiring, rehiring, promotion, pay increase, and awarding of back pay. Figure 4 plots the basic data.[47] It should be noted that the series is not consistent over time. In 1975–76, the annual reports added a category denoting cases that were disposed of through court action. According to the reported statistics, the number of settlements grew throughout most of the first two decades after the FEPC/DFEH was established.

There was a noticeable drop in the number of settlements from 1974–75 to 1976–77. The reason for this decline appears to have been a lack of adequate resources. While the number of new complaints

Figure 3: Annual Number of Race- and Gender-Based Complaints to California's Fair Employment Practices Commission (1960–1966)

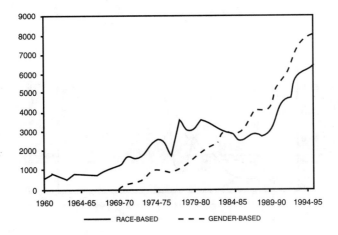

Source: Annual reports, State of California Fair Employment Commission.

increased by 237 percent from 1968–69 to 1974–75, FEPC/DFEH funding in constant dollars increased by only 61 percent. Normalizing funding by the number of new claims shows that resources declined by approximately two-thirds. As a consequence of these developments, the FEPC/DFEH developed a sizable backlog of unsettled cases. From 1971–72 to 1973–74, the number of active cases jumped from 3,434 to 6,373, and continued to climb, reaching 13,300 by 1977–78. The growing numbers indicate that a funding-constrained FEPC/DFEH was overwhelmed by the escalating number of new complaints, and this impaired the organization's ability to settle cases. The increase in the budget starting in the mid-1970s, as seen in Figure 4, along with an internal reorganization and expansion of the staff in 1976–77, eventually allowed the FEPC/DFEH to reduce the number of active cases. While the funding per new complaint did not reach the level of the mid-1960s, the FEPC/DFEH probably gained some efficiencies and effectiveness through economies of scale. There certainly was enough renewed vitality that the FEPC/DFEH was able to reduce the backlog and win an increasing number of settlements. By 1981–82, the number of settlements reached an all-time high of 2,284.

Unfortunately, the budget stopped growing in the early 1980s, and actually declined in real dollars. From 1980–81 to 1992–93, funding fell by 33 percent. This decline in resources may account for the decrease in the number of settlements, which dropped to the 1,800 to 2,000 range for much of the 1980s. The 1990s were no better, and in fact, the number of settlements dropped over a third to the 1,110 to 1,200 range. The drop in FEPC/DFEH settlements is not due to lack of complaints, which increased during much

Figure 4: Number of Settlements of Race- and Gender-Based Claims, and Funding of California's Department of Fair Employment and Housing (1960–1996)

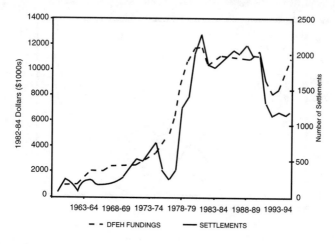

Source: Annual reports, State of California Fair Employment Commission; annual California Governor's Budget.

of this period, particularly in the 1990s. As indicated by the events in the 1970s, funding is a crucial determinant of the FEPC/DFEH's effectiveness. By the early 1990s, funding per new complaint was at only one-third of its level during the late 1970s and only one-quarter of its level during the mid-1960s. During this most recent period of limited funding, the FEPC/DFEH has failed to fulfill its obligation to investigate and resolve complaints in a timely manner, according to a report by the state auditor.[48] Given the resource constraints on the FEPC/DFEH, many complainants sought other avenues for remedies. In 1981–82, only 555 claimants elected to seek relief through the courts. A decade later, 3,756 did. For the most recent year for which we have data (1995–96), 8,944 individuals initiated court actions.

Conclusion

For most of the post–World War II era, California has been blessed with a growing economy, which has generated jobs for an increasingly diverse labor force. Despite an extremely severe and protracted recession during the early 1990s, California is once again seeing better days. Unfortunately, racial and gender disparities in wages and earnings persist. We are at a crossroads about what should be done to alleviate these disparities. Voter approval of Proposition 209, for example, represents a growing doubt about the efficacy of programs that were depicted by the proposition's proponents as giving unfair preferences to minorities and women at the expense of white men. Resentment, too, may play a part: There is some evidence that white men believe that they have been victims of reverse discrimination. The FEPC data show an increase in the number of race-based complaints filed by whites, most of which are probably filed by white men since there is a separate category for gender-based complaints. By 1995–96, there were 635 such complaints statewide.

There are, however, two important points to note. First, complaints by white men are not a recent phenomenon. The number of white claims has increased steadily ever since FEPC's establishment, with fluctuations that reflect the business cycle. If there are "angry white men," they have been with us for a long time. Second, the relative number of claims by white men is low. In 1980–81, 3.5 percent of all claims were filed by whites. If discrimination against this group has become more prevalent over the subsequent 15 years, we would expect the relative share to be larger, especially given the current political climate, in which it is more acceptable to claim to be a victimized white man. In 1995–96, 3.7 percent of all claims were filed by whites—hardly the figure one would expect based on the heightened discussion of this issue in political forums and the media.

Trends in funding for the FEPC/DFEH are troubling in light of continued racial and gender disparities and discrimination. Most Californians, including a number of those opposing affirmative action, acknowledge the need to fight discriminatory practices and to ensure "real" equal opportunity. Unfortunately, achieving this goal will not be easy, given the recent history of reduced state support for enforcement of antidiscrimination laws. The FEPC/DFEH's core mission is to fight discriminatory employment practices, but its capacity has been weakened seriously since the early 1980s, with resources reaching a historic low during the 1990s. A state constitutional prohibition against race-, gender-, or national origin–based affirmative action programs would continue this trend of further limiting remedies for racial and gender inequality and discrimination in the labor market.

Notes

1. In this paper, "race" refers to non-Hispanic whites, African Americans, Hispanics, and Asian Americans. For convenience, the terms whites and non-Hispanic whites are used interchangeably.

2. For convenience, "Fair Employment Practices Commission" refers to the commission as well as to the Department of Fair Employment and Housing, which carries out the commission's day-to-day operations. See Chapter 2 for a history of the commission and the department. The data on complaints of employment

discrimination come primarily from the published annual FEPC reports. Data for the 1990s come from unpublished departmental fact sheets.

3. These estimates are based on data from the Public Use Micro Samples (PUMS) for the 1960, 1970, 1980, and 1990 decennial censuses (U.S. Department of Commerce, Bureau of the Census, Census of Population and Housing) and the March 1995 Current Population Survey (U.S. Department of Commerce, Bureau of the Census). The 1 percent PUMS was used for 1960; two 1 percent PUMS were used for 1970, thus creating a combined 2 percent sample; and the 5 percent PUMS were used for 1980 and 1990. The data for 1940 and 1950 are taken from Ong, Chapa, Schink, et al.,"Socio-Economic Trends in California" (Sacramento: California Employment Development Department, 1986). There are inconsistencies across decades. For example, the earlier censuses included individuals as young as 14 years of age in the labor-force counts, but later censuses raised the age limit to 16 years of age. Despite these differences, the numbers do provide a reasonable overview of long-term trends.

4. The national figure is based on statistics reported in the "Economic Report of the President" (1996).

5. The figures for the reporting years are 10.4 percent in 1960, 9.1 percent in 1970, 9.7 percent in 1980, 10.9 percent in 1990, and 10.1 percent in 1995.

6. These figures are for 1970, 1980, and 1990 only.

7. The groups are created by using two variables: race and Hispanic origin. To develop exclusive categories, the following rule is used: All African Americans and Asian Americans are classified by their racial categories without regard to Hispanic origins; the Hispanic category includes those of Hispanic origin who are either white or other by race. The dominant group is defined as non-Hispanic whites, which includes all whites who are not of Hispanic origin. In the vernacular, this group is also known as Anglos. It should be noted that the definition for Hispanic origin changed in 1970. In 1960, this group included persons with a Spanish surname. In 1970, the census used the Spanish-surname category and Spanish-origin category, which included people who self-identify as Mexican, Puerto Rican, Cuban, Central or South American, or other Spanish. Spanish descent is available for only one of the 1970 1 percent PUMS. Our combined 2 percent sample includes both categories. For 1980, 1990, and 1995, Spanish origin is used. The Asian American category has also changed over time to encompass more Asian ethnic populations and Pacific Islanders.

8. The March 1995 CPS is based on a relatively small sample. The total number of employed civilians in the sample is 5,694 persons, of which 9.5 percent are Asian/Pacific Islanders. When the CPS weights are used to derive estimates of all employed civilians, that percentage declines to 8.4 percent. Unlike the weights in the PUMS, which are based on the census, the CPS weights are based on estimates of the 1995 population. We suspect that the weights are outdated and too low for Asian/Pacific Islanders; thus the estimate for this group is artificially low. Based on past population trends, it is likely the real figure is closer to 10 percent.

9. See comments in note 8.

10. California's female share in 1995 was slightly lower than the national figure, probably because of the relatively larger number of Latinas, who tend to have a lower labor-force participation rate than other racial groups.

11. The findings presented in this paper are consistent with those reported by Martin Carnoy and Richard Rothstein ("Hard Lessons in California: Minority Pay Gap Widens Despite More Schooling, Higher Scores" [Working paper of the Economic Policy Institute: Washington, DC, 1996]). That study examines the "minority pay gap" in California for the period from 1979 to 1995, using a different criterion for their sample. For the early 1990s, they find no evidence of a closing of the gap, and in some cases, even a growing gap.

12. Francine Blau and Lawrence Kahn, "Rising Wage Inequality and the U.S. Gender Gap," *American Economic Review* 84 (2): 23–28 (1994); Martin Carnoy, *Faded Dreams: The Politics and Economics of Race in America* (Cambridge, England: Cambridge University Press, 1996); Gregory DeFreitas, *Inequality at Work: Hispanics in the U.S. Labor Force* (New York: Oxford University Press, 1991); Claudia Goldin, *Understanding the Gender Gap: An Economic History of American Women* (New York: Oxford University Press, 1990); Jonathan Leonard, "Wage Disparities and Affirmative Action in the 1980s," *American Economic Review* 86 (2): 285–289 (1996); James Smith and Finis Welch, "Black Economic Progress After Myrdal," *Journal of Economic Literature* 27: 519–564 (1989).

13. The primary criterion used to identify individuals in the private sector is class. Although all four censuses identify those employed in the private sector, only the 1990 census differentiated between the for-profit and nonprofit sectors. For greater consistency across decades, industries dominated by nonprofit employers are excluded: educational institutions, libraries, residential care facilities, social services, museums, art galleries, zoos, labor unions, religious organizations, and membership organizations.

14. Earnings data are for the year prior to the decennial census. Only income from paid employment is used. For 1969 and 1959, income data are recorded in hundreds of dollars. Current values are translated into constant 1989 dollars using the CPI-U index. The average hourly wage is estimated by dividing annual earnings by the total number of hours worked in the prior year. The 1980 and 1990 PUMS report the exact number of weeks worked and average hours per week for the prior year. The 1960 and 1970 PUMS report the number of weeks worked by categories, and the midpoints are used in the calculations. For these last two PUMS, only the number of hours worked in the week prior to the enumeration was collected, and the data are reported by category. The midpoints are used as a proxy for the average hours worked in the prior year.

15. In these models, the log of earnings and the log of wages are dependent variables. The set of independent variables includes the years of schooling, potential years of labor-market experience, and its squared value. Potential years of labor-market experience is defined as age minus the years of schooling minus six. Dummy variables for the racial or gender categories are used to capture unexplained group effects. The models that examine the gender gap use the same set of independent variables. The models do not include the potential effects of geographic location, sample selection bias, family composition, and spousal income. Although it is desirable to use much more complex models, limited time and resources preclude such an effort for this report. There are substantial inconsistencies in the data across decades, and it would require a major effort to reconcile the differences so that the models would be consistent across census years.

Although the models used here are relatively simple, the findings for men are consistent with models that include additional independent variables (geographic location and family characteristics) and that allow for group-specific returns to education and experience. See, for example, Paul Ong, "Uncertain Economic Progress: Racial Inequality Among Californian Males, 1940–1980," in Sucheng Chan, ed., *Income and Status Differences Between White and Minority Americans: A Persistent Inequality* (Queenston, Ontario: The Edwin Mellen Press, 1990), pp. 29–55. Moreover, the findings on trends in the gender gap for California are similar for those reported for the nation as a whole.

16. In neoclassical microeconomics, the prevailing wage under perfect competition is set at the equilibrium point where the supply curve of labor intersects the demand for labor. At this point, the wage is equal to the marginal monetized contribution of the last unit of labor. Even under imperfect competitive conditions, the wage level is tied to the marginal contribution of labor, although there is rent collected by either workers or employers, or both.

17. Racial disparity fluctuates over the business cycle, but this is not an issue in the analysis. All four years occurred during the expansionary part of the business cycle. The census does not collect information on nonwage benefits, such as health insurance and pension plans. In general, benefits became more common through the 1960s and early 1970s; however, there has been a retrenchment since the late 1970s. Not including benefits creates a downward bias in what can be observed as compensation; the effects on intergroup comparisons are less severe. In general, benefits are correlated with wages and earnings: higher-paid jobs are more likely to offer better benefits packages.

18. The geometric mean is the mean of the log of wages. This measure is widely used because wages do not exhibit a normal distribution, but the values of the log of wages do. The geometric mean is close to the median value. The log of wages is also used in economic analysis because returns to investments in human capital, like returns to investments in financial capital, should theoretically yield a proportionate return to an individual's investment, regardless of the size of that investment. Analysis based on the log of wages (and earnings) is consistent with this concept. Minority-to-white ratios are estimated by first taking the difference between the geometric means for two groups, and then calculating the exponential value of that difference.

19. The term "1970s" refers to the change between 1969 and 1979. Clearly, there are year-to-year changes that are not captured by decennial data. The term 1970s, and its equivalence for the other decades, should not be interpreted as literally meaning that the decade-to-decade change holds for every year.

20. There are exceptions to this societal rule. Historically, those with severe disabilities are exempt from these expectations. This attitude has become less pervasive, but they are still not subject to the norms applied to the able-bodied. There are also neighborhoods and communities where decades of poor and declining job opportunities have undermined the norm, and joblessness has become an accepted (although not necessarily desirable) part of life (William Wilson, *The Truly Disadvantaged: The Inner City, the Underclass, and Public Policy* [Chicago: University of Chicago Press, 1987]).

21. Jacob Mincer and Solomon Polachek, "Family Investments in Human Capital Earnings of Women," *Journal of Political Economy* 82: S76–S108 (1974).

22. William T. Bielby and James N. Baron, "A Woman's Place Is with Other Women: Sex Segregation Within Organizations," in Barbara F. Reskin, ed., *Sex Discrimination in the Workplace: Trends, Explanations, Remedies* (Washington, DC: National Academy Press, 1984); Goldin, *Understanding the Gender Gap*; Joyce P. Jacobsen, "Sex Segregation at Work: Trends and Predictions," *The Social Science Journal* 31 (2): 153–169 (1994); Ruth Milkman, *Gender at Work: The Dynamics of Job Segregation by Sex During World War II* (Urbana: University of Illinois Press, 1987).

23. Barbara R. Bergmann, "Occupational Segregation: Wages and Profits When Employers Discriminate by Race or Sex," *Easter Economic Journal* 1: (April/May 1974); Kevin C. Duncan and Mark J. Prus, "Starting Wages of Women in Female and Male Occupations: A Test of the Human Capital Explanation of Occupational Sex Segregation," *The Social Science Journal* 29 (4): 479–493 (1992); Paula England, "The Failure of Human Capital Theory to Explain Occupational Sex Segregation," *The Journal of Human Resources* 17 (3): (1982); Barbara F. Reskin and Heidi I. Hartmann, eds., *Women's Work, Men's Work: Sex Segregation on the Job* (Washington, DC: National Academy Press, 1986); Donald J. Treiman, and Heidi I. Hartmann, eds., *Women, Work, and Wages: Equal Pay for Jobs of Equal Value* (Washington, DC: National Academy Press, 1981).

24. This comparison underestimates the gender difference at any one point in time because the percentages are based on workers. Since the labor-force participation rate for women is lower, the overall proportion of all working-age women who worked FT/FY is considerably lower than the comparable proportion of all working-age men. On the other hand, since there has been a secular increase in the female participation rate, the gender gap in FT/FY among all working-age people has declined more sharply than indicated by the comparison.

25. The analysis is based on the occupational categories reported in the 1970 and 1990 Public Use Micro Samples for California. The gender composition of an occupation is based on all employed females as a percent of all employed persons. The extent of occupational segregation may be even higher than the figures reported in the text because the statistics are based on broad occupational categories that can obscure higher levels of segregation among subcategories and among firms for the same occupation.

26. In 1970, 30 percent of non-Hispanic white women were in an occupation where females comprised at least 90 percent of the workforce; in 1990, 17 percent of non-Hispanic white women were in an occupation where females comprised at least 90 percent of the workforce.

27. The source of the inequality is crucial in the policy debate. Sources outside the labor market, such as inequality in educational opportunity, point to policies to improve public institutions such as public schools. Inequalities generated by discriminatory policies within the labor market, however, point to policies covering hirings, promotion, and pay. It is the author's opinion that both discrimination from sources outside the labor market and labor-market discrimination exist at a level such that both types of policies are warranted.

28. For the seminal work on this, see Gary Becker, *The Economics of Discrimination* (2nd ed.) (Chicago: The University of Chicago Press, 1971).

29. For an internal labor-market explanation, see Peter Doeringer and Michael Piore, *Internal Labor Markets and Manpower Analysis* (Lexington, MA: Health

Lexington Books, 1971); for a job queue model, see Lester Thurow, *Poverty and Discrimination* (Washington, DC: The Brookings Institution, 1969); for a statistical discrimination model, see Edmund Phelps, "The Statistical Theory of Racism and Sexism," *American Economic Review* 62: 659–661 (1972).

30. David Card and Alan Krueger, "School Quality and Black-White Relative Earnings: A Direct Assessment," *Quarterly Journal of Economics* CVII (1): 151–200 (1992); Bill Rodgers, "What Does the AFQT Really Measure: Race, Wages, Schooling and the AFQT Score" (Unpublished manuscript, Department of Economics, College of William and Mary, 1994).

31. Treiman and Hartmann, *Women, Work, and Wages*; Evelyn Blumenberg, "Gender Politics, Local Labor Markets, and Women's Economic Status: The Case of Comparable Worth" (Ph.D. dissertation, Department of Urban Planning, UCLA, 1995).

32. Another potential factor is occupational segregation. Moreover, the sex composition of occupations is itself partially a product of sexist views of gender roles in the workplace.

33. Gary Orfield, Susan Eaton, and the Harvard Project on School Desegregation, *Dismantling Desegregation: The Quiet Reversal of* Brown v. Board of Education (New York: New Press, 1996).

34. Chinhui Juhn, Kevin M. Murphy, and Brooks Pierce, "Accounting for the Slowdown in Black-White Convergence," in M. Kosters, ed., *Workers and Their Wages* (Washington, DC: AEI Press, 1991), pp. 107–143.

35. Robert H Topel, "Regional Trends in Wage Inequality," *American Economic Review* 84: 17–22 (1994).

36. David G. Blanchflower and Richard B. Freeman, "Unionism in the United States and Other Advanced OECD Countries," *Industrial Relations* 31 (1): 56–79 (1992); Richard B. Freeman and James L. Medoff, *What Do Unions Do?* (New York: Basic Books, 1984).

37. Bennett Harrison and Barry Bluestone, *The Great U-Turn: Corporate Restructuring and the Polarizing of America* (New York: Basic Books, 1988); Frank Levy and Richard J. Murnane, "U.S. Earnings Levels and Earnings Inequality: A Review of Recent Trends and Proposed Explanation," *Journal of Economic Literature* 30 (3): 1333–1381 (1992); Paul Ong and Evelyn Blumenberg, "Income and Racial Inequality in Los Angeles," in Allen Scott and Edward Soja, eds., *The City: Los Angeles and Urban Theory at the End of the Twentieth Century* (Los Angeles: University of California Press, 1996), pp. 311–335; Deborah Reed, Melissa Glenn Haber, and Laura Mameesh, *The Distribution of Income in California* (San Francisco: Public Policy Institute of California, 1996).

38. George J. Borjas, Richard B. Freeman, and Lawrence F. Katz, "On the Labor Market Effects of Immigration and Trade," in George J. Borjas and Richard B. Freeman, eds., *Immigration and the Workforce: Economic Consequences for the United States and Source Areas* (Chicago: University of Chicago Press, 1992), pp. 213–244; Howard Wial, "Immigration and the Distribution of Earnings" (Washington, DC: U.S. Department of Labor, Immigration Policy and Research Working Paper Series, 1994).

39. Paul Ong and Abel Valenzuela, "The Labor Market: Immigrant Effects and Racial Disparities," in Roger Waldinger and Mehdi Bozorgehm, eds., *Ethnic Los Angeles* (New York: Russell Sage Foundation, 1996), pp. 165–191.

40. In fact, a large majority of Californians registered to vote believe that "discrimination is still common," and only a small minority believe otherwise. The data here are from a *Los Angeles Times* survey reported in an article by Dan Morain, September 19, 1996, p. A1 ("The Times Poll: 60% of State's Voters Say They Back Prop. 209"). The survey asked questions regarding opinions on Proposition 209. The responses indicate that 41 percent believe that "discrimination is still common, but affirmative action has simply gone on too long," and another 37 percent believe that "we need to continue affirmative action because discrimination is still common." Only 13 percent believe that "affirmative action is no longer needed because discrimination has been largely eliminated." While public opinion cannot be taken as evidence of reality, these opinions are important in shaping public policy.

41. David Neumark, Roy Blank, and Kyle Van Nort, "Sex Discrimination in Restaurant Hiring: An Audit Study" (Cambridge, MA: National Bureau of Economic Research, Working Paper No. 5024, 1995).

42. Joleen Kirschenmanand Kathryn Neckerman, " 'We'd Love to Hire Them, But . . .' ": The Meaning of Race for Employers," in Christopher Jencks and Paul Peterson, eds., *The Urban Underclass* (Washington, DC: The Brookings Institution, 1991), pp. 203–232.

43. Roger Waldinger, "Who Makes the Beds? Who Washes the Dishes? Black/Immigrant Competition Reassessed" (Unpublished manuscript, Department of Sociology, UCLA, 1992).

44. African Americans filed a vast majority of the race-based charges, and Hispanics filed a large majority of the ancestry-based charges. The race-based complaints include complaints by whites, but these have been excluded from the statistics reported in Figure 3. The issue of complaints by whites is addressed later in the text (see "Conclusion") Most of the complaints are against private-sector employers, although there are also complaints against governmental agencies. Unfortunately, those complaints cannot be separated out from most of the data. The number of claims filed against the state was limited, in large part because the state Personnel Board did not allow state workers to file charges through the FEPC/DFEH. The policy was in effect until 1985, when the California Supreme Court ruled that the state Personnel Board did not have the authority to impose such a prohibition.

45. In their reports, the FEPC/DFEH does not break down race- and ancestry-based complaints by gender. Minority men might file a disproportionate share of the complaints because minority women can file either a race-based complaint or a gender-based complaint, depending on the nature of the perceived problem.

46. The published FEPC/DFEH reports do not break down gender-based complaints by race. It should be noted that while minority women can file either a race-based or gender-based complaint, non-Hispanic white women are more likely to file a gender-based complaint.

47. Figure 4 uses two separate scales so that both sets of data can be displayed. The left scale denotes the number of settlements, and the right scale denotes the level of funding in constant dollars.

48. Ken Chavez, "Some Say State's Anti-Bias Law Not Working," *Sacramento Bee* (January 20, 1997), p. A1.

Chapter 4

The Impact of Affirmative Action on Public-Sector Employment in California, 1970–1990

M. V. Lee Badgett[1]

Assessing the potential impact of a dramatic change in public policy—such as the proposed elimination of affirmative action in public-sector employment in California if Proposition 209 is upheld in court—is a difficult task, requiring some prediction about the future behavior of individuals whose actions depend on a number of factors in addition to public policy. One way to approach the question is to look carefully at the history of recent affirmative action policy and its impact. Thus this study considers the impact of eliminating affirmative action on the race and gender composition of state and local employment in California by looking back at the apparent impact of *implementing* the affirmative action policy and using the past to predict the impact of *removing* the policy. In the context of this paper, affirmative action refers to the results-oriented efforts to eliminate discrimination in employment that federal regulations require for federal contractors according to Executive Order 11246, issued by President Johnson in 1965.

Employers in the public and private sectors have faced many of the same economic and social constraints over the last four decades. In particular, openly discriminatory practices that kept women and people of color out of certain jobs—generally the higher-paying, more stable, and more prestigious jobs—were common in both the public and private sectors at least into the 1960s. But as public opinion and public policy shifted toward a conviction that employment discrimination based on race and sex was wrong, employers were required to adjust their hiring and compensation practices.

Public-sector employers (outside the South, at least) were expected to adjust more quickly to a policy of nondiscrimination, and the first nondiscrimination policies applied only to the public sector, as discussed in the review of U.S. and California affirmative action policies, laws, and programs in Chapters 2 and 3. Federal-government policies had led the way toward the Civil Rights Act of 1964, which forbade race and sex discrimination in employment, and toward affirmative action. In 1941, President Franklin D. Roosevelt issued the first executive order forbidding racial discrimination in the federal government and by defense contractors. The combination of relatively early policy changes combined with the role of political pressure in shaping the public-sector workforce led to the expectation of greater gains for women and people of color in obtaining jobs in federal, state, and local government.

When the goals of nondiscrimination laws and policies were reinforced by affirmative action, which required not just the ending of discriminatory practices but also positive efforts to seek out qualified female and minority applicants, government employers were expected to carry out such efforts more vigorously, since government agencies were themselves responsible for enforcement of these policies. However, because public employers generally faced no competition in the provision of government goods and services, and because entrenched interests could succeed in monopolizing certain jobs for particular race and/or gender groups, some economists expected that government performance in equal employment opportunity hiring could, in fact, lag behind that of the private sector.[2]

This study begins with a review of economic and political-science studies of the impact of affirmative action and equal employment opportunity policies on public-sector employment. Overall, these studies clearly found that government employers tend to hire more women and people of color and to pay them more than do private-sector employers. But although public employers appear to have *better* hiring practices than private-sector employers, evidence remains that in the public sector women and people of color are still at a disadvantage compared to white men.

The remainder of the chapter looks specifically at California for evidence of the public employers' success in ending discrimination. Drawing on decennial census data, we examine the race and gender composition of state- and local-government employment for evidence of the impact of affirmative action. Much of the increase in public-sector hiring of women and people of color over the last two decades reflects big shifts in the composition of the workforce, which have also affected private-sector employment. In a closer comparison of the employment patterns of state and local employers with private employers in California, we find that the public sector is more likely than the private sector to hire women and men of color as well as white women, particularly in managerial and professional jobs. Since private employers often face less stringent requirements for conformity with equal employment opportunity laws (and perhaps more lenient enforcement of these requirements), differences in employment composition are probably at least partially the result of government employers' more active efforts to hire women and people of color.

The chapter concludes with a discussion of the likely impact of the elimination of current public-sector affirmative action programs: a reduction in public-sector employment opportunities for female and minority managers and professionals.

Existing Studies of Public-Sector Employment Patterns

Over the last three decades, economists and political scientists have analyzed federal, state, and local workforces for evidence of employment discrimination against women and people of color (often focusing on blacks). Using government personnel data, decennial census data, and monthly government surveys, these analysts have compared the workplace positions of people with similar education, experience, and other characteristics that tend to influence labor-market success to see if race, ethnicity, or gender matter over and above the more appropriate factors.

The findings from many different studies have been remarkably consistent, revealing racial and gender differences in incomes and employment patterns. In the federal sector, the earliest studies showed that women and nonwhites (the racial category used in those studies) earned less than men and whites, respectively.[3] More recent studies still reveal differences by race, ethnicity, and gender that are unexplained by differences in education and experience. Lewis, for instance, showed that among federal white-collar workers, white women, Asian American men and women, black men and women, and Latino men and women all earned less than white men with the same education, college major, age, and years of federal service.[4] Kim and Lewis found that Asian American men and women still face a "grade gap" in the civil-service structure compared to white men and women.[5] Studies of state-government employment, which have mainly examined the impact of gender, have found a similar pattern: Women earn less than men and are less likely to be employed in high-level positions.[6]

While the persistence of the disadvantaged position of women and people of color in public-sector employment can be discouraging, the picture is mitigated somewhat by two other perspectives. First, being a woman or a person of color is *less* disadvantageous in the public sector than in the private sector. In other words, although women and minorities in public-sector jobs earned less than white men, those wage differences were smaller than in the private sector.[7] Women who were state or local employees also fared better in earnings relative to white men than did their private-sector counterparts.[8] Using national data from 1979, Blank found that women were more likely to be in the state and local sector than comparable men, and nonwhite workers more likely to be in the federal sector than were comparable whites.[9]

Second, the positions of women and people of color in the public sector have improved, although some disadvantage remains. Several studies of white-collar and higher-grade federal employees found improvements over time. Kellough and Kay found a notable increase between 1962 and 1980 in the rate of white women's gains after affirmative action in the form of goals and timetables became federal policy, but no clear gain for black federal workers.[10] Studying a later period, 1976–1986, Lewis observed growing shares of white-collar federal jobs going to white, Asian American, Hispanic, and black women, as well as somewhat higher shares for minority men, with white women gaining the most.[11] And although he found salary gaps by race and gender that were not explained by differences in worker characteristics, the gaps declined over the decade studied. Lewis and Kim saw the gains for Asian American workers continue through 1992, and the grade differences between white and Asian American men largely disappear for those with college degrees.[12] White women's rapid gains were not completely matched by Asian American women's gains, however, and the position of Asian American women worsened relative to white women with comparable education.

Studies of state employment also document improvement for women and people of color over time. Kelly et al. compared career advancement among upper- and middle-level male and female managers. They found evidence that women advanced somewhat faster than did men, but far more men occupied elite positions. Women earned less than men in the 1970s and the 1980s, but the salary gap had closed a bit by the 1980s. In the California departments studied, women earned 60.4 percent of what men earned in 1975, but 74.3 percent in 1985.[13] Bullard and Wright compared male and female state-agency heads from 1964 to 1988. Women held more such positions in 1988 (18 percent compared to 2 percent in 1964), and salaries were almost equal.[14] Lewis and Nice documented a decline in occupational segregation by race and gender in state employment between 1981 and 1987.[15]

What were the factors that improved the position of women and people of color in the public sector? Borjas found that the race and gender composition of the "constituency" served by a federal agency was correlated with employment in the agency. Agencies serving mostly women, for instance, would hire more women. He also found that blacks were better represented in agencies that had responsibility for enforcing equal opportunity laws and provisions.[16] Kellough and Kay suggested that affirmative action policy mattered in the federal sector.[17] Lewis and Nice found that states with less conservative but more urban and better-educated populations had less segregation of minorities or white women into particular occupations.[18] Bullard and Wright found evidence that women were able to circumvent the glass ceiling in state government, and that female heads of agencies were more often appointed by governors than by independent boards.[19]

Those explanations all hint at the role of policy in reducing discrimination, which should have improved the position of women and people of color in the public sector. However, other analysts have suggested different interpretations of existing patterns and change. First, the unexplained differences in earnings and employment may not be evidence of discrimination requiring further policy attention. Some have argued that there might be unobserved differences between workers that matter for labor-market success and might be correlated with race or gender. For instance, if the quality of education provided for blacks or Latinos is poorer than that available to most whites, then blacks and whites could have the same years of education but very different sets of skills. So any difference that appears to be related to race is not discrimination in the labor market but in educational opportunity. However, some evidence suggests that these "unobserved differences" might not be very important in the public sector. Borjas found that the earnings disadvantage faced by women in federal agencies was closely correlated with the disadvantage for blacks. As Borjas pointed out, this correlation means that blacks and women are either both facing discrimination or lack similar unobserved skills. But it is difficult to attribute the wage differences to unobserved skill differentials, at least in terms of the usual explanation for those differences, given that white women typically attend the same schools as white men.[20]

Another possibility remains. Discrimination is almost always thought of as a "demand-side" issue. That is, employers choose employees based on race, ethnicity, or gender. An alternative interpretation, though, is that the differences seen in these surveys reflect some "supply-side" difference if workers in certain groups are more likely to seek employment in a particular sector. For instance, a black might prefer a government job over a private-sector job. Although employees' preferences for one sector over another might depend on certain characteristics of the job, such as the fact that government jobs are more stable, one has to propose a reason for thinking that members of a particular race and/or gender group would *systematically* value those factors more highly than people in other groups. The most logical explanation for the preference for public-sector employment among women and people of color is that they perceive or expect that they will be treated more fairly and will have greater opportunities for advancement than in the private sector. So even if this supply-side phenomenon does contribute to the patterns seen in the literature, we should think of it as linked to public employers' greater commitment to ending discrimination or promoting opportunities for women and people of color.

Furthermore, if the supply-side hypothesis is true, we would also expect to see lower relative wages for women and people of color in state and local government employment. The fact that we see higher public-sector wages for those groups, measured both as lower discrimination penalties (discussed earlier) and as higher earnings levels (see Chapter 1), suggests that a demand-side effect must be overwhelming changes in supply, pushing up wages even as more people enter the public sector.

To summarize, numerous studies have found the public sector more welcoming to women and people of color than the private sector in terms of wages and career advancement, providing a big incentive to seek jobs in the public sector. Almost all of the routes by which the public sector is said to have become more welcoming—political, ideological, or legal—involve affirmative action policy, either as a vehicle for change or indirectly as an impetus for change.

Public-Sector Employment in California

Two large gaps in the existing literature make it difficult to evaluate the potential impact of eliminating affirmative action programs in California. First, most of the studies on the impact of affirmative action and equal opportunity policies and on the representativeness of state workforces do not focus on specific states. This first issue might not be so serious were it not for the second problem: It is not clear what the impact of implementing affirmative action was on the race and gender composition of public-sector employment. To measure precisely the impact of a policy we must have a control group that is not subject to the policy to compare with the policy-affected employer. Studies of affirmative action in the private sector have compared companies that are federal contractors and are *required* to practice affirmative action with companies that are not contractors and are therefore not obliged to use affirmative action. (But even this comparison has problems—see Badgett and Hartmann.[21]) If we do not know how affirmative action has affected the composition of California public employment, we will have a hard time predicting the impact of removing affirmative action policies.

For the public sector, the closest thing to a control would be the composition of the workforce *before* affirmative action was implemented. As Thomas and Garrett discuss in Chapter 2, the state of California did not require its agencies to submit written affirmative action plans with hiring goals until Governor Reagan issued an executive order in 1974. Similarly, federal law did not include state and local governments in antidiscrimination law until 1972. Thus, if affirmative action policy is effective beyond a simple policy of nondiscrimination, then the main effects would have been seen in the 1970s. Of course, the problem is that other influences on employment change over time, too, such as the available labor supply and the occupational composition of the state's workforce. Also, detailed information on the composition of California's state and local government workforces is not available for every year.

The U.S. Census of Population, conducted every 10 years, provides the most detailed information on California residents, allowing a close look at public-sector employment. For this study, the data in the figures and table were drawn from the Public Use Micro Samples (PUMS) for the 1970, 1980, and 1990 censuses. The 1980 and 1990 samples represent 5 percent of California residents, and the 1970 sample, 1 percent. With the census data, we can compare individuals employed in the private sector with those employed in the public sector. For the most part, the focus here will be on private, state, and local employment, with employees of the state's higher-education institutions not included with other state employees since they are subject to different employment policies and systems. (Unfortunately, the census does not include data on specific departments of state and local employees.) The primary race/gender groups examined are white men and women, black men and women, Asian American men and women, and Latino men and women. The group of Native Americans and of those listing some other racial group on the census form are very small groups and so are left out of most calculations. (See the Appendix on page 100 for the construction of the race/ethnicity categories.)

The census data confirm several patterns in California that were found in the studies cited earlier. First, compared to the private sector, state and local employers were relatively big employers of certain protected groups. Figures 1A–1C present the race and gender composition of private-, state-, and local-sector employment in 1990. A comparison of the three pie charts shows that white women, black men, and black women made up a greater percentage of state and local employment than of private-sector employment. For example, 2.7 percent of private-sector workers were black women, while more than 6 percent of state and local workers were black women. Latina women and Asian American men and

Figures 1A–1C: California Employment Composition by Gender, Race/Ethnicity, and Sector (1990)

A

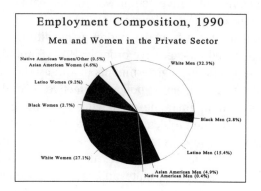

B

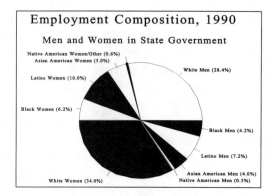

C

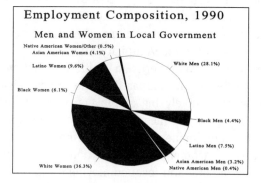

Source: Author's Calculations from PUMS data for 1990.

women were more evenly spread across the three sectors, while Latino men were much more likely to be in the private sector.

A second clear pattern concerns the dramatic change in the state and local workforces. White men's share of employment in state government dropped by 19 percentage points from 1970 to 1990 and by 11 percentage points in local government. White women's shares dropped also, but less dramatically. Latinos showed the greatest growth in the public sector, with men adding 4 percentage points and women almost 8 percentage points to their shares of state employment, with comparable gains in local government. Black women's share of state employment rose by 3 percentage points, and Asian American men and women gained steadily over the two decades as well.

Were these increases in public employment for women and people of color *purely* the result of affirmative action? Probably not, since we observe similar changes in private-sector employment: White men's share of private-sector employment fell by 18 percentage points from 1970 to 1990. Latino men and women gained 9 and 5 points, respectively. Asian American men and women more than doubled their small share of private-sector jobs. The similarities in changes across sectors suggest that either affirmative action was working across the board, or some other major factor occurred, such as a shift in the racial and ethnic composition of the labor force. Both scenarios are plausible, but the size of the shift requires a much larger structural change in the available labor force than could be accomplished simply from affirmative action. As Paul Ong discusses in Chapter 3, California's workforce has grown increasingly diverse in terms of race, ethnicity, and gender since World War II, with the growth of the Latino and Asian American workforce accelerating after 1970. Thus the simple change in public-sector employment composition over time is not very revealing about the impact of affirmative action.

Another way to think about the affirmative action efforts of state and local governments would be to compare them with those in the private-sector workforce. In the private sector, only firms with federal and/or state contracts are *required* to have affirmative action plans, including goals and timetables, but all private firms with more than five employees (15 according to federal law) are prohibited from discrimination based on sex or race. (Noncontractors are allowed and encouraged to have affirmative action plans.) All state- and local-government employers, however, must use affirmative action in hiring. One useful measure for a comparison of public- and private-sector workforces involves comparing a group's share of overall employment to its share of employment in a particular sector. For instance, in 1990 white men made up 31.8 percent of the workforce. They claimed 32.1 percent of private-sector employment but only 28.3 percent of state and 27.9 percent of local employment. A simple way of summarizing the representativeness of the sectors is to divide the sectoral employment share by the total employment share (see Dometrius and Sigelman[22]). Thus in 1990 white men had a "representativeness ratio" of 1.01 in the private sector and 0.89 and 0.88 in the state and local sectors, respectively. Ratios under 1 suggest underutilization of a group, and ratios over 1 suggest disproportionate hiring of a group.

Figure 2 plots the representativeness ratios for 1970, 1980, and 1990 for six race/gender groups, showing that the representativeness of sectors varies by group. Latino, white, and Asian American men were best represented in the private sector in all three censuses (white and Latino men are not shown; black men are shown in 2A). Black men, however, were best represented in local-government jobs, with representation in the state government increasing steadily over the two decades. For women, the private sector employed Latinas (Fig. 2E) and Asian American women (Fig. 2F) proportionately, but hired fewer than expected white women and black women. Representation of white women was high in state and local employment in all three censuses (Fig. 2C). Public-sector representativeness rose dramatically for Latinas and for black women (Fig. 2D) in the 1970s, with ratios approaching 2 for black women in 1990.

This overview of sectoral employment demonstrates that, compared to the private sector, state and local governments have a relatively heavy demand for women in general and for black men. Significant gains for black workers and for Latinas in the 1970s suggest some role for affirmative action, since changes in the overall labor-force composition are controlled for with the representativeness ratio and since the private sector faced the same shifts in labor-force composition.

Access to Managerial and Professional Jobs

Another important way of evaluating personnel practices for fairness involves studying access to higher-paying and more prestigious positions, such as managerial and professional jobs. Recent research attention to high-level jobs has asked whether women and people of color bump up against a glass ceiling in their career progress. While that term often refers to the highest levels of managerial jobs, access to *any* managerial or professional job is not to be taken for granted. Sometimes access is internal, as individuals move up job ladders into managerial positions; sometimes access is external, especially for professionals whose training qualifies them for a particular position. The literature cited earlier (see note 6) points out that women and people of color are still less likely to be in high-level positions than men or whites with the same characteristics. Again, for purposes

Figures 2A–2F: California Employment Representativeness Ratios by Gender, Race/Ethnicity, and Sector (1970–1990)

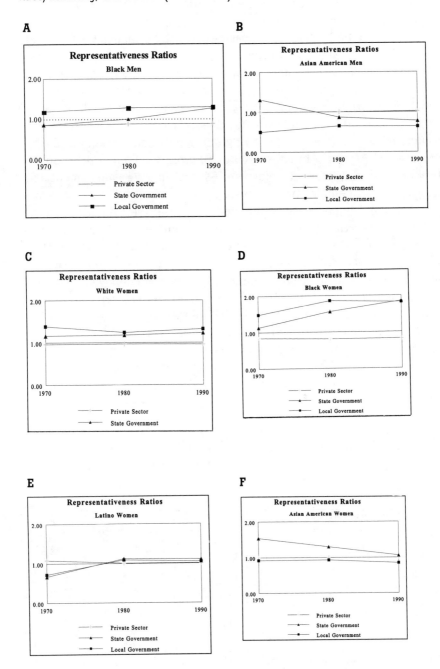

Source: Author's Calculations from PUMS data for 1970, 1980, and 1990.

of comparison, the private sector offers a scenario involving less enforcement and policy effort for promoting and hiring female and minority managers and professionals.

The representativeness ratio measure can also be applied here. Figures 3A–3H chart the ratios for managerial and professional hiring in each sector over time. The patterns are similar to the overall patterns. Among men, the state and local sectors employed black male managers and professionals at a higher rate than did the private sector—that is, black men's ratios in state and local employment exceeded 1—while the private sector was more likely to hire men in other groups. State and local governments also disproportionately hired women of all groups, although the ratio for Asian American women's employment fell to 1 in state employment and below 1 for local employment in 1990.

The ratios simply measure progress relative to the overall pattern of California employment, but give no sense of how women and people of color fare relative to others in the same sector. Since the base for the ratios is the group's overall percentage of managers and professionals in the labor force, systematic discrimination by all kinds of employers that lowers the total percentage of Latinas, for example, in managerial or professional jobs would not be reflected in the ratios.

Another angle on this question of access, then, is to ask whether employees with similar productive characteristics are treated similarly within each sector with regard to managerial or professional employment. If women or people of color are treated in the same way as white men,

Figures 3A–3B: California Professional/Managerial Employment Representativeness Ratios by Gender, Race/Ethnicity, and Sector (1970–1990)

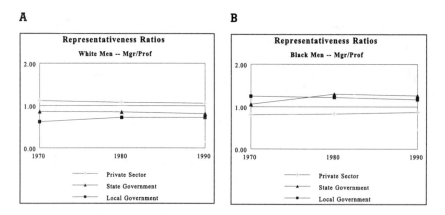

Source: Author's Calculations from PUMS data for 1970, 1980, and 1990.

Figures 3C–3H: California Professional/Managerial Employment Representative-ness Ratios by Gender, Race/Ethnicity, and Sector (1970–1990)

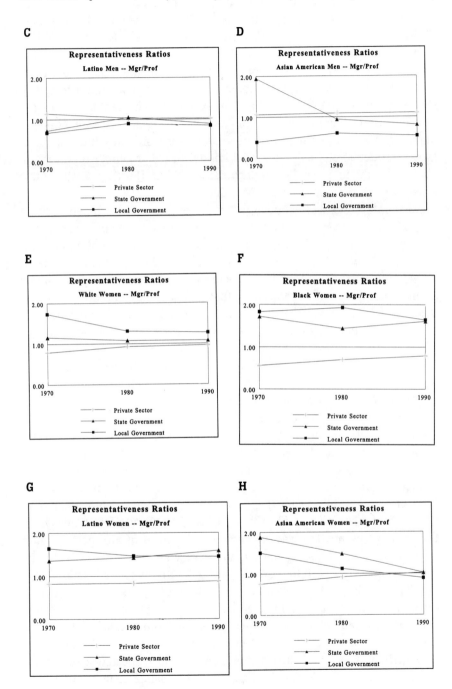

Source: Author's Calculations from PUMS data for 1970, 1980, and 1990.

then they should be as likely as white men to be in managerial or professional jobs when they have similar qualifications.

The census provides variables that are likely to be related to the qualifications and productivity of workers: education, age (which would be related to work experience), citizenship, marital status, English proficiency, and disability status. People with more education and experience, and without a work-limiting disability or limited English language ability, should be more likely to be in high-level jobs. The key test is to see whether controlling for these factors removes the effect of being female or minority. The statistical procedure that I used estimates the impact of those productive factors plus the individual's race or gender on the probability of being in a managerial or professional job. (Further details of this procedure are provided in the Appendix.)

Separate statistical models are used for men and women. Within which sector—the state and local sectors combined or the private sector—did women and men of color have more access to managerial and professional jobs? Table 1 shows the impact of being in a particular racial or ethnic group on the probability of being in a managerial or professional occupation. Each value represents the change in probability related to race. (The calculations are described in the Appendix.) For example, in 1970 a black man with some college experience was less likely than a white man with the same characteristics to have a managerial/professional job in the private sector; being black reduced his probability of having such a job by 3.5 percentage points. Black men in the state/local sector in 1970 were less disadvantaged, with only a 0.3 percentage-point drop in probability related to race.

In general, for both men and women of color, state-/local-sector employment presented fewer race-related barriers to managerial and professional jobs. For most groups and in most years, the race-related disadvantage was much smaller in the public sector than in the private sector. Over time, the public-sector disadvantage for women of color relative to white women shrank considerably and, as of 1990, was less than half of 1 percentage point. Both sectors show some impact of affirmative action for women of color, as the disadvantage grew smaller with each decade (except for 1970 to 1980 for Latinas), although the biggest reduction came in the 1970s. By 1990, race was all but irrelevant for determining women's access to professional and managerial jobs in the public sector. For men of color, the disadvantage was more stable, with some decline in the 1970s and a disturbing increase in the 1980s in both the public and private sectors. Perhaps this retrenchment for men of color reflected a decline in effort from President Reagan's Department of Justice in promoting affirmative action at the state and local levels in the 1980s.[23]

Table 1: Effect of Race on Probability of Being in a Managerial or Professional Job by Race/Ethnicity and Gender (1970–1990)

Ethnicity/ Gender	1970 Private	1970 State/ Local	1980 Private	1980 State/ Local	1990 Private	1990 State/ Local
Men						
Black	-0.035*	-0.003*	-0.023*	-0.004*	-0.027*	-0.015*
Latino	-0.031*	-0.002	-0.019*	-0.001	-0.029*	-0.005*
Asian American	-0.010*	-0.000	-0.013*	-0.002*	-0.017*	-0.012*
Women						
Black	-0.110*	-0.021*	-0.039*	-0.009*	-0.010*	-0.001*
Latina	-0.009*	-0.003	-0.048*	-0.006*	-0.015*	-0.000
Asian American	-0.126*	-0.055*	-0.066*	-0.045*	-0.020*	-0.004*

*Significantly different from zero at the 5 percent level.

Source: Author's calculations from PUMS data for 1970, 1980, and 1990.

While similar direct comparisons between white men and white women are not possible with these particular models, an indirect comparison shows a clear improvement in a white woman's chances of holding a managerial or professional job, given her sector of employment. (A direct comparison would use the statistical model on a combined sample of only white men and white women to see whether gender makes any difference.) In 1970, a 38-year-old married white woman with some college, English proficiency, U.S. citizenship, and no disability was 15 percent less likely than a white man with the same characteristics to be in a managerial or professional position in the private sector, but she was only 4 percent less likely to hold one in the public sector. White women's private-sector opportunities appeared to increase: By 1980 she was only 4 percent less likely to hold a managerial job, and by 1990 her chances were roughly equal. But in the public sector in 1990, this representative white woman was roughly 5 percent *more* likely than a similar white man to be in the top occupational category. Managerial and professional women have been in greater demand, and in demand for a longer period of time, in the public sector than in the private sector.

The Potential Impact of Eliminating
Public-Sector Affirmative Action Programs

Overall, the census data for California reveal several important features of public-sector employment in the state:

*   From 1970 to 1990, white, black, and Asian American women were overrepresented in state-government jobs and, except for Asian American women, in local-government jobs. From 1980 to 1990, Latinas also were overrepresented in the public sector. Among men, blacks were overrepresented in local government over these two decades, and in state government since 1980.

*   Overrepresentation of white, black, and Latina female managers and professionals was particularly pronounced in the public sector. Until 1990, Asian American female managers and professionals were also overrepresented in the public sector.

*   More detailed comparisons within the private and public sectors (Table 1) suggest that women and men of color have greater access to managerial and professional jobs in the public sector, where they also face less race-related disadvantage than do their white counterparts with similar productive characteristics.

*   In the 1980s, men of color lost ground as they became less likely to be managers or professionals in the public sector compared to similarly qualified white men (Table 1).

*   White women appear to have been in greater demand for managerial and professional jobs in the public sector than have white men.

What do these comparisons suggest about the impact of the potential elimination of public-sector affirmative action programs in California? The answer depends first on the role of affirmative action in enhancing opportunities for women and people of color in the public sector, and second on the response of government employers to the removal of those affirmative action policies.

Several factors related to the timing of the gains of some race/gender groups suggest that affirmative action influenced the composition of the public-sector workforce. After the state and federal governments began to require affirmative action plans of state and local agencies in the early 1970s, the representation of Latina and black women increased dramatically (Figs. 2E and 2D). Also, access to managerial and professional jobs (after adjusting for individual characteristics) increased for women of color in the 1970s (although improvement was stronger for Asian American women in the 1980s) (Table 1). The different timing of effects for men and for women—with women of color continuing to gain in the 1980s while progress for men of color was reversed—is difficult to interpret. Perhaps more affirmative action attention was paid to women in the 1980s than to men, with some visible court cases upholding cases concerning affirmative action for women (e.g., *Johnson v. Transportation Agency of Santa Clara County*) and questioning some cases more closely related to men (e.g., *Firefighters Local Union No. 1794 v. Stotts*). In other words, perhaps women of color gained in the 1980s because of sex-related affirmative action rather than race-related affirmative action.

The other reason to suspect that affirmative action had an effect relates to the finding of greater public-sector access for women of color and some men of color relative to the private sector. As noted earlier, only some private-sector firms are required to have affirmative action plans. The greater access to all public-sector jobs for women in general and for higher-level positions in particular (which perhaps best measures an employer's commitment to affirmative action) compared to the private sector suggests some difference on the employer-demand side of the labor market rather than on the supply side, a difference that both sectors potentially share.

In thinking, then, about how the elimination of public-sector affirmative action programs would be likely to affect the race and gender composition of public-sector employment in California, the private sector might provide the best guide. Two possible scenarios emerge. First, the enactment of Proposition 209 could eliminate the strong results-oriented kind of affirmative action requirement for public employers, leaving public employers in a position similar to the private-sector firms that are not now federal contractors. Or second, if federal law requires the state—or, more likely, only some state agencies or departments—to practice some form of affirmative action, the state would be placed in the position of a federal contractor subject only to federal monitoring. The private-sector calculations in this study combine those employers who practice affirmative action along with those who do not, so those calculations are not a precise guide for either scenario. But both scenarios are likely to result in a reduced demand for women and people of color by the public sector, since one removes the affirmative action requirement and the other removes a level of enforcement and political accountability.

The effect of a reduction in demand depends on the overall state of the economy, the ability of the labor market to adjust, and the occupations of the individuals "displaced." Some female and minority group workers will probably shift toward the private sector either because they cannot obtain jobs in the public sector or because they no longer desire jobs in a public sector that does not practice affirmative action as it did previously. In a strong labor market with low unemployment, many of the workers who would have been employed in the public sector would be readily absorbed into the private sector, especially if some private-sector workers shift to the public sector. However, the shift for people of color and for women is likely to result in lower wages, as suggested by the preponderance of literature comparing wage gaps in the public and private sectors. Also, the statistical probability (probit) models from this study (see the appendix) suggest that some individuals who would have been hired for managerial or professional jobs in the public sector will not be able to obtain comparable jobs in the private sector, resulting in underemployment for some female and minority managers and professionals. Unfortunately, it would be unwise to predict how large these changes would be based on the census data. However, the direction of change—a loss of opportunities for women and people of color—is clear, even if the magnitude of the change is not.

Appendix

Data and Analytical Method

Coding of Race/Ethnic Groups
The U.S. Census uses two different ways of constructing racial and ethnic groups. All individuals are asked two questions, which varied somewhat on the three different censuses examined here. Basically, one question asks the respondent his or her race, and the other asks whether the respondent is of Hispanic origin. Thus people of Hispanic origin could be of any "race": white, black, Native American, Asian American, or "other." In fact, most people of Hispanic origin in California list "other" as their racial category. To create mutually exclusive groups for purposes of this analysis, all people of Hispanic origin who reported race as white or other were classified as Latino. All people of Hispanic origin of another racial category (black, Native American, or Asian American) were classified as belonging to the reported racial category.

Subsamples Used

Self-employed workers were excluded in all calculations. Figures 1 and 2 used data for all employed Californians in private, federal, state, and local sectors, even though all subgroups were not presented. Figures 3 and 4 and the probit equations for Table 1 did not include people in farming occupations and sales occupations, since very few of those workers are found in the public sector.

Use of Probit Procedure

The probit procedure is designed for use when the value of the dependent variable, or variable to be explained, is either 0 or 1. In this case, the dependent variable equals 1 when an individual is in a managerial or professional occupation within the sector, and 0 when an individual is in any other kind of occupation. The procedure is somewhat like a multiple regression procedure, in that it generates coefficients reflecting the influence of the independent variables on the probability of being in a managerial or professional job. The coefficients are not directly interpretable, however, requiring the use of some representative individual to serve as a baseline for calculating the impact of changes in the independent variables on the probability of being in a managerial or professional job. For this paper, the baseline person is of average age (which is a few years younger for private-sector workers), a U.S. citizen, proficient in English, nondisabled, and with some college experience. For further details on this procedure, see Maddala.[24]

The probit models were run on employed individuals in the three sectors, with people in sales and farm occupations excluded from the subsample to increase comparability. Full results are available from the author.

Notes

1. I would like to thank William Harris for research assistance, Paul Ong for help with the 1970 data, and Richard Robinson of CIESIN (Consortium for International Earth Science Information Network) for help with the 1980 and 1990 data.

2. Thomas Sowell, *Markets and Minorities* (New York: Basic Books, 1981).

3. George J. Borjas, "The Politics of Employment Discrimination in the Federal Bureaucracy," *Journal of Law and Economics* 25: 271–299 (1982); Arthur J. Corazzini, "Equality of Employment Opportunity in the Federal White-Collar Civil Service," *The Journal of Human Resources* 7 (4): 424–445 (1972); Mark R. Killingsworth and Cordelia W. Reimers, "Face, Ranking, Promotions, and Pay at a Federal Facility: A Logit Analysis," *Industrial and Labor Relations Review* 37 (1):

92–107 (1983); James E. Long, "Employment Discrimination in the Federal Sector," *The Journal of Human Resources* 11 (1): 86–97 (1976).

4. Gregory B. Lewis, "Progress Toward Racial and Sexual Equality in the Federal Civil Service?" *Public Administration Review* 48: 700–707 (1988).

5. Pan Suk Kim and Gregory B. Lewis, "Asian Americans in the Public Service: Success, Diversity, and Discrimination," *Public Administration Review* 54 (3): 285–291 (1994).

6. Angela M. Bullard and Deal S. Wright, "Circumventing the Glass Ceiling: Women Executives in American State Governments," *Public Administration Review* 53 (3): 189–202 (1993); Rita Mae Kelly, et al., "Public Managers in the States: A Comparison of Career Advancement by Sex," *Public Administration Review* 51 (5): 401–412 (1991); Sharon P. Smith, "Government Wage Differentials by Sex," *Journal of Human Resources* 11 (2): 185–199 (1976).

7. Smith, "Government Wage Differentials by Sex"; Long, "Discrimination in the Federal Sector"; Nelson C. Dometrius and Lee Sigelman, "Assessing Progress Toward Affirmative Action Goals in State and Local Government: A New Benchmark," *Public Administration Review* 44: 241–246 (1984).

8. Smith, "Government Wage Differentials by Sex."

9. Rebecca Blank, "An Analysis of Workers' Choice Between Employment in the Public and Private Sectors," *Industrial and Labor Relations Review* 38: 211–224 (1985).

10. James E. Kellough and Susan Ann Kay, "Affirmative Action in the Federal Bureaucracy: An Impact Assessment," *Review of Public Personnel Administration* 6 (2): 1–13 (1986).

11. Lewis, "Progress Toward Racial and Sexual Equality?"

12. Kim and Lewis, "Asian Americans in the Public Service."

13. Kelly et al., "Public Managers in the States."

14. Bullard and Wright, "Circumventing the Glass Ceiling."

15. Gregory B. Lewis and David Nice, "Race, Sex and Occupational Segregation in State and Local Governments," *American Review of Public Administration* 24 (4): 393–410 (1994).

16. Borjas, "Politics of Employment Discrimination."

17. Kellough and Kay, "Affirmative Action in the Federal Bureaucracy."

18. Lewis and Nice, "Race, Sex and Occupational Segregation."

19. Bullard and Wright, "Circumventing the Glass Ceiling."

20. George J. Borjas, "The Measurement of Race and Gender Wage Differentials: Evidence from the Federal Sector," *Industrial and Labor Relations Review* 37 (1): 79–91 (1983).

21. M. V. Lee Badgett and Heidi I. Hartmann, "The Effectiveness of Equal Employment Opportunity Policies," in Margaret Simms, ed., *Economic Perspectives on Affirmative Action* (Washington, DC: Joint Center for Political and Economic Studies, 1995).

22. Dometrius and Sigelman, "Assessing Progress."

23. Bureau of National Affairs, *Affirmative Action Today: A Legal and Practical Analysis* (Washington, DC, 1986).

24. G. S. Maddala, *Limited-Dependent and Qualitative Variables in Econometrics* (Cambridge: Cambridge University Press, 1983).

Chapter 5

Federal-Contractor Status and Minority Employment: A Case Study of California, 1979–1994

William M. Rodgers III

Affirmative action policies in employment date back to World War II initiatives developed during the Roosevelt administration. The measures were intended to induce the cessation of discriminatory practices in defense contracting.[1] In 1961, Kennedy's Executive Order 10925 further established standards for firms that did business with the federal government.[2] During that year, the OFCC (now the OFCCP) was created to address contract compliance in the public sector. However, it was not until Executive Order 11246, issued by President Johnson, that language satisfying antidiscrimination designs through affirmative action means was included. The language of President Johnson's Order was consistent with the mandate of Title VII of the Civil Rights Act of 1964.[3]

In 1969, the Nixon administration continued affirmative action efforts with the Philadelphia Plan. This plan required affirmative action measures for construction firms and unions with federal contracts and established precedents concerning executive domain over enforcement of antidiscrimination policies. The Philadelphia Plan, with its requirements for low bidders, became a precedent through its extension to all firms holding contracts with federal, state, and municipal governments. Its major contribution was the application of goals and timetables to achieve target levels of minority employment.[4] This plan would later apply to policies specific to the construction industry as well as to firms with government contracts in general.

These earlier efforts were political in nature and satisfied symbolic purposes rather than real goals. Though early affirmative action and anti-discrimination measures lacked teeth, they were the first steps toward addressing sensitive issues, exploring the underlying causes of discrimination, prompting voluntary action, and, most relevant to the context of this study, working to develop machinery that would be the roots for later policies.[5]

The ramifications of these early policies varied with the administrations following Nixon's. Since 1980, federal affirmative action programs have faced growing criticism. Responding to differential treatment of the issue by various states and municipalities, the Carter administration centralized the process of enforcement. In doing so, it weakened administrative efficacy in the short term. For ideological and budgetary considerations, the Reagan administration weakened the scope and size of antidiscrimination enforcement and affirmative action. Supreme Court appointments by Presidents Reagan and Bush created a conservative court that put further restrictions on voluntary actions and applications of affirmative action.[6] Though severely limited by judicial precedents and hampered by Republican budget allocations, the Clinton administration has defended affirmative action and expanded the efforts of the OFCCP and EEOC.

Those opposing such programs argue that the federal Civil Rights Act of 1964 has been distorted into government-sanctioned discrimination. Legislation is therefore needed to prevent state and local governments from discriminating against or granting preferential treatment to any individual or group on the basis of race, sex, color, ethnicity, or national origin in public employment, public education, or public contracting. One potentially controversial program in the area of public contracting is the federal government's use of Executive Order 11246 (issued by President Johnson in 1965) to award contracts to firms who agree to develop affirmative action plans that increase their applicant pools and employment of minorities and women. The intended effect is to increase minority and female employment in establishments that have such contracts, and a potential indirect effect is to increase the product and labor-market competition faced by firms with lower minority and female representation.

There is an absence of detailed information on the impact of this policy because the federal government has cut resources devoted to monitoring the effort of public contractors. This decline, which started in the early 1980s, is consistent with the findings reported by Leonard[7] and Anderson[8] that document a sharp fall in federal enforcement activity since the first Reagan administration. They are also consistent with the results in Rodgers and Spriggs,[9] which found that federal-contractor status contributed more to improving the representation of nonwhite workers in firms *after* the Reagan administration than it did during that administration.

The aim of this chapter is to specify the impact of federal-contractor status on the participation of minorities and women in the national workforce in California, based on Rodgers and Spriggs' model.[10] However, this chapter focuses exclusively on examining the ability of federal-contractor status to explain racial and ethnic differences in California's employment patterns at the business-establishment level. I compare the racial, ethnic, and gender employment distributions of contractor and noncontractor establishments contained in the state's Employer Information Report EEO-1 files. The evidence suggests that contractor status continues to contribute positively to improving the representation of California's nonwhite workers. Along with contractor status, the results show that an establishment's county of location, major industry, and occupational structure influence the ethnic/racial composition of its workforce. Most of these factors contribute more to explaining the variation in the workforce than does contract status. The comparison between the United States and California drives home the importance of state-level studies because, as will be demonstrated, California's racial and ethnic labor market differs from the national aggregate.

The chapter is organized as follows: The next two sections describe the data about California federal contractors and provide a set of stylized facts—an overview culled from the data—about the impact of federal contracting in California on the employment shares of different ethnic/racial groups between 1979 and 1994. The final two sections respectively report the results of a regression analysis (the methodology is described in the Appendix) and provide an interpretation of the results and a conclusion.[11]

The Data

Data for this study come from the U.S. Department of Labor, Office of Federal Contract Compliance Programs, and Employer Information Report EEO-1 files for selected years from 1979 to 1994.[12] This period was selected on the basis of the overall condition of the U.S. and California economies across two comparable business cycles. In 1979 and 1989, the state and national economies were at similar points in the business cycle. The state and national unemployment rates had reached their lowest points in the cycle: California's unemployment rates in 1979 and 1989 were 6.2 percent and 5.1 percent, respectively, and the national unemployment rates were 5.8 percent and 5.3 percent. The data for 1982 and 1992 capture the effects of each recession. Both California's and the nation's unemployment rates had reached their peaks in these years.[13] Finally, the data for 1984, 1988, and 1994 capture the California economy during each recovery.

The EEO-1 files include private establishments that are required to file an annual report, which contains information on the racial, ethnic, and gender distribution of an establishment's labor force. All establishments with at least 100 employees are required to file a report. Establishments with at least 50 employees are required to file if they fall into one of the following categories: establishments that are federal contractors, establishments that are first-tier subcontractors (direct subcontractors to the primary federal contractor) and have at least $50,000 in contracts, or establishments that act as a depository of federal funds in any amount or as an issuing and paying agent for U.S. Savings Bonds and Notes. Before 1983, the minimum establishment size for contractors was 25 employees. To maintain comparability across years, I excluded establishments with fewer than 50 employees in the years prior to 1983.[14] Because of the criteria for reporting, the EEO-1 files do not include all private establishments. A comparison with data from the Bureau of Labor Statistics indicates that the employment reported in the EEO-1 files covers less than half of total private-sector employment, with variations across years and industrial sectors. At the national level, the coverage rates typically range from 40 to 50 percent. The coverage rates for California are lower, averaging between 36 and 37 percent of total private employment in this state for the study period. The rates for California vary considerably across industrial sectors, from a high of 66 percent for transportation to a low of 9 percent for construction.

Several trends stand out in California's EEO-1 data. Panel A of Table 1 shows that after 1979 the fraction of California federal-contractor establishments reporting any Asian Americans (men or women) and Hispanic women increased significantly. The growth was distributed equally throughout the period from 1979 to 1994. The proportion of such establishments reporting at least one African American (man or woman) and one Hispanic man increased modestly. Panel B of Table 1 reports the presence of minorities in the headquarters of multiestablishment firms. The headquarters data exhibited patterns similar to those found in panel A for all establishments. For example, in the headquarters the greatest increase was shown by Asian Americans and Hispanic women. Compared to the national-level data in Rodgers and Spriggs[15] and Rodgers[16] that span from 1979 to 1992, the only major difference was in the proportion of establishments that reported at least one Asian American and one Hispanic. The changes in the proportions were quite similar to one another.[17]

Table 2 profiles the share of California employment for each racial, ethnic, and gender group. Among federal contractors, the most striking result was the decline in the whites' share of employment from 1979 to 1994: White men's share in establishments fell 8 percentage points; white women's, 5 percentage points. The employment shares of Asian Americans

Table 1: Percentage of California Establishments with Minority and Women Employees by Federal-Contractor and Noncontractor Status (1979–1994)

Race/ Ethnicity	1979 (%)	1982 (%)	1989 (%)	1992 (%)	1994 (%)	Percentage Point Change
PANEL A: ALL ESTABLISHMENTS						
Contractors						
Black Men	79	78	78	80	79	0
Black Women	67	69	70	73	71	4
Hispanic Men	91	90	92	93	93	2
Hispanic Women	84	85	89	90	91	7
Asian Men	74	76	80	85	85	11
Asian Women	64	69	74	78	79	15
Noncontractors						
Black Men	70	72	73	72	74	4
Black Women	63	65	69	67	69	6
Hispanic Men	88	90	91	93	94	6
Hispanic Women	83	87	90	92	93	10
Asian Men	68	72	76	77	78	10
Asian Women	66	69	74	75	76	10
PANEL B: HEADQUARTERS						
Contractors						
Black Men	65	66	62	62	63	-2
Black Women	68	71	65	66	66	-2
Hispanic Men	76	77	75	76	78	2
Hispanic Women	80	83	80	83	83	3
Asian Men	73	74	78	78	79	6
Asian Women	72	78	78	79	80	8
Noncontractors						
Black Men	55	57	57	57	58	3
Black Women	56	58	62	62	63	7
Hispanic Men	73	74	75	75	76	3
Hispanic Women	74	77	80	80	82	8
Asian Men	62	66	69	72	72	10
Asian Women	64	68	75	77	77	13

Source: Author's tabulations from the EEO-1 files.

and Hispanics increased by 3 to 4 percentage points. The shifts raised the Asian American share to approximately 5 percent of total employment, and the Hispanic male and female shares to just over 14 percent and 9 percent, respectively. The share of black employment remained at 3 to 4 percent.

Table 3 shows employment shares within the headquarters of multi-establishment firms in California. The employment share of white men among the contractor firms fell here also, while Asian American shares

Table 2: Percentage Share of California Employment Under Federal Contractors and Noncontractors by Race/Ethnicity and Gender (1979–1994)

PANEL A: MEN

Race/ Ethnicity	1979 (%)	1982 (%)	1989 (%)	1992 (%)	1994 (%)	Percentage Point Change
Under Contractors						
White	42	40	35	35	34	-8
Black	4	4	4	4	4	0
Asian American	3	3	5	6	6	3
Hispanic	10	11	13	13	14	4
Under Noncontractors						
White	33	32	29	27	27	-6
Black	3	3	3	3	3	0
Asian American	3	3	4	4	5	2
Hispanic	13	11	14	16	16	3

PANEL B: WOMEN

Race/ Ethnicity	1979 (%)	1982 (%)	1989 (%)	1992 (%)	1994 (%)	Percentage Point Change
Under Contractors						
White	29	28	27	25	24	-5
Black	3	4	4	4	4	1
Asian American	2	3	4	5	5	3
Hispanic	6	7	8	8	9	3
Under Noncontractors						
White	33	36	32	31	30	-3
Black	4	3	3	4	4	0
Asian American	3	3	4	5	5	2
Hispanic	8	8	9	10	11	3

Source: Author's tabulations from the EEO-1 files. The samples consisted of private establishments that met the following requirements: (1) establishments with at least 100 employees; or (2) establishments with at least 50 employees that either had a federal contract or first-tier subcontract worth $50,000 or more, acted as depositories of federal funds in any amount, or acted as issuing and paying agents for U.S. Savings Bonds and Notes.

increased, and black and Hispanic shares remained almost constant. The low minority shares within the headquarters of multiestablishment firms can partially be explained by the fact that most headquarter jobs are white-collar; however, they also provide information about who is within the heart of corporate America. The evidence is consistent with that found in the U.S. Department of Labor's 1995 glass ceiling study.[18]

Table 3: Percentage Share of California Employment in Headquarters of Federal Contractors and Noncontractors by Race/Ethnicity and Gender (1979–1994)

PANEL A: MEN

Race/ Ethnicity	1979 (%)	1982 (%)	1989 (%)	1992 (%)	1994 (%)	Percentage Point Change
Under Contractors						
White	42	40	38	38	37	-5
Black	3	3	2	2	2	-1
Asian American	3	4	6	7	7	4
Hispanic	6	6	6	7	7	1
Under Noncontractors						
White	40	39	35	33	32	-8
Black	2	2	2	2	2	0
Asian American	3	4	4	5	5	2
Hispanic	9	8	8	8	9	0

PANEL B: WOMEN

Race/ Ethnicity	1979 (%)	1982 (%)	1989 (%)	1992 (%)	1994 (%)	Percentage Point Change
Under Contractors						
White	34	34	33	31	30	-4
Black	4	4	3	3	3	-1
Asian American	4	5	6	6	7	3
Hispanic	5	6	6	6	6	1
Under Noncontractors						
White	34	35	35	35	34	0
Black	3	3	3	3	3	0
Asian American	3	4	5	6	7	4
Hispanic	6	6	7	7	8	2

Source: Author's tabulations from the EEO-1 files. The samples consisted of the headquarters of private multiestablishments with at least 50 employees that either had a federal contract or first-tier subcontract worth $50,000 or more, acted as depositories of federal funds in any amount, or acted as issuing and paying agents for U.S. Savings Bonds and Notes.

Disaggregating the data by broad industry categories reveals the source of the decline in the share of white employment in California and the source of Hispanic and Asian American employment growth. Manufacturing industries ended the 1970s with 30.8 percent of employment, but their share fell during the 1980s and early 1990s. Between 1979 and 1994, employment in durable manufacturing fell from 18.8 percent to 12.4 percent, and from 12 percent to 7.7 percent in nondurable manufacturing.

California's employment growth occurred in the retail-trade and business-services industries. The share in retail trade increased from 24 percent of establishments in 1979 to 29.3 percent in 1994; the share in business services jumped from 5.2 percent in 1979 to 15 percent in 1989 (before falling to 11.7 percent in 1994). Health services also showed a modest increase. Compared to the national data, the shifts in California's manufacturing industries were much greater. U.S. manufacturing (durable and nondurable) fell from 29.1 percent to 26 percent. The national retail sector's share remained at approximately 28 percent; however, the share in business services more than doubled, from 4 percent to 9.3 percent. The share in health services almost doubled.

The industries in which the share of white employment fell the most were durable manufacturing, nondurable manufacturing, retail trade, business services, and health services. From 1979 to 1994, the share of white men's employment fell 5 to 9 percentage points in durable manufacturing, 6 to 11 points in nondurable manufacturing and retail trade, and 5 to 7 percentage points in business services. The employment share of white women fell by 1 to 3 points in manufacturing and business services, and 9 to 12 points in retail trade and health services. The large gain of Asian Americans can be attributed to an increase in their shares in manufacturing, retail-trade, and business-services industries. Hispanic gains were in nondurable manufacturing, retail-trade, and health-services industries. California's and the nation's patterns were virtually identical, differing only in their size: The losses for whites and gains for Asian Americans and Hispanics in the national data were smaller than in California.

Stylized Facts About Federal Contractors

This section focuses on establishing a set of facts about employment differences by race, ethnicity, and gender between federal contractors and noncontractors between 1979 and 1994. The presence of a federal contract was associated with an increased number of establishments that reported having any African Americans and Asian American men. Table 1 shows that for all California establishments, the gap between the proportion of contractors and noncontractors having any African American male employees was 5 to 9 percentage points. The gap for African American female employees was 1 to 6 percentage points, and 4 to 8 percentage points for Asian American men. Starting in 1992, Asian American women benefited from the presence of federal contracts. For Hispanics, federal contracting seems to have done little to increase their presence.

At the national level, the gaps between the proportion of contractors and noncontractors having African American employees were virtually the same as in California. The proportion of Asian American women employed by contractors was the same as by noncontractors. Hispanic men benefited from the presence of federal contracts, while Hispanic women seem not to have benefited.

Panel B of Table 1 contains calculations of the presence of minorities and women in the headquarters of multiestablishment firms in California. Federal contracts raised the likelihood that minority workers were hired. In 1979, the contractor-noncontractor gap for women and minorities was 8 to 12 percentage points; however, during the 1980s, the gap narrowed. At the national level, the gap also narrowed. What generated these results? A shift in employers' preferences with regard to filling minority slots may have occurred, or a difference in response to corporate restructuring that resulted in relatively greater outsourcing and layoffs of minorities by contracting firms than by noncontracting firms. This result clearly deserves further investigation. Mar and Ong provide indirect evidence that stereotypes about a group's work ethic, both positive and negative, influence the hiring and firing decisions of employers.[19] In particular, African Americans are hurt by the stereotypes and Asian Americans are helped.

Table 4 reports race or ethnicity employment shares by contract status. The shares are not differentiated by gender. This permits a direct comparison of the unadjusted contractor-noncontractor difference to the regression-adjusted difference. The most salient observation is that even with the fall in the share of white men's employment during the 1980s and early 1990s, whites still had a larger share of employment in establishments that had federal contracts when compared with the total shares for minorities. In 1979, the gap for whites between contractor and noncontractor establishments was 5 percentage points, and in 1994, 1 percentage point. Asian and African Americans are the only demographic groups whose shares of employment were higher in establishments with federal contracts; however, these differences were quite small. Depending on the year, the difference between the shares of Hispanics (men and women) for contractors versus noncontractors ranged from 1 to 5 percentage points. The national trends were not as stark: The white share in contractor establishments exceeded the noncontractor share by only 0.4 to 0.9 percentage points, and the shares of African Americans, Hispanics, and Asian Americans were virtually the same for contractors as for noncontractors.

Disaggregating the data by industry reveals why white men's employment shares, though decreased, were larger in establishments with contracts, and why Hispanic men's employment shares (also decreased) were lower. In durable manufacturing, white men's shares under contractors were 9 to 12 percentage points higher than under noncontractors. These

Table 4: Percentage Share of California Employment Under Federal Contractors and Noncontractors by Race/Ethnicity (1979–1994)

Race/ Ethnicity	1979 (%)	1982 (%)	1989 (%)	1992 (%)	1994 (%)	Percentage Point Change
Under Contractors						
White	71	68	62	60	58	-13
Black	7	8	8	8	8	1
Asian	5	6	9	11	11	6
Hispanic	16	18	21	21	23	7
Under Noncontractors						
White	66	68	61	58	57	-9
Black	7	6	6	7	7	0
Asian	6	6	8	9	10	4
Hispanic	21	19	23	26	27	6

Source: Author's tabulations from the EEO-1 files. The samples consisted of private establishments that met the following requirements: (1) establishments with at least 100 employees; or (2) establishments with at least 50 employees that either had a federal contract or first-tier subcontract worth $50,000 or more, acted as depositories of federal funds in any amount, or acted as issuing and paying agents for U.S. Savings Bonds and Notes.

gaps were significantly higher than the differences in Table 2 (which provides a profile of the share of California employment for each racial, ethnic, and gender group), where the gaps were between 6 and 9 percentage points. White men's higher shares in establishments with contracts can also be attributed to differences within the business-services industry, where white men have had a high historical predominance even in the noncontractor sector. The contractor-noncontractor differential in business services partially explains why the shares of white women under contractors were smaller than the shares under noncontractors: The share of white women in noncontractor business-services establishments was 8 to 13 percentage points below the share of white women in contractor establishments. The source of Hispanic men's employment gap according to the employer's contract status was the durable manufacturing industry, where their share of employment under contractors was 10 to 14 percentage points below their share under noncontractors.

The Separate Effect of Contractor Status

A major reason why white men had a disproportionately high share of the federal-contractor workforce and minorities a disproportionately small share is that the procurement process is dominated by the defense, energy, and construction industries. A more careful look at the effect of the enforcement of affirmative action through Executive Order 11246 requires controlling for establishment characteristics, such as industrial classification, geographic location, and occupational structure. In the case of California, controlling for these characteristics is especially important because they contain information on the large structural changes that occurred in the state's labor market during the 1980s and early 1990s. This study used a multivariate technique to estimate the separate effect of contracting status.

Table 5 presents the estimated coefficients (ß) for the multivariate model, which indicates the effects of the federal-contracting variable on each group's employment share. The columns containing the partial derivatives (ΔP) translate the coefficients into estimates in percentage points of the gap in each group's employment share for contractors versus noncontractors.[20] The analysis used EEO-1 data for 1979, 1982, 1984, 1988, 1992, and 1994. Controlling for California establishment characteristics (e.g., industrial classification, geographic location, and occupational structure) was quite important because these factors may be correlated with the racial and ethnic composition of the labor force at the establishment level.

Evaluating the model at the mean proportion of the U.S. workforce (estimated from the EEO-1 files) that was white, I found that federal-contractor status lowered the white share in California by 1.4 percentage points for 1982 (from a mean of 67.6 percent) and by 1.2 percentage points for 1994 (from a mean of 57.3 percent). In other words, the impact of federal-contractor status decreased marginally over this period. The national-level results for whites over roughly the same period show that federal contracting also lowered the white share, but the size of the effect increased: from 0.70 percentage points in 1982 to 1.42 percentage points in 1992.[21]

Federal-contractor status positively and significantly affects the share of an establishment's workforce that is African American and Asian American. For African Americans, federal-contractor status raised their share by 1.7 percentage points in 1982 (from a mean of 7.7 percent) and by 1 percentage point in 1994 (from a mean of 7.4 percent). For Asian Americans, federal-contractor status raised their share by 0.8 percentage points in 1982 and 1994 (from a mean of 7 percent in 1982 and 11.5 percent in 1994). At the national level, throughout the period of analysis, federal-contractor status raised the African American share from 0.83 to 1.36 percentage points (evaluated at mean proportions of 10.3 percent and 11.7 percent), and the Asian American share by 0.2 percentage points (from means of 1.6 percent and 2.6 percent).

To the extent that the establishment characteristics adequately capture aspects of labor demand, labor supply, and institutions, federal-contractor status tended to decrease the proportion of Hispanic workers in an establishment's workforce. This result held only in 1979, 1982, 1984, and 1994.

Table 5: Logit Estimates of the Impact of Federal-Contractor Status on Employment in California by Race/Ethnicity (1979–1994)

	1979[1]		1982[2]		1984		1988		1992		1994	
	ß[3]	ΔP[4]	ß	ΔP	ß	ΔP	ß	ΔP	ß	ΔP	ß	ΔP
White	0.020 (0.019)	0.4	-0.063 (0.018)	-1.4	-0.035 (0.018)	-0.8	-0.085 (0.016)	-2.0	-0.100 (0.015)	-2.4	-0.047 (0.014)	-1.2
Black	0.136 (0.024)	1.0	0.213 (0.023)	1.7	0.170 (0.023)	1.3	0.155 (0.020)	1.2	0.166 (0.018)	1.2	0.141 (0.017)	1.0
Asian	0.015 (0.023)	0.1	0.115 (0.023)	0.8	0.097 (0.023)	0.7	0.056 (0.020)	0.3	0.121 (0.018)	1.2	0.079 (0.017)	0.8
Hispanic	-0.097 (0.020)	-1.4	-0.065 (0.019)	-0.9	-0.076 (0.019)	-1.1	0.014 (0.017)	0.2-	-0.016 (0.015)	-0.3	-0.049 (0.015)	-0.9

1. The 1979 model includes all of the variables except the dummy variables for metropolitan location.

2. The 1982 model was re-estimated without the metropolitan controls. The results were identical to those reported above that contain the metropolitan location information.

3. Estimated coefficient for the effect of the federal contracting variable on racial/ethnic group's employment share.

4. Translation of ß into *percentage-point* estimate of the employment-share gap for contractors versus noncontractors.

Source: Author's calculations from EEO-1 files. For a description of the method, see Appendix. Standard errors of the coefficient are in parentheses.

For the latter three years, federal-contractor status lowered the share by 0.9 percentage points for 1982 and 1994 (from means of 17.7 percent and 23.6 percent) and by 1.1 percentage points for 1984 (from a mean of 18 percent). One potential explanation for the decline is the contribution of less skilled immigrants to California's economy. If these new workers, both documented and undocumented, had a higher likelihood of being employed in noncontractor establishments, then my inability to control for the supply of immigrants could explain the estimated negative effects of federal contracting. This explanation probably does not account for all of the difference. In an analysis of national data, Rodgers and Spriggs[22] and Rodgers[23] also found that federal-contractor status lowered the Hispanic share of employment. Because Hispanics are much more dispersed at the national level, we would not expect this result. Clearly, the unexpected finding of a lower Hispanic share at both the state and national levels should be studied in greater detail.

The pattern of the partial derivatives (ΔP) for whites, African Americans, and Asian Americans in Table 5 suggests that federal-contractor status had less of an impact on their employment shares during the late 1980s. This deterioration in the impact of federal-contractor status coincides with the sharp cutbacks in federal spending and contracting, particularly in the defense industry. Although small in an absolute sense, the reductions were nontrivial for African Americans and Asian Americans. African Americans constituted 7 percent to 8 percent of California's employees by EEO-1 statistics. As a result, they bore the brunt of the restructuring. The share for Asian Americans also declined, but their share in contracting recovered faster than that of African Americans. Ong and Lawrence found identical results to these for African Americans and similar results for Asian Americans. Their study of California's aerospace industry revealed that African Americans were disproportionately affected by the decline in federal spending and contracting, particularly those employed in the defense industry. The experience of Asian Americans was similar to that of whites.[24]

Summary and Conclusions

Federal-contractor status raises the employment shares of African Americans and Asian Americans who work in California. Relative to the mean shares of African Americans and Asian Americans in the workforce, its impact is nontrivial. As of 1994, African Americans constituted just over 7 percent of California's employees according to EEO-1 statistics, and Asian Americans, 11.5 percent. Thus the estimated federal-contractor effect of 0.7 to 1 percentage point represents a large relative shift in each group's share of the workforce. Federal-contractor status appears to lower the employment shares of whites and Hispanics. I attribute the result for Hispanics to my inability to adequately control for the supply of immigrant labor to the California economy.

For whites, the largest demographic group in the California economy, the negative effect of federal-contractor status is relatively small. Whites make up 57 percent of the state's employment, according to EEO-1 statistics; the estimated effect of federal-contractor status is a reduction of 1.2 percentage points in employment. Thus the federal-contractor program has its intended employment effect, while at the same time the program diffuses its costs across society. Furthermore, the federal-contractor program may help to allocate workers across firms in an economically more efficient fashion than would be the case without such a program. It places minorities and women in work environments that are potentially less discriminatory, thus eliminating economic losses associated with artificial racial and gender barriers. The program may also help to increase competition with firms that discriminate.

How do these results compare to the national analysis performed in Rodgers and Spriggs[25] and Rodgers?[26] What lessons can be learned from this exercise? First, given that the estimated federal-contractor effects are similar across these three studies, and African Americans constitute a larger share of the U.S. workforce compared to California's, the direct effects found nationally for this group appear to be smaller than those found in California. Second, I also found that, nationally, federal-contractor status is associated with lower employment shares of whites and Hispanics. For Hispanics, inadequate control for the supply of immigrant labor can explain only part of the result. For whites nationally, the estimated negative effect of federal-contractor status is even smaller than in the context of California: Whites made up 78 percent of U.S. employment in 1992 and experienced a reduction of 1.4 percentage points, versus 59 percent and 2.4 percentage points in California.

In the case of California, evaluation of the federal-contractor program at the state level appears to strengthen the importance of the program in raising the share of minority employment. The shift in employment due to the presence of contracts is nontrivial; however, the majority population is still large enough that the costs of the program are distributed broadly across society.

Appendix

Methodology

A linear specification of a binomial logit of a racial or ethnic group's proportion of employment in California establishments was estimated using the establishment's county of location, metropolitan location, establishment type, federal-contractor status, major industry, and occupational structure. Separate regressions were estimated for each race or ethnic group for each year. To correct for heteroscedasticity, weighted least squares was used.

The following description provides a more detailed explanation of the methodology. The log-odds ratio for the rth race/ethnic group in the ith establishment in year t is defined by the following equation:

$$E[\ \ln(\frac{P_i}{1-P_i})|\ X_i] = X_i'\beta$$

where P_i is the ith establishment's share of employment for the rth race/ethnic group, $\ln[P_i/(1-P_i)]$ is the ith establishment's log-odds ratio, X_i is a k x 1 vector of predictor variables for the ith establishment, and β is a k x 1 vector of parameters. The notation $E[\ln(P/(1 - P)|X]$ denotes the mean of the conditional distribution of the log-odds ratio given X. To correct for heteroscedasticity, the regressions are weighted by $[n_i/(P_i(1 - P_i)]^{.5}$, where n_i denotes the ith establishment's number of employees.

The regression also includes as an independent variable a dummy (dichotomous) variable that denotes whether an establishment has a federal contract (1 for yes, 0 for no). The specification for metropolitan residence includes dummy variables for central city location and rural location, and a dummy variable that denotes whether the establishment's metropolitan location is unidentifiable. The excluded metropolitan group is suburban location. Three indicator variables for establishment type are added. They denote whether the establishment is a stand-alone company or an entity of a multiestablishment company. Headquarter establishments are the excluded group.

The following industry dummy variables are added: agriculture, mining, construction, durable manufacturing, nondurable manufacturing, transportation, wholesale trade, retail trade, finance, insurance, real estate, personal retail services, business services, entertainment, and health. Durable manufacturing is the excluded group. The occupational structure of the establishment is modeled as the shares of the establishment's workforce employed as professionals, technicians, sales workers, office and clerical workers, craft workers, operatives, laborers, and service workers.

Officials and managers are the excluded group. Finally, 18 county dummy variables are added. Dummy variables are included for counties that have at least 1 percent of total employment (Contra Costa, Fresno, Kern, Los Angeles, Orange, Riverside, Sacramento, San Bernardino, San Diego, San Francisco, San Joaquin, San Mateo, Santa Barbara, Santa Clara, Sonoma, Stanislaus, and Ventura). An additional dummy variable is included that equals 1 if the county's share of total employment is less than 1 percent, and 0 if the county's employment is at least 1 percent. Establishments located in Los Angeles County are the excluded group.

The ability of the model to explain variations in the share of a particular racial (or ethnic) group varied, as indicated by an analysis of R-squares (R^2's) and partial R^2's, which indicate the portion of the variation explained by the model as a whole or by a subset of independent variables. Several striking results emerged from the analysis. First, from 1982 to 1994, the ability of labor demand, labor supply, and institutional measures to explain the variation in each race or ethnic group's share of employment rose over time. A significant amount of variation exists across the R^2 values for each group. The model using the white share as the dependent variable explained 37.1 percent of the variation for 1982 and 44.2 percent for 1994. For the Hispanic share, the model explained 43.1 percent for 1982 and 50.3 percent for 1994. Only 14 percent and 17.1 percent of African American and Asian American employment, respectively, could be explained for 1982; the respective values in 1994 were 16.2 percent and 21.5 percent.

The predictors of employment for whites were an establishment's occupational structure, county of location, and industry. These predictors did not change over time. For blacks, county of location and industry were the most important. For them, the importance of county decreased over time, with industry and occupational structure growing in importance. Asian American workers' employment was best explained by county and industry measures. For them, geographic importance also declined over time, while that of industry grew. Finally, Hispanic employment was best explained by occupational structure, industry, and an establishment's county of location. The relative importance of these measures was fairly stable over time. More detailed results are available from the author.

Notes

1. Roosevelt's action was a response to the threat of black workers to march on Washington.

2. The standards were enforced by the OFCC (and, later, the OFCCP) through contract reviews, which resulted in (1) a conciliation agreement or (2) debarment

from federal contracting. The reviews reconcile the affirmative action plan submitted by the federal contractor and the gap in full utilization. This gap was determined by comparing the available labor market and the particular firm's labor distribution (with respect to both general employment and promotional status), a procedure termed "utilization analysis." If a major discrepancy existed, it was incumbent on the firm develop a conciliation agreement (an affirmative action plan to remedy the situation) or risk the threat of debarment. Debarment, for both the Kennedy administration and executive tenures to follow, was rarely, if ever, utilized. The number of reviews and extent of enforcement depended (and depends) on the resources available to the enforcement mechanisms of the U.S. government, most notably the OFCCP and the EEOC.

3. Title VII established the EEOC, a commission with informal power to respond to individual complaints of discrimination and seek conciliation. The commission first worked with firms, unions, etc. in an effort to settle disputes and, if necessary, pursued action through the courts. The commission received more formal power in 1972, when it was first permitted to seek out egregious offenders and proceed with class action suits.

4. Bernard Anderson, "The Ebb and Flow of Enforcing Executive Order 11246," *American Economic Review* 86(2): 298–301 (1996).

5. The 1971 *Griggs v. Duke Power* case advanced the notion of the need to deal with structural discrimination. A group was said to have suffered disparate impact if its employment was affected by job requirements found to be immaterial to performance, even if no overt discrimination was in practice per se. The case spurred the re-evaluation of the hiring and promotional practices of many businesses and educational institutions and set new standards for federal contractors. Recent movements in the business sector indicate that, to a certain extent, political and consumer pressures (both local and global) also spur advancements toward equality, albeit for less than noble reasons. Businesses in the private sector have also shown an interest in protecting themselves from liability and satisfying the demands of a growing labor market. This demand is future-oriented, as most U.S. firms have noted the trend toward changing demographic conditions by developing their attractiveness as an employer and their efficiency as a firm.

6. The current standard of strict scrutiny is now applied to all government programs. Strict scrutiny requires narrowly tailored objectives to meet specific remedial needs and typically does not permit race-based preferences without qualification (i.e., definitive evidence of corresponding socioeconomic differentials created by persistent and overt discriminatory practices). For a detailed discussion of cases heard during the Bush administration, see Samuel Rabinove's chapter in Donald Altschiller, ed., *Affirmative Action* (New York: H. W. Wilson Company, 1991); for a comprehensive review of pertinent case history, see "Affirmative Action Report to the President."

7. Jonathan Leonard, "Wage Disparities and Affirmative Action in the 1980s," *American Economic Review* 86 (2): 285–289 (1996).

8. Bernard Anderson, "The Ebb and Flow of Enforcing Executive Order 11246," *American Economic Review* 86 (2): 298–301 (1996).

9. William M. Rodgers III and William E. Spriggs, "The Effect of Federal-Contractor Status on Racial Differences in Establishment-Level Employment Shares: 1979–1992," *American Economic Review* 86 (2): 290–293 (1996).

10. Ibid.

11. Additional tables containing statistics beyond those in this study may be obtained directly from the author.

12. The data are not public; access was provided by the Office of Federal Contract Compliance Programs through special arrangements.

13. The national and the California unemployment rates were 9.2 percent and 9.9 percent, respectively, in 1982, and 7.2 percent and 9.3 percent in 1992.

14. Before 1983, establishments that had at least 25 employees, but had either a federal contract or a first-tier subcontract worth $50,000 or more, acted as depositories of federal funds in any amount, or acted as issuing and paying agents for U.S. Savings Bonds and Notes, were required to file reports to the EEOC. After 1983, the minimum was increased to 50 employees. This increase in size requirements on which establishments are required to file a report led to a growing inability to capture large segments of employment. The above requirements clearly exclude small single-establishment employers and multiestablishment employers whose entities have small workforces. The data obtained under the new minimum requirement of 50 indicate that minorities are less represented in smaller firms.

15. Rodgers and Spriggs, "Effect of Federal-Contractor Status."

16. William M. Rodgers III, "Racial Differences in Employment Shares—New Evidence from the EEO-1 Files," in Samuel L. Meyers, ed., *Civil Rights and Race Relations in the Post-Reagan-Bush Era* (Westport, CT: Praeger, 1997).

17. The proportion of establishments reporting at least one Asian American (man or woman) was approximately 30 percent in 1979 and 40 percent in 1992. The proportion of establishments reporting at least one Hispanic was between 42 percent and 53 percent in 1979 and 51 percent to 60 percent in 1992.

18. U.S. Glass Ceiling Commission, "Good for Business: Making Full Use of the Nation's Human Capital" (Washington, DC: Department of Labor, 1995).

19. Don Mar and Paul M Ong, "Race and Rehiring in the High-Tech Industry," *The Review of Black Political Economy* 22 (3): 43–54 (1994).

20. The change in the probability of observing an individual of a particular racial or ethnic group associated with the kth dummy variable is
$$\Delta P_k = [1 + \exp(-X'\beta - \beta_k)]^{-1} - P$$
where $X'\beta = \ln[p/(1 - P)]$ and P equals the average share in the sample, and βk is the logit coefficient for the kth variable.

21. The models were evaluated at mean proportions of 82 percent for 1982 and 77.8 percent for 1992.

22. Rodgers and Spriggs, "Effect of Federal-Contractor Status."

23. Rodgers, "Racial Differences in Employment Shares."

24. Paul M. Ong and Janette R Lawrence, "Race and Employment in California's Aerospace Industry," *The Review of Black Political Economy* 23 (3): 91–99 (1995).

25. Rodgers and Spriggs, "Effect of Federal-Contractor Status."

26. Rodgers, "Racial Differences in Employment Shares."

Chapter 6

The California Civil Rights Initiative: Which Firms Stand to Lose and How Much?

Darrell L. Williams

Introduction

California possesses the largest and most viable small-business community in the nation. According to the U.S. Census Bureau, in 1987 there were 1.8 million small businesses operating in California with total annual revenues equal to $246 billion.[1] A nontrivial share of California small-business revenues are derived from sales to state and local governments, accounting for nearly one-fifth of the total revenues of all small businesses in California. Moreover, nearly 15 percent of all California small businesses (or one in seven) sold goods or services to state and local government entities.[2]

Based on these aggregate statistics it is apparent that state/local government sales are an important, if not vital, source of California small-business revenue. What is less apparent is the importance of sales to state/local governments for California small businesses that are owned by women and minorities, an issue of fundamental concern in light of the potential impact of the California Civil Rights Initiative (CCRI) on procurement practices. As will be discussed below, the implication of arguments on both sides of the CCRI debate is that women-owned business enterprises (WBEs) and minority-owned business enterprises (MBEs) that benefit from so-called affirmative action policies will face fewer procurement opportunities after CCRI is adopted. However, all firms will not be uniformly affected; some firms will experience significantly greater disruptions and loss of sales than others. This posits the question, which firms are most likely to be affected, and by how much? Analyzing the distributional consequences of reducing state/local procurement opportunities for WBE and MBE firms is the goal of this study.

The focus on the distributional issues—that is, the "how important" and "which firms" questions—is justified in part by the fact that both sides agree that the expected effect of CCRI is to reduce the procurement-contracting opportunities for WBE and MBE firms, albeit for different reasons. According to proponents of CCRI, adoption of the initiative will reduce WBE and MBE contracting opportunities because under the current policy WBE and MBE firms are afforded preferential treatment in the bidding process that enables them to compete effectively against more productive firms. Without such preferential treatment in the bidding process, the less productive WBE and MBE firms that have been awarded government contracts under the current policy would lose the bidding competition to superior firms. In contrast, opponents of CCRI argue that its adoption will reduce WBE and MBE contracting opportunities because under the current policy WBE and MBE firms receive protection against discrimination and unfair competition in the selection of government contractors, protection that CCRI would eliminate. As a result, fewer WBE and MBE firms will be awarded contracts.

Thus, in spite of philosophical differences—proponents suggest the number of WBE and MBE contractors is artificially high under the current policy and opponents suggest that the number is correct or possibly too low—the implication of both sides of the issue is that the expected effect of the CCRI is to decrease WBE and MBE procurement opportunities (either by the elimination of preferential treatment or by reducing protections against discrimination and unfair competition). Given the absence of disagreement about the direction of the effect, it is reasonable to limit this analysis to an assessment of its potential magnitude and apportionment.

The analysis below focuses on the potential for lost sales to *existing* WBE and MBE firms. Because government contracting relationships are often long-term and there are frequent repeat purchases, the focus on lost sales to existing businesses is a useful indicator of the future impact of CCRI.[3] However, the risk of lost sales is by no means the only likely effect of CCRI on WBE and MBE firms, and it is not necessarily the most important. There are also likely to be incentive effects that may affect the rate at which *new* businesses are created and/or the rate at which existing businesses expand. These incentive effects are not taken into account in the analysis that follows, even though their magnitude may be large and significant.[4]

Despite the limitations noted above, it is important to identify the characteristics of WBE and MBE firms in California that are state/local contractors and as a result are at risk of losing revenue in the post-CCRI era. The results of this study indicate that the vast majority of WBE and MBE firms derived none of their revenue from state/local government procurement. Moreover, the proportion of WBE and MBE firms that rely heavily on sales to state/local government is small. These results suggest that any effect of CCRI on existing firms may be limited to a small proportion of the WBE and MBE business populations and that those firms that are likely to be affected have other sources of revenue. However, there is evidence that a disproportionately large fraction of the top MBE firms are at risk of being adversely affected in the post-CCRI era.

Finally, it should be emphasized that the narrow focus of this analysis does not inform several critical issues of contention in the CCRI debate, such as: Are the number of WBE and MBE firms too low as a result of historical discrimination? And, if so, are affirmative action–type policies the most effective policy instrument for eradicating discriminatory effects? While these issues are crucially important, they are beyond the scope of this study. The reader should therefore resist the temptation to infer conclusions about the broader issues of economic efficiency and societal welfare from the analysis that follows.

After a brief description of the data, the empirical results are presented. These are followed by a summary and concluding remarks.

About the Data

The data used in this study were taken from the Characteristics of Business Owners (CBO) database, which is compiled by the Enterprise Statistics Division of the U.S. Bureau of the Census. The CBO database is based on a nationwide survey of 125,000 small-business owners that filed federal tax returns in 1987. Due to the exceptionally high response rate (approximately 70 percent), the CBO database contains about 90,000 observations on United States small-business owners.

The sample used in this study was constructed by first creating a subsample of all firms in the CBO database that were operating in California in 1987. To be included in the analysis, data on the percentage of 1987 gross sales revenues to state and local governments was required. Therefore, firms in which the owners failed to report this information were eliminated. The final sample consists of 3,838 California small businesses.

The Empirical Results

Table 1 reveals that 7.2 percent of women-owned firms, 12.6 percent of minority-owned firms, and 16.4 percent of nonminority small businesses sold goods or services to state/local governments in 1987. This suggests that, relative to nonminority firms, WBE and MBE firms participate in government-procurement transactions at a lower rate.[5] In fact, the vast majority of WBE and MBE firms (89.7 percent and 85.6 percent, respectively) sell exclusively to private, nongovernmental customers.[6] Table 1 further reveals that, on average, California state/local government contractors are larger, employ more workers, and are more experienced than noncontractors for WBE, MBE, and nonminority firms alike.

Some readers will be tempted to interpret the low procurement participation rates for WBE and MBE firms as an indication of discrimination. No such conclusion is possible on the basis of these summary data alone, since they do not take into account such factors as production costs and output quality that may explain disparities in participation rates. But whatever else these low participation rates might suggest, they clearly indicate that the potential harm to *existing* businesses from CCRI is limited to a small (but certainly nontrivial) proportion of WBE and MBE

Table 1: A Comparison of State/Local Government Contractors and Noncontractors in California (1987)

	WBE Firms	MBE Firms	Nonminority Firms
Firms That Are State/Local Contractors	7.2%	12.6%	16.4%
Mean Sales (Thousands)			
Contractors	$617.8	$362.5	$504.2
Noncontractors	$264.7	$268.0	$405.4
Mean Assets			
Contractors	$118.6	$106.4	$94.4
Noncontractors	$60.9	$66.5	$75.6
Mean Number of Employees			
Contractors	4.0	3.8	4.4
Noncontractors	3.3	2.9	3.7
Mean Firm Age			
Contractors	12.6	7.1	9.6
Noncontractors	8.6	6.9	9.2
New Entrants That Are State/Local Gov't Contractors	7.0%	13.2%	19.4%

Source: Author's computation based on the CBO database, 1987 (U.S. Department of Commerce, Bureau of the Census, Enterprise Statistics Division).

firms.[7] However, any optimism resulting from this fact is tempered by the knowledge that, even though the proportion of the potentially affected firms is small, the affected firms appear to be an important part of the WBE and MBE firm populations. More will be said about this below.

Table 1 also provides data on new entrants (firms that had been in business no more than one year in 1987). Procurement opportunities may be more important in the early stages of firm development if they provide a protected market to start-ups. If so, procurement participation rates are expected to be higher for new entrants than for mature firms. This would be the case, for example, if the small business produced an intermediate good, such as an equipment component; private-sector customers of the intermediate good are less likely than government purchasers to buy from a firm that does not have an established reputation for quality.[8]

The last row of Table 1 provides the proportion of new entrants that are contractors. Among MBE and WBE firms, state/local contracts are not substantially more or less prevalent than within the population generally. In contrast, state and local government contractors are overrepresented among nonminority new entrants, where they represent 19.4 percent of new entrants. Nonminority entrants are more likely to be awarded a government contract than MBE entrants, and two times more likely than WBE firms.

A closer examination of state/local government contractors is provided in Table 2. In absolute dollar amounts, WBE firms had greater sales to state/local governments than either MBE firms or nonminority firms, despite the fact that WBE firms are the least likely to sell to state/local governments (see Table 1). The average MBE firm sold only $55,300 in goods and services to state/local governments, far less than any other group. The large differences in average dollar revenues across firm subsamples does not translate into substantial differences in the percentage of revenues attributable to government sales. State/local government revenues account for between 16.6 and 18.9 percent of revenue, on average. These data suggest that scale of operation is an important determinant of procurement opportunities.

While comparisons of group averages are informative, averages may hide important differences in the distribution of government revenue across groups. For example, some small businesses may specialize in serving government customers because they produce to specification or simply because they were awarded a government contract that utilizes all available capacity. A policy change that reduces the likelihood of being awarded a contract is expected to have a disproportionately large effect on WBE and MBE firms that specialize in sales to government, in contrast to firms that have a more diversified customer base.

As an indication of the degree of specialization in government markets, Table 2 reports the percentage of firms in each subpopulation that derives

Table 2: Characteristics of State/Local Contracting Firms (in Millions and Percents)

	WBE Firms	MBE Firms	Nonminority Firms
Mean Procurement Dollar Revenue	$84.3	$55.3	$77.4
Mean Percent State/Local Contracting Revenue	$18.7	$17.7	$16.6
Percent of Firms for Which State//Local Contracting Represents at Least 50% of Revenue	1.7%	6.6%	3.1%
Percent of State/Local Contractors That Are Also Federal Contractors	20.1%	43.7%	41.8%
Mean Sales	$617.8	$362.5	$504.2
Mean Assets	$118.6	$106.4	$94.4
Mean Number of Employees	4.0	3.8	4.4

Source: Author's computation based on CBO database, 1987.

at least 50 percent of its total revenue from government sales. While the proportion of firms is generally small, MBE firms are two times more likely than nonminority firms to rely heavily on (derive at least 50 percent of their revenue from) government sales. This suggests that for the 6.6 percent of MBE firms that specialize in government sales, a regulatory change could jeopardize their survival prospects if their physical and human capital are not transferable at a low cost to supplying private-sector customers.

More information on the degree to which firms rely on government procurement is provided in Table 3, where the subsample of California state/local vendors is split according to the proportion of sales to government. Firms are classified within one of two categories: (1) firms for which state/local government sales represent less than 25 percent of total firm revenues, and (2) firms with government sales equal to 25 percent or more of total firm revenues. The basic rationale is that firms that rely on state/local government sales for 25 percent or more of their total sales are more susceptible to a policy change that reduces the probability of receiving a government contract. A cutoff of 25 percent of government revenues is chosen in order to facilitate comparisons with a national sample of small-business vendors.[9] Small sample sizes prevent reporting averages for WBE firms separately.

Generally, less-diversified small businesses (those with government sales equaling 25 percent or more of total sales) are smaller than diversified small businesses. These size differences are not large, but they nevertheless fail to indicate that the larger firms are substantially more

Table 3: California Small Businesses that Sell to State/Local Government (1987)

	Under 25 percent of revenues from government	25 percent or more of revenues from government
A. *MBEs Only*		
Mean gross revenues	$383,223	$291,952
Mean sales to state/local governments	$27,534	$149,982
Mean number of employees	4.0	3.1
Mean years in business	7.3	6.5
Firms in this group as a percentage of MBE government vendors	77.2%	22.7&
B. *WBEs and MBEs*		
Mean gross revenues	$509,300	$255,224
Mean sales to state/local governments	$38,900	$126,761
Mean number of employees	4.4	2.4
Mean years in business	7.9	10.8
Firms in this group as a percentage of MBE/WBE government vendors	71.6%	28.4%
C. *Nonminority Firms*		
Mean gross revenues	$513,283	$459,347
Mean sales to state/local government	$41,056	$255,816
Mean number of employees	4.7	3.0
Mean years in business	8.0	17.6
Firms in this group as a percentage of MBE government vendors	83.1%	16.9%

Source: Author's computation based on CBO database, 1987.

vulnerable to CCRI. Nor does it appear that the more experienced MBE firms are at greater risk from CCRI; on average, diversified firms are about one year older than undiversified firms. However, there is evidence that the more experienced WBE firms stand to lose more than will less experienced WBE firms. Finally, consistent with the results in Table 2, WBE and MBE firms are more likely to depend heavily on sales to state/local governments than nonminority firms. For example, 28.4 percent of all MBE

Table 4: Percent of Top Quartile of Firms by Employment, Experience, and Assets That Sell to State/Local Government

	MBE Firms	WBE Firms	Nonminority Firms
Percent of All Firms That Are State/Local Contractors	7.2	12.6	16.4
Percent of Top Quartile of Employers That Sell to State/Local Governments	13.4	5.0	15.9
Percent of Firms with at Least 10 Employees That Sell to State/Local Governments	14.8	14.7	20.0
Percent of Top Quartile of Firms with the Largest Revenues That Sell to State/Local Governments	16.6	15.4	25.9
Percent of Top Quartile of Firms with the Largest Assets That Sell to State/Local Governments	25.7	20.7	31.9
Percent of Firms with at Least 10 Years in Business That Sell to State/Local Governments	13.6	12.6	12.9

Source: Author's computation based on CBO database, 1987.

and WBE firms depend heavily upon government sales, compared to 16.9 of all nonminority firms.

Table 4 offers an assessment of the potential risks to the most successful WBE and MBE firms from a different perspective. It reports the fraction of the most successful firms that are state/local contractors and therefore at risk of lost revenues as a consequence of CCRI. This was accomplished by first identifying the top firms within each of the small-business subpopulations (MBE, WBE, and nonminority) in three different categories: employment, size, and experience (for instance, all WBE firms were ranked according to number of employees and then the top 25 percent were identified). Then the fraction of the top firms in each category that were state/local contractors was computed. The results are reported in Table 4.

For comparison, the first row of Table 4 contains the percentage of all firms that are state/local contractors in each population segment—WBE, MBE, and nonminority firms, respectively (see Table 1). This number is properly interpreted as the (unconditional) probability that a firm from a particular population segment will be affected by CCRI. Hence, there is a 7.2, 12.6, 16.4 percent probability that a MBE, WBE, or nonminority firm will be affected by CCRI.[10]

For MBE firms, 13.4 percent of the top quartile (top 25 percent) of firms in terms of employment are state/local contractors, compared to 7.2 percent of all MBE firms. This suggests that the top MBE employers are nearly two times more likely to be affected by CCRI than a randomly chosen MBE firm. The largest MBE firms, measured in terms of revenues and assets, are also more likely to be affected by CCRI than a randomly chosen MBE firm. For example, MBE firms with the most assets are three times more likely to be affected than would be the case if an MBE firm was picked at random. More experienced MBE firms are also more likely to be affected than the typical firm.

For WBE firms, the top firms are only slightly more likely to be at risk. For example, WBE firms with at least 10 years' experience are no more likely to be at risk than a randomly chosen WBE firm. The one exception is that WBE firms with the most assets are at a somewhat greater risk than a WBE firm chosen at random.

These data suggest that the distributional consequences of a policy change that reduces state/local contracting opportunities to WBE and MBE firms are not uniform. The most successful firms are generally more likely to sell to state/local government entities, and therefore are at greater risk of being adversely affected by a policy change. Concerns about the adverse effects being disproportionately placed on the most successful firms appears to be greatest among MBE firms.

Concluding Remarks

This chapter reported data for a sample of 3,838 California firms drawn from a national sample of small businesses compiled by the U.S. Census Bureau to assess the potential impact of the CCRI on WBE and MBE firms. The approach was direct and simple: to identify characteristics of California state/local contractors for the purpose of highlighting segments of the WBE and MBE small-business population that stand to lose the most if CCRI significantly reduces the state/local procurement opportunities of these firms. The analysis takes as given the contracting positions of existing WBE and MBE firms and makes no claims regarding the "correctness" of existing contract allocations.

The main conclusions are:

1. Procurement participation rates of WBE and MBE firms are low; the vast majority of WBE and MBE firms do not sell to state/local governments.

2. Procurement participation rates of new entrants are not significantly different from those of older incumbent firms.

3. Compared to WBE and MBE noncontractors, state/local contractors are larger on average and employ more persons.

4. The top WBE and MBE employers are at slightly greater risk due to the policy change, but these top employers do not appear to rely heavily on state/local government revenues.

5. Firms that specialize in selling to the government (i.e., derive a substantial share of their revenue from government sales) represent a small proportion of WBE and MBE firms.

6. A disproportionately large fraction of the top MBE firms are state/local contractors and are therefore at a substantial risk of being adversely affected by a policy change that reduces their procurement opportunities.

These results suggest areas for concern, especially regarding the top MBE firms, but only similar results from a more thorough analysis should precipitate alarm. There are a number of mitigating factors that were not addressed here. For example, even though the most successful firms are more likely to be adversely affected, they are also more likely to survive a setback. And even if these firms experience a significant reduction in revenue from state/local government customers, the impact of such a reduction on a particular firm will depend on the cost to the firm of penetrating alternative market segments. The cost of serving alternative customers will depend, in turn, on whether or not there exists private-sector demand for the firm's output. If not, then the cost of switching physical capital and skills to the production of goods and services for which there is private-sector demand will determine the impact of the policy change. In many cases, it may be possible to replace sales to California state/local governments by supplying federal governments, or by supplying state/local governments other than those in California. The economic relevance of these factors and others are empirical issues worthy of future research.

Notes

1. The Characteristics of Business Owners (CBO) Survey is published by the U.S. Census Bureau every five years. At the time of this study, the 1987 data was the most recent; the 1992 survey had not yet been published.

2. Small businesses are defined as firms with annual revenues between $250,000 and $10 million in 1987 dollars.

3. Of course, WBE and MBE firms are unlikely to lose all procurement opportunities, so the direct effects will be less than actual sales to state/local government; a determination of how much less must await a post-CCRI period that is sufficiently long to ensure that reasonable estimates of the actual effects can be obtained.

4. To the extent that CCRI reduces expected procurement opportunities, it will reduce the incentive to create new WBE and MBE firms. The effect of lost procurement opportunities on entry decisions is ignored below. This intentional oversight is the result of data limitations and the limited scope of this analysis. It should not be interpreted as an indication that these effects are not important. To the contrary, a basic rationale offered by Presidents Nixon and Kennedy for their Executive Orders mandating affirmative action in government procurement is that these policies would encourage the creation of minority businesses.

5. The reader is cautioned against inferring a cause from these data. The low rates of participation for WBE and MBE firms are consistent with any of the following causes: (1) rejection by procurement authorities for legitimate reasons such as the submission of more favorable bids by rival firms; (2) rejection by procurement authorities because of racial/gender bias against WBE and MBE firms; or (3) a decision by WBE and MBE entrepreneurs not to compete for procurement sales.

6. The proportions do not add up because some firms sell to federal government entities.

7. The small share of WBE and MBE firms that are minority vendors may be a consequence of the type of competitive disadvantage cited by critics of CCRI. Even if these numbers doubled to account for downward bias, they suggest that the lion's share of the minority- and women-owned business population will not be directly affected by CCRI. Of course, data on actual sales do little to inform us about the fairness of the procurement process as measured by the probability of being awarded a contract conditional on meeting selection criteria.

8. For example, consider a computer maker that purchases some of its internal parts from a small business. If the small business sells shoddy parts, customers will penalize the computer maker by reducing its expected sales into the future. State/local government entities frequently have a monopoly in their market. The absence of close substitutes for the product makes switching by customers difficult if not impossible. If the public transit system had purchased the shoddy products, public transit passengers may have little choice but to continue using the service despite any poor performance caused by the shoddy parts. A similar analysis applies to other markets where the products and services of small businesses are used as inputs (i.e., are intermediate goods) by other (larger) businesses or by state/local government entities.

9. Timothy Bates and Darrell Williams, "Preferential Procurement Programs and Minority-Owned Businesses," *Journal of Urban Affairs* 17 (1): 1–17 (1995).

10. The effect on nonminority firms is likely to be positive, assuming that state/local demand for goods and services does not decrease after CCRI is implemented.

Chapter 7

Affirmative Action Programs for Minority- and Women-Owned Businesses

Tom Larson

Affirmative action programs have been developed for employment, education, and government contracting. Government contracting programs aimed at increasing the use of minority- and women-owned business enterprises (MWBEs) are the least known of these programs among the public, but have been more carefully studied than any other type of affirmative action program since 1989. In 1989, the U.S. Supreme Court ruled, in *City of Richmond v. J. A. Croson Co.*, that affirmative action programs for minority-owned business enterprises (MBEs) must pass "strict scrutiny"; that is, state and local laws creating racial preferences must be narrowly tailored to achieve a compelling government interest (see Chapter 2 for more details on this ruling). The *Croson* decision lead to numerous studies of set-aside[1] programs and contracting outcomes in order to satisfy the Court's requirements for a legal program, and also to changes in programs, providing a rich set of data for analysis. This chapter examines data on contracting by the city of Los Angeles and reviews other studies of government contracting and set-aside programs. The impacts of local-government set-aside programs are assessed by examining changes in the use of WBEs and MBEs associated with the establishment, presence, or weakening of program requirements.

The main hypothesis examined below is that a city with an MWBE affirmative action program increases its use of MWBEs. This hypothesis appears to be confirmed by the data on contracting. The core of the analysis is based on data for the years 1978–1991 for the city of Los Angeles. The major findings are that more MWBEs obtained business contracts after a preference program was implemented, and that fewer MWBEs did in the post-*Croson* era. A review of other California post-*Croson* studies reinforces the conclusion that targeted programs are critical in helping MWBEs receive a fair portion of government contracts. This study also found that jurisdictions without affirmative action programs have extremely low utilization rates[2] of MWBEs; jurisdictions that moved from a race- and gender-neutral approach to a targeted approach increased MWBE utilization; and that the *Croson* ruling has undermined these programs and reduced MWBE participation.

Self-Employment Among Minorities

The development of federal governmental programs to aid minority- and women-owned firms has been based on a recognition that both groups suffer from a large gap in business ownership relative to white men on a national level. Not only are there large differences in self-employment rates, but relative to firms owned by non-Hispanic whites, black- and Latino-owned firms tend to have much lower average sales and to employ fewer workers. Many minority firms consist only of the owner or the owner and his or her family. They are usually privately held, operate in heavily urban areas, and are in industries in which these groups have traditionally been present, such as housecleaning, janitorial services, auto repair, barber and beauty services, and auto dealerships. These are often the traditional mom-and-pop stores. Such operations generally earn low profits and have high failure rates.[3] Historically, there has been a lack of development of large-scale enterprises in both the black and Latino communities. Not many years ago, the list of the largest black-owned firms in America was dominated by auto dealers. In recent years, however, larger minority-owned firms have been developed, and now more such firms are found in industries in which they traditionally have not had a presence.[4]

Minority and female underrepresentation in business ownership is also a problem in California. Table 1 shows self-employment rates by race and gender for decennial years from 1940 to 1990. Between 1940 and 1970, there was a downward trend in self-employment for all but two race/gender groups, which paralleled the national trend of this period. Black and Latino male self-employment rates fell from 1940 to 1960, rose only slightly after 1960, fell between 1970 and 1980, and rose after 1980. The rates for Asian Americans fell from 1950 to 1980. The extremely high Asian American self-employment rates of 1940 and 1950 correspond to a period when Asian Americans faced great labor-market discrimination and used self-

Table 1: Self-Employment in California as a Percentage of the Labor Force by Ethnicity and Gender (1940–1990)

Gender/ Ethnicity	1940	1950	1960	1970	1980	1990
Men						
Asian American	24.4	25.7	19.7	15.1	11.5	12.3
Black	9.9	4.9	4.2	5.6	5.2	6.2
Latino	8.9	8.4	6.1	6.3	5.4	6.9
White	19.5	18.3	12.7	11.4	14.5	15.7
All	19.0	17.3	12.0	10.7	12.4	12.5
Women						
Asian American	8.1	12.9	6.1	4.8	5.2	7.6
Black	7.3	2.8	3.8	3.0	2.2	3.5
Latina	11.2	4.5	3.1	2.7	2.5	5.4
White	10.3	8.2	5.8	5.4	6.6	9.3
All	10.2	7.7	5.5	5.0	5.6	5.8

Sources: For 1940–1970: Paul Ong, et al., "Socio-Economic Trends in California" (Sacramento: California Employment and Development Department, 1986). For 1980 and 1990: author's estimates using Public Use Micro Samples (5 percent PUMS), (U.S. Department of Commerce, Bureau of the Census).

employment as an alternative. The need for self-employment may have simply declined among Asian Americans after 1950.

Nationally, self-employment rates began to rise after 1970. We see this post-1970 rise in California among whites, but not among minorities (except for Asian American women) until after 1980. In percentage-point increase and absolute numbers, however, the post-1980 rise in self-employment among minorities lagged behind the rise in white self-employment. There is reason to be concerned about overall business-formation rates in the state now that minorities are on the verge of becoming the majority. In Los Angeles County, blacks and Latinos already constitute a majority of the population, but are only about half as likely as whites to be self-employed. Such low self-employment rates among groups that are becoming the new majority of the population suggest that new business formation will lag in the future unless the rates for Latinos and blacks can be increased substantially.[5]

While there is a large gap between white and minority levels of business ownership since 1970, minority firms have generally grown in size, become more diversified, and are more successful than in the past. One reason for the growth of minority-owned firms in nontraditional industries and for the development of larger black firms in traditional industries (such as construction) is said to be the widespread use of government and corporate minority set-aside programs.[6] The use of set-aside programs became important only in the late 1970s.[7]

Business Set-Asides and Economic Efficiency

While it has been argued that increasing the usage of MWBEs will improve the level of efficiency in a market by increasing competition, it has also been argued that setting aside contracts for MWBEs will lead to higher costs and thus higher prices. In those markets where no MWBEs are being used and contracts are largely awarded through an "old boys' network," opening up the market to MWBEs could be expected to lower prices and improve efficiency. However, setting up and monitoring an affirmative action program does require administration costs. In addition, a loss in efficiency could result when large numbers of contracts are awarded to very young MWBE firms, and few are awarded to experienced white firms. Which effect has been greater cannot be conclusively determined by current evidence, but there is little evidence that government contracting has ever been conducted in ideally competitive markets. It is not clear that society is faced with a trade-off between fairness and efficiency in having to decide whether or not to have affirmative action programs for MWBEs. The most common practices of government contracting, even in the absence of affirmative action programs, appear to restrain competition and favor firms owned by whites, and therefore are noncompetitive and inefficient by nature. Our real choice may be whether to have a system that is both unfair and inefficient, or have it replaced with a system that is fair, but inefficient.

Twenty-five years ago, MWBEs did not receive government contracts in any significant numbers; many contracts were likely to go to the same firms year after year. In 1972, less than one-sixth of 1 percent of federal contract dollars were awarded to MBEs.[8] Studies done in the 1980s and 1990s reveal that even in California, in cities with large minority populations, MWBEs were virtually excluded from public-contract awards (see the discussion of Sacramento below). The entry of MWBEs into government contracting as a consequence of preference programs has caused this entire area to be subject to careful court scrutiny, and this in itself is likely to add to the care with which contracts are let out, resulting in an increase in efficiency. Reviewing how set-aside programs are established shows that the use of MWBEs requires more attention to how all contracts are treated and how and even whether bidding processes are conducted.

Economic theory implies that economic discrimination acts to increase production costs. Most economists argue that discrimination itself is inefficient and robs society of resources.[9] While employer discrimination has been explicitly linked to inefficient forms of market behavior, discrimination that restricts businesses from competing is clearly suspect of reducing economic efficiency, just as any form of restraint of trade is viewed as reducing efficiency. Even if affirmative action programs are ended, efficiency may be increased by ending practices that limit competition and pose unfair barriers to MWBEs getting contracts.

Barriers to Self-Employment

The ability to be self-employed is important to both individuals and society for at least three reasons. Self-employment is an important alternative to wage employment; it can provide opportunity when wage employment is restricted or undesirable. Self-employment is also an important outlet for entrepreneurial talent, and entrepreneurship is often viewed as a factor of production as important to the economy as land, labor, or capital. Finally, an increased level of business formation among minorities holds out hope for less employment discrimination, since minority-owned firms are known to be more likely to hire minorities than are white-owned firms.

The self-employment gaps between whites and minorities (reported in Table 1) reflect a variety of factors. Light and Rosenstein[10] have described the decision to be self-employed as affected by three types of factors: affinity, capability (resources), and labor-market disadvantage. The decision to be self-employed can also be based on a comparison of opportunities, with some better than others. Labor-market disadvantage is just one way of evaluating comparative opportunities. Conditions of market demand will determine which and how many of the self-employed can expect to remain in business.

Some people may have an affinity for entrepreneurship because they live in an environment where entrepreneurship is practiced and valued. If one's family and family friends have their own businesses, this is likely to help cultivate affinity and to help socialize individuals for self-employment. Socialization is not just accomplished through knowing people who have businesses, though; otherwise men and women would be equally likely to be self-employed. Affinity only partly explains the supply side of self-employment. For instance, we observe among Korean immigrants in the United States very high rates of self-employment, yet self-employment rates are low in Korea. Both resource availability and comparative opportunities are important in explaining why groups start producing entrepreneurs.

Starting or acquiring a business requires financial resources, so entry can be expected to be affected by personal and family wealth as well as by education and training. Asset differences between whites and blacks or Latinos are large and may be expected to be important sources of differences in self-employment rates. However, many businesses can be started up with only a few hundred or a few thousand dollars, amounts well within reach of most blacks and Latinos. Business knowledge and experience may be far more important than financial assets, but also are not equally shared among the races.

The construction industry provides a useful illustration of the problem of acquiring business knowledge. This industry is often examined in disparity studies and is reviewed in the case studies below. In order to do business, it is necessary in many industries to have regular contact with others in the industry. Knowing industry insiders or having mentors can be very useful in learning the details of doing business. Family and friends can be helpful if they are involved in an industry. This kind of close relationship can also act as a barrier for those who are trying to break into an industry.

Acquiring specific business knowledge requires the ability to directly learn a business. In construction, many contractors begin as construction workers (carpenters, painters, or electricians) and learn how to develop a business based on their trade skills. Unfortunately, for many years the construction trades were virtually closed to minorities and women. A combination of nepotism and discrimination prevented generations of blacks and women from learning the basics of the industry. In the case of construction firms, exclusion has been particularly unfortunate because the industry lends itself to entrepreneurship. Construction firms can be formed without high capital costs and any skilled worker can become a contractor. Many firms begin as a second job and expand as owners exploit opportunities for larger jobs.

Today, there are many minority workers (mostly black and Latino) in construction and the number of minority firms has greatly expanded in the last 20 years. However, most minority construction firms have remained small. Often minority firms get work only from other minorities and are unable to bid on large projects. Because minority-owned construction firms tend to be young, they have less experience and weaker financing. They also have greater problems finding qualified workers (who tend to work with larger firms) and in developing management skills. Because of many years of minority exclusion in the industry, whites tend to have the qualifications needed for large jobs, but rarely will work for black-owned firms. Robert Glover reports that in the 1970s, black-owned construction firms had trouble finding qualified black supervisors (due to the years of industry exclusion), while white supervisors tended to be reluctant to work for black-owned firms.[11]

Labor-market disadvantage is an old explanation for entrepreneurship, with Jewish entrepreneurship in Europe and the United States as a classic example. In California, Chinese self-employment was rooted in a history of labor-market exclusion. In a study of Atlanta in the 1980s, Koreans cited labor-market disadvantage as a reason for becoming storekeepers.[12] Immigrants may face disadvantages in the labor market due to language difficulties, a lack of recognition of foreign degrees and credentials, cultural differences, or discrimination. A reduction of wage- and salary-employment opportunities can also promote efforts at self-employment. Several studies have found that self-employment rises when the unemployment rate rises.[13]

On the other hand, for some groups, other labor-market opportunities may be more inviting. Some groups may face discrimination both as employees and as business owners. Blacks appear to suffer from both forms of discrimination, although opportunities have generally improved more in public employment than in private. Robert Boyd has found that in metropolitan areas where blacks have received rising shares of public-service employment, black self-employment has lagged.[14]

On the demand side, a major explanation offered for the black-white self-employment gap is the effect of customer discrimination and discrimination from other businesses. If many white consumers have a strong preference for buying from other whites, the returns to self-employment would be less for blacks than for whites of the same skill.[15] It is the presence of customer discrimination that provides an important basis for seeking protection for groups who face discrimination in self-employment. For blacks, severe customer discrimination may provide an important reason why self-employment is not seen as much of an alternative to salaried employment.

Overall, there are higher rates of self-employment in California. In 1980, the self-employment rate for non-Hispanic whites was 8.5 percent in the United States and 8.8 percent in 28 large Standard Metropolitan Statistical Areas (SMSAs), but it was 12 percent in Los Angeles, 12.1 percent in Orange County, 12.7 percent in San Diego, 10.8 percent in San Francisco, and 11.2 percent in San Jose. Minority self-employment rates were closer to national averages than non-Hispanic white rates, which means that local minorities are less able to benefit from overall strong general demand conditions.

The above economic analysis indicates that a variety of factors can influence self-employment. Self-employment is not simply the result of innate propensities, but is influenced by supply and demand factors that can be altered. Self-employment rates for women and minorities are not "natural" or constant: There is evidence that certain barriers affect the level of self-employment, and thus the elimination of these barriers can be an effective technique for increasing the numbers of self-employed people. The principle barriers may be: (1) lack of information and business knowledge (part of which may reflect discrimination); (2) lack of assets (again, part of which may reflect discrimination); and (3) discrimination in self-employment (by customers or suppliers). Economic theory indicates that set-aside programs can be effective by simply promoting fair entry into markets and emphasizing technical-assistance programs in order to overcome weak business backgrounds among blacks, Latinos, and poor immigrants.

Government Policies on Minority-Owned Businesses

Discrimination in employment by race or gender is subject to both state and federal legislation, but firms that discriminate in their dealings with other firms are not governed by any such federal laws, while evidence suggests that state laws are ineffective. Suggs points out that "no federal statute ever has been adopted specifically to bar racial discrimination in private commercial transactions between two business firms."[16] While both federal and state laws protect employment rights and have been used with effect, there is no comparable protection for minority- or women-owned firms that encounter discrimination. While business-to-business discrimination occurs in both the private and the public sector, remedies have been largely directed toward firms doing business with the public sector. Rather than relying on general prohibitions of discrimination, governments have designed programs aimed at assisting minority firms and at opening up government procurement contracting to minority-owned firms.

The 1960s saw the initial development of government programs to assist minority enterprises, and in the 1970s "black capitalism" became a catchphrase. In 1969, Nixon created the Office of Minority Business Enterprises (OMBE) in order to help develop minority enterprises. In the 1960s and early 1970s, low-interest or guaranteed loans were used to help minority businesses—but this strategy had, at best, limited success. In 1973, only 740 loans were made to blacks under Small Business Administration (SBA) programs. Many loans were for refinancing older loans, many were to established firms, and some were never actually disbursed. Bates characterized the early SBA programs as ineffectual, while others claimed the programs were politicized and corrupt.[17] By 1973, there were numerous investigations of robbery, extortion, and fraud in the minority business programs.[18]

An alternative strategy to assist MWBEs is to increase their participation in government contracting. Government expenditures on goods and services are a sizable share of GDP. In California alone, state and local governments spent $1.9 billion on construction in fiscal year 1991–92. For the entire country, the value of government contracts (federal, state, and local) was about $450 billion, or 10 percent of the GDP in 1990.[19] The trend toward privatizing government work promises to increase the value of government contracting.

Historically, however, MWBEs have received few contracts from government agencies.[20] Public-agency MWBE affirmative action programs were established to address this underrepresentation. The intent of government affirmative action programs is to set goals or establish preferences for awarding contracts to minority contractors and subcontractors. The purpose of the set-aside goal is to aid minority firms in getting started and to assist their further development, either by providing initial government contracts or by helping them establish contacts with larger firms.

Set-aside goals have been justified as a way to increase the size of the minority enterprise sector, to help develop minority communities, and to help develop larger minority middle classes.[21] The National Association of Minority Contractors (NAMC) argues that set-asides are useful because they "increase productive capacity and competitiveness among contractors." Some set-aside programs establish goals for MWBE participation, some simply promote preferences for MWBEs, some seek to encourage MWBEs by allowing "discounts" on bids by MWBEs, and some programs eschew set-asides and preferences and rely on race- and gender-neutral programs that focus on business training. Examples of each of these approaches are found in California.

Affirmative Action for Large Corporations Facing Discrimination

While there is current debate over the use of affirmative action programs for minorities and women, the use of this concept is not limited to economic minorities within the United States. The term "managed trade" has been used in U.S. demands that Japan open its domestic markets to American firms. Demands have been made for specified market shares—in essence, set-asides for large American firms.[22] In some discussions of the economics of discrimination, race has been compared to a trade barrier, where skin color acts as a tariff on trade.[23] Robert Suggs argues that trade barriers erected by Japan against U.S. firms have parallels to race as a trade barrier and observes that set-asides have been proposed for both cases. In both cases there has been debate over whether the simple removal of formal restraints would be adequate to increase market share. It has been argued that Japanese business success results from a partnership of giant conglomerates and government bureaucrats, with informal agreements as effective as any government decree in barring American firms from penetrating Japanese markets. Altering formal restrictions would not have much impact on trade where informal agreements remain powerful. This view has been the basis for U.S. demands for managed trade, where market shares are reserved for American firms.[24]

If it is difficult or impossible for American Fortune 500 corporations to do business in Japan because of discriminatory customs, the barriers must be even more daunting for MWBEs in the U.S. economy in the face of discrimination. Just as federal government efforts to increase Japan's importation of U.S. semiconductor parts have been successful in helping American corporations in Japan, affirmative action programs taken collectively may have had more impact on MWBEs than any other program. Since 1970, minority firms have grown in number, size, and diversity. One reason for the growth of minority-owned firms in industries in which they traditionally have not had a presence, and for the development of larger black firms in industries in which they traditionally have (such as construction), is likely the widespread use of government and corporate minority set-aside programs.[25] The use of set-aside programs became important only in the late 1970s,[26] and there has been a rapid growth in the number of minority-owned firms since then.

Croson and Its Aftermath

Despite, or perhaps because of, the achievements of MWBE programs, the strategy has faced significant opposition. In January 1989, the United States Supreme Court rendered a major decision regarding the use of set-aside programs: *Croson*.[27] The city of Richmond, Virginia, had established a program to set aside some business for minority contractors. Majority prime contractors were required by city ordinance to provide 30 percent of the contract to MBEs. Croson Co. was a contractor that was the sole bidder for a city contract. Croson sought a waiver from the 30 percent set-aside requirement, but was denied. Then, failing to comply with the ordinance, Croson lost the contract. Subsequently, Croson sued, claiming the requirement was unconstitutional, and the case was ultimately decided by the Supreme Court. In the *Croson* decision, the Court ruled that municipalities may use programs to correct the effects of identified, systemic racial discrimination within its clearly defined market areas. But the presence of discrimination had to be demonstrated and programs had to be "narrowly tailored" to address discrimination. *Croson* did not address WBE programs, but lower courts have used *Croson* as a guide for how WBE programs should be tailored as well.

While the Court found that Richmond could legally have a program to aid MBEs, the program in place was found to be illegal, having violated the equal protection clause of the Fourteenth Amendment. The Court required that a study be done to demonstrate that discrimination was a problem and that race-neutral measures were not adequate to produce relief. The Court further insisted that discrimination be demonstrated in individual markets and for specific groups. While oral evidence of discrimination could be used to identify discriminatory behavior, statistical evidence needed to be gathered to demonstrate an actual disparity between the availability[28] and the utilization of MBEs. The Court also allowed assessment of the impact of barriers that would cause minority-firm formation to be reduced[29] in order to determine whether there had been past discrimination in that market.

Armed with both anecdotal evidence and statistical proof that minority firms are harmed by discrimination, government agencies can proceed to create MBE affirmative action programs if other remedies are not adequate. For instance, if a lack of capital is all that prevents MBEs from being competitive, then a race-neutral program to assist firms in gaining access to capital would be appropriate. Programs with set-aside goals can only be continued as long as disparities exist, requiring continual monitoring.

Since the *Croson* ruling, lower courts have reviewed numerous programs with set-aside goals and preferences, finding some unconstitutional and upholding others. The threat of legal challenge has forced state and local governments to review and often revise or discard existing programs. Those governments that want to establish programs now know they must follow the *Croson* guidelines and carefully tailor their programs.

The *Croson* decision led a number of local and state governments to abandon their MWBE programs, while others proceeded to conduct post-*Croson* disparity studies that addressed the Court's requirements for proof of harm from discrimination. One deterrent to providing or continuing a set-aside program is the expense of doing a disparity study. These studies cost from $60,000 to more than $1 million, depending on the database requirements and complexity of the study.

In California, several cities and counties and some large government agencies have conducted disparity studies. Several of these studies are examined in the following sections in order to assess the impact of such affirmative action programs—and their discontinuation or modification in light of *Croson*—on both minority contracting and self-employment and on the use of MWBEs by state and local governments. The focus is on the experience of several different cities and counties, primarily in California. Appendix A for this study (see page 153) contains summaries of the California disparity studies reviewed below.[30] Only the city of Los Angeles data are original in this report.

MWBE Contracting with the City of Los Angeles

The city of Los Angeles procures more than $1 billion in goods and services annually. This sum can have a significant impact on minority business opportunities directly (through the choice of contractors) and indirectly (through expenditures in local communities). Mayor Tom Bradley created an MWBE program by issuing Executive Directive No. 1-B on March 4, 1983. At the time, no study of MWBE contracting with the city had been done, and the city lacked consistent standards for documenting and reporting contracts. Each city department was directed to develop an 11-point program for contracting and bidding procedures that would help raise the level of MWBE participation. The plans were to include outreach, monitoring, reporting, and the provision of information and technical assistance to MWBEs. In addition to the stated program directions and goals, there is one further reason to expect minority firms to have improved their business with the city of Los Angeles during the period that the program existed: As mayor, Bradley, an African American, had the influence and willingness to implement this program.

A clear test of the impact of the Los Angeles affirmative action program is to compare MWBE contracting before, during, and after the program. Data are available for 1978–1991, all years during which Mayor Bradley was in office. The data include all available contracts for all city departments, agencies, and subdivisions. Many departments kept contracts for only a few years before discarding their files, so the database is only reasonably complete for recent years for all departments. While the records of contracts are largely complete for recent years, important vendor information such as ethnicity, gender, and major industry is often missing. The numbers cited must be viewed as estimates. A detailed description of the methodology of collecting the data and of estimating the percentage of local-government contracts obtained by minority- or women-owned businesses—utilization of MBEs or WBEs—is provided by Larson, Ochoa, and Levine.[31]

As shown in Figure 1, utilization of MWBEs increased dramatically with the establishment of Bradley's program. Utilization is based on either the number or the value of contracts awarded. For minorities, utilization in value terms (the percentage of the total dollar value of all contracts) increased from 2.2 percent to 11.8 percent. All three minority groups experienced an increase in the value of contracts: double for Asian American–owned firms (from 1.5 percent to 3 percent), more than tenfold for black- and Latino-owned firms (from 0.3 to 3.6 percent and from 0.3 to 5.2 percent, respectively). For women-owned firms, utilization increased at an even higher rate, from 0.3 to 8 percent.

Following the *Croson* decision, the city's set-aside program was modified. A new directive, 1-C, stated that the city would continue its policy of outreach to MWBEs, but the language was modified to indicate that only reasonable steps would be taken and that all firms would have equal opportunity to compete for contracts. The city continued to request that prime contractors seek out qualified minority subcontractors and demonstrate "good-faith" efforts to do so. A failure to make good-faith efforts could be the basis for withdrawal of a contract. This attempt to maintain an MWBE program proved to be only partially successful. Utilization of Asian American–owned firms continued to rise, albeit modestly, from

Figure 1: Utilization Rates (in Contract Dollars) for Minorities and Women in the City of Los Angeles

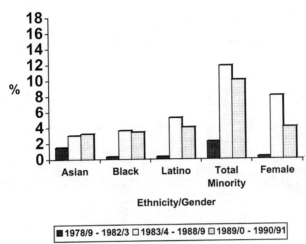

Source: Tom Larson, Eduardo Ochoa, and Ned Levine, "MWBE Contracting with the City of Los Angeles" (Unpublished manuscript, California State University, Los Angeles, 1996).

3 percent prior to *Croson* to 3.2 percent after *Croson*. This group is the least disadvantaged minority (although some Asian Americans must be considered disadvantaged, such as those of Vietnamese and Cambodian descent). The proportion of all contracts awarded to black-owned firms declined moderately, from 3.6 percent to 3.4 percent, while the decline for Latino-owned firms was larger, from 5.2 percent to 4 percent. For all minorities, the utilization rate dropped from 11.8 percent to 10 percent. The decline for women-owned firms, however, was significantly larger, both in absolute and relative terms. The utilization rate of women-owned firms was cut in half, from 8 percent to only 4 percent.[32]

Despite the initial marked increase in MWBE utilization in Los Angeles as a result of the Bradley program, a problem of underutilization relative to availability remained. Table 2 documents the disparity. In Table 2, the city's utilization of MBEs is compared to the availability of MBEs in the market area for Los Angeles. Availability was derived from the 1990 Census of the Population; "major occupation" was used to identify the self-employed. The table compares contract shares against shares of self-employment. The difference between the share of contracts awarded and the share of self-employment is the disparity. The data cover all industries and the construction industry separately. The construction industry is relatively easy to define and thus can easily be compared across time and across cities. Other industries are also analyzed in disparity studies, but have not been included here for the sake of brevity and because of large differences in

Table 2: City of Los Angeles Disparities for All Industries and the Construction Industry: MWBE Contract Shares (1987–1990)

Ethnicity/Gender	Availability (%)	Utilization (%)	Disparity
All Industries			
Asian American	12.9	5.6	-7.3
Black	4.4	5.9	1.5
Latino	19.8	7.7	-12.1
Minorities (total)*	37.2	19.2	-18.0
Women	31.0	16.1	-14.9
Construction Industry			
Asian American	6.7	6.8	0.1
Black	4.4	7.3	2.9
Latino	22.7	16.9	-5.8
Minorities (total)	33.8	31.0	-2.8
Women	6.4	11.5	5.1

* For the cities studied, Native American contractors and subcontractors were often too small a group from which to make statistical inferences. Therefore, except for tables in Appendix A for Oakland and Richmond, the numbers for Native Americans are included under total minorities.

Source: Larson, Ochoa, and Levine, "MWBE Contracting with the City of Los Angeles."

industry groupings outside construction. (For this reason, the data in Appendix A are taken exclusively from the construction industry.)

The disparity analysis shows that even by the late 1980s, and before the *Croson* decision, minority-owned firms were less likely to be utilized than were white-owned firms, after adjusting for availability. The numbers for all industries reveal large disparities for firms owned by Latinos, women, and Asian Americans, although no disparity for black-owned firms. (Many studies have found that there is a large disparity for black-owned firms, but this is not the case for Los Angeles.)

The above analysis did not take into account that discrimination has likely discouraged minority-firm formation. One striking finding is the low number of black- and Latino-owned firms compared to the number owned by whites and Asian Americans. This may reflect long-term patterns of discrimination that have created barriers to firm formation. In the construction industry there are several barriers to minority firm formation. First, in previous decades few minorities were allowed to join labor unions, thereby reducing the training opportunities necessary for becoming a contractor. Second, the so-called old boys' network has put minority firms at a disadvantage when competing with white-owned firms. Third, financial institutions have been less likely to loan funds to minority-owned firms, making it difficult for them to get bonded or to expand. Fourth, experienced and skilled white workers have tended to work for white-owned firms, thus reducing the talent available to minority firms.

Table 3: Disparity Estimates Based on Potential Availability for All Industries, City of Los Angeles: MWBE Contract Shares (1988–1992)

Ethnicity/Gender	Potential Availability (%)	Utilization (%)	Disparity
Asian American	14.9	5.6	-9.3
Black	7.9	5.9	-2.0
Latino	31.9	7.7	-24.2
Minorities (total)	54.3	19.2	-35.1
Women	39.9	16.1	-23.8

Source: Larson, Ochoa, and Levine, "MWBE Contracting with the City of Los Angeles."

Because of the almost certain (but usually unmeasured) impact of discrimination on availability, Larson, Ochoa, and Levine[33] explored the use of alternative estimates of availability in the hypothetical absence of discrimination. Their analysis indicates that the self-employment rate of minorities is lower than that of whites, after comparing individuals of the same education, experience, and other observable characteristics. Table 3 reports "potential availability" where potential availability is the hypothetical number of minority firms in the absence of discrimination that prevents women and minorities from becoming self-employed. Potential availability reflects the likelihood of self-employment in a world where women and minorities are treated the same as whites or males, but still have observed levels of education and assets (the full set of control variables are listed in Appendix B). They concluded that after adjusting for discrimination, the disparity rate for women is higher, and almost doubles for each minority group. For blacks, the disparity rate based on the estimated availability is -2 percentage points, rather than the positive 1.5 percentage points based on the unadjusted availability rate, as shown in Table 3.[34]

Effects of Establishing and Weakening Local-Government Set-Aside Programs in Other Jurisdictions

The observed effects for Los Angeles of first establishing an MWBE program and then weakening it are not limited to this one local government. A review of disparities for other jurisdictions provides evidence that supports the importance of affirmative action programs on MWBE participation in public contracting. It also finds that in the absence of such programs MWBEs are underutilized, race-neutral programs are ineffective, and the *Croson* ruling has had a broad chilling effect.

In 1990, a disparity study in Tallahassee, Florida, revealed that MBE prime contractors and subcontractors had received no city contracts in the years 1973–1975. Tallahassee began a set-aside program for construction projects in 1983. By 1987, MBEs were being awarded 24 percent of all annual construction contracts (prime contractors and subcontractors combined). The 1990 Tallahassee disparity study found that black firms had been underutilized as contractors despite being "able to do the work."[35] MWBEs registered a similar striking advance in New Haven, Connecticut, in roughly the same period. Before instituting its program, New Haven had awarded less than 1 percent of its contracts to MWBEs. Within a few years after instituting set-aside goals, MWBEs were being awarded 25 percent of the city's annual contracts.

A 1998 Urban Institute study reviewed 58 disparity studies from across the country, including several from California. The institute's major findings were: (1) there are substantial disparities between the availability and utilization of minority-owned firms in government contracting (based on availability, MBEs receive only 57 percent of the expected value of MBE contracts); (2) disparities exist for MBEs in all industries, with the smallest disparities in construction subcontracting; (3) disparities are greater in cities that do not have have affirmative action programs. In cities with no program, MBEs receive only 45 percent of the value they should expect to receive of contracts (compared to 57 percent in cities with programs).[36] The Urban Institute results indicate that the present study, by focusing on construction contracts, presents a more optimistic picture of the prospects for MBEs receiving government contracts (without intervention in the form of affirmative action).

A number of studies of California cities report dramatic changes in the awarding of contracts to MBEs and WBEs after an affirmative action program was instituted. Often the programs had to be refined, as in the case of San Jose, the third-largest city in California. In 1970 the San Jose city council passed Resolution 37160 to encourage prime contractors to hire workers and subcontractors in a nondiscriminatory manner with regard to race; in 1973 the resolution was broadened to include gender. In 1977 the council took further steps, believing that previous resolutions hadn't been successful in promoting equality in the use of minority contractors. New resolutions were passed in 1983 and 1987. The 1987 resolution required MWBEs to be certified, and made prime contractors subject to greater scrutiny in their efforts to attract MWBE subcontractors. Financial penalties for false information or failure to follow the program were added.[37]

Data on prime contractors and subcontractors in the San Jose construction industry illustrate the effects of refining the MWBE program. In fiscal year 1981–82, more than 90 percent of all prime construction contracts and more than 96 percent of all contract dollars were awarded to firms owned by white men. Only three prime contracts were awarded to minority-owned firms in 1981–82, and none were awarded to women-owned firms. By 1987–88, white male–owned firms received only 79 percent of all prime contracts, but over 90 percent of all contract dollars.

It would be expected that subcontractors would be more affected by the city's program than prime contractors, and this appears to be the case. Among subcontractors, in 1981–82, white men received more than 81 percent of all contracts; in 1987–88, less than 56 percent. The disparity for minority prime contractors was reduced from 33 percentage points in 1981–82 to 15 percentage points in 1987–88. The disparity for women prime contractors disappeared. The disparities for both minority subcontractors (as a whole) and women subcontractors also disappeared. In each year, black-owned prime contractor and subcontractor firms experienced a disparity between availability and utilization, and no Asian American–owned firms were used as prime contractors in 1987–88. The main reason that overall usage of minority-owned firms was large and increased dramatically is the number of Latino-owned firms that were awarded contracts. A second reason for the decrease in disparity is due to the lower availability of black-owned construction firms in 1987 (down from 10 percent of available firms in 1981 to 5 percent in 1987).

Where there were no programs, the utilization of both MBEs and WBEs was found to be low relative to availability. In 1993–94, MWBEs had only an 8 percent share of all contracts in Orange County, 11 percentage points below their availability. In San Diego, the MWBE share was 4 percent, 13 percentage points below their availability.[38]

The use of race-neutral programs alone does not appear to help MWBEs, as illustrated by the case of Sacramento. Four agencies that were studied by MGT Consultants[39] had race- and gender-neutral policies in place during the years studied (1982–1991). In construction, more than 90 percent of all prime contracts and subcontracts went to white male–owned firms in every year that was studied. In no year did black-owned firms receive a single construction contract. Even though the availability of minority-owned construction firms grew from 1982 through 1990, there was little change in the number of contracts awarded to minority-owned firms. There was also little change in the number of contracts going to women-owned firms, and almost all of the women-owned firms receiving contracts were owned by whites. Very few subcontracts went to minority-owned firms. Data for the city of Sacramento are reported in Appendix A, but each of the four agencies studied (city, county, transit district, redevelopment agency) had similar numbers. While only construction industry data are reported below, the findings were similar in each industry/category studied (professional services, other services, and purchasing expenditures). The great disparities in

Sacramento were accompanied by the consultants' conclusion that Sacramento's program, which relied on race-neutral policies, was a weak one.

After 1989, a number of MWBE affirmative action programs were abandoned or weakened, allowing further assessment of whether the programs had really had an impact on the use of MWBEs. As a result of the *Croson* decision, a number of municipalities discontinued their set-aside programs. Consequently, the use of MWBEs fell considerably in cities such as Atlanta; Richmond, Virginia; Tampa, Florida; and Philadelphia.[40] MWBE utilization decreased from 37 percent to 24 percent in Atlanta, from 32 to 11 percent in Richmond, and from 25 to only 3.5 percent in Philadelphia. In Tampa, MWBE utilization essentially disappeared, decreasing by 99 percent.

Despite the program changes necessitated by the *Croson* ruling, not all cities experienced a reduction in MWBE utilization. Oakland has had an MWBE program since 1979, when the city council passed Resolution 57926 C.M.S., which established the Minority Business Enterprise Program. Initially, the program was for MBEs. When it was revised in 1982, WBEs were included. A set-aside goal of 30 percent was established for MBEs, with an additional goal of 50 percent set aside for small businesses. The goal for WBEs was a 5 percent set-aside, and 50 percent of these also were to be small businesses. The city's policy was to award contracts to the "lowest responsible bidder" who has achieved or made a good-faith effort to achieve the program's goals. The program focuses more on subcontractor opportunities than on prime contractors, and requires MWBE certification. Oakland continued its program after *Croson* and increased the share of contracts awarded to MWBEs in the 1990s. In a comparison of the figures for 1991–92 to those for 1993–94, the minority disparity was reduced from -15.8 to -7.7 percentage points.[41] In neither period was there a disparity for WBEs. Oakland's experience shows that it is possible to run an effective MWBE program in the post-*Croson* era.

Most disparity studies do not permit a comparison of contracting in different time periods. Often this is due to a lack of older contracts. Sometimes this reflects a small budget for the study. Both San Francisco and Richmond have set-aside programs and have conducted disparity studies, but we are unable to assess the impact of the programs over time. The San Francisco and Richmond studies show that both cities have significant disparities, despite majority minority populations and strong minority political representation in both cities.

Conclusions and Policy Implications for MWBE Programs

Since about 1970, self-employment rates have been increasing in the United States. The overall self-employment rate in California has also grown and exceeds the national average. Among minorities and women in this state, self-employment rates remain substantially lower than among whites and men, but have been generally rising since about 1980. Despite growth since 1980, minority self-employment rates are surprisingly low, particularly for Latinos and blacks, but also for some Asian groups, such as Vietnamese, Cambodians, and Filipinos. Self-employment rates for blacks and Latinos remain so far below those for whites that California's overall rate of business formation may slow down, curbing future economic growth.

The major factors responsible for low self-employment rates among minorities are: (1) discrimination (whether by the customer, supplier, or financier); (2) low average levels of human capital and financial assets; and (3) lack of knowledge of business entrepreneurship.[42] Firm formation among blacks and Latinos appears to be especially affected by the above factors, but Asian Americans are also affected by disparate treatment

While discrimination has been found to be a serious problem for minority- and women-owned firms,[43] there is no effective legal prohibition against customers, suppliers, and financial institutions basing purchasing or lending decisions on the race or gender of the owner of a firm. State laws prohibiting discrimination against firms appear to be ineffective, and there are no federal regulations governing the private sector. Thus, the primary tools for redressing discrimination between firms have been: (1) lending programs designed for MWBEs and small businesses; (2) technical assistance programs for MWBEs and small businesses; and (3) affirmative action programs for MWBEs (as well as for disadvantaged business enterprises [DBEs], veterans, or the disabled). Neither lending programs nor technical assistance programs, by themselves, have been shown to have significant impact on assisting MWBEs.

In the absence of effective laws barring discrimination between firms, MWBE affirmative action programs are presently the only effective redress for such discrimination between firms. As we have shown in this chapter, an analysis of California disparity studies indicates that MWBE affirmative action programs have had an important positive effect on minority- and women-owned businesses. Proposition 209's mandate that all affirmative action programs in California be discontinued would include the dismantling of MWBE affirmative action programs.

The disparity studies summarized in Appendix A provide a wealth of statistical evidence and personal testimony from business owners supporting the argument that discrimination has had a chilling effect on minority- and women-owned enterprise, even in California in the 1980s and 1990s.

Nevertheless, since the failure of "black capitalism" programs of the 1970s, and despite the limiting effects of the *Croson* decision, programs to combat discrimination in public contracting have been effective in increasing the number of public contracts awarded to MWBEs. Today, many public programs also seek to promote small businesses and provide technical assistance to MWBEs. Technical assistance programs, in combination with affirmative action programs, can be expected to help MWBEs develop, since a lack of entrepreneurial background is part of the explanation for low levels of MWBE firm formation. However, acting to improve the supply of MWBEs (through technical assistance programs) while ignoring ways of raising demand for them (such as through affirmative action programs) has not proven to be an effective remedy. Two good examples of raising demand for MWBEs through affirmative action programs were those enacted by the cities of Los Angeles (1983–1989) and San Jose (1987).

Moreover, simply encouraging self-employment among minorities and women will do little for MWBE development if it results in just more mom-and-pop retail stores. Government contracts that have a high dollar value affect a larger scale of business, one that has seen very few MWBEs in the past. By enabling MWBEs to obtain some or more of such contracts, affirmative action programs have begun to change this picture. Thus affirmative action has not only been able to provide opportunities for more MWBEs, but also to provide MWBEs with opportunities outside the area of traditional mom-and-pop enterprises. The development of substantive businesses can be encouraged through these programs. This can bring more businesses into markets and open up competition, and promises, ultimately, to provide the lowest prices possible. Abuses and inefficiencies may continue to occur in the form of "fronts" and because of practices of accepting higher bids from MWBEs (which remains rare in California), but appropriate affirmative action programs (ones that can be legally defended in light of the *Croson* decision) can promote both fairness and efficiency.

Because of *Croson* and other court decisions, MWBE affirmative action programs are both carefully and strictly regulated today. Current law requires narrow tailoring of programs where detailed studies have demonstrated disparities. Set-aside programs are much more closely regulated than are employment programs. If public opposition to affirmative action is based on feelings that unqualified minorities are being granted an unfair share of opportunities, the strict scrutiny that MWBE affirmative action programs have been subject to since 1989 should alleviate such concerns. Public programs to promote the use of MWBEs are required by law to be carefully tailored to meet proven areas of discrimination by industry and by ethnicity. Programs must then be monitored and are subject to discontinuance once disparities are eliminated. Programs that are seen as unfair to majority firms can and do end up in court. A greater public awareness of how carefully these programs are constructed and run may reduce fears of reverse discrimination among the majority population. The availability of redress through the court system for white-owned firms has contributed to the careful construction of programs.

This study has found an affirmative action approach (targeted programs for MWBEs, or set-asides) that appears fair and that works, but remains little-known among the general population. Overall, affirmative action programs have opened important business opportunities to minorities and women in California and promise to aid in the development of minority communities. Furthermore, the formation and development of MWBEs in California can make an important, if not crucial, contribution to overall economic growth. At the same time, the record does not show that white-owned firms are unfairly being foreclosed from business opportunities. White self-employment has grown even as minority and women's self-employment has grown in California.

In the aftermath of Proposition 209, successful programs that survived post-*Croson* scrutiny have been discontinued. Once 209 was enacted, San Jose ended its successful program. San Jose continued to require prime contractors to do outreach, but even that requirement has been challenged in court.[44]

Appendix A

Summary of Disparity Studies for Selected California Cities and Counties

The key elements for statistical analysis in a disparity study are the estimation of MWBE availability, utilization, and market areas. Once the availability and utilization rates for a group in an industry for a given market are estimated, the disparity is calculated. It may be given as the simple difference between availability and utilization or by a comparison of the two, with availability defined as parity.

Utilization refers to the proportion of contracts, in terms of either the number or the dollar value, awarded to MBEs or WBEs by a government agency. In this study, utilization is reported in terms of the percentage of the total number or total value of contracts entered into by the agencies.

Poor recordkeeping means that it is not always possible to have accurate counts of agency contracts, but most studies try for complete counts rather than samples. This may simply limit the years that can be analyzed, as older records are generally harder to find or to code correctly in terms of ethnicity, gender, industry, or even dollar amounts.

Availability is a measure of the relative availability of MWBEs. There are different ways to estimate availability, and a wide variety of numbers are possible. The *Croson* decision is generally interpreted to require very narrow tailoring of set-aside programs. At one extreme, this would mean identifying those individual firms that had been excluded from getting contracts in the past because of clearly identified instances of discrimination based on race or gender and then giving them preference in the future. At the other extreme, one could estimate all firms that are capable of providing goods or services, whether or not they have ever bid on an agency's contracts, plus all those potential firms that did not come into existence because discrimination was great enough to discourage firm formation.

There are three common types of data used to estimate availability: Economic Census data, Census of the Population data, or various lists of contract bidders and MWBEs. The most conservative approach is to use contract-bidder lists. These are lists of firms that have actually participated in the process of bidding for agency contracts. If discrimination is a problem, many firms may not be on such lists because they do not expect to be awarded contracts or may be excluded from such lists because of discrimination in the first place. The problem of discrimination will be underestimated if bidder lists are used as the basis of measuring firm availability. Lists of MWBEs that are maintained by various organizations may augment the bidder lists. Some of these lists are of certified MWBEs; other lists rely on self-identification.

The Economic Census not only counts all firms, based primarily on IRS records, but also includes the Survey of Minority-Owned Business Enterprises (SMOBE) and the Survey of Women-Owned Business Enterprises (SWOBE). These surveys generally include all single proprietorships, partnerships, and type S corporations (corporations with fewer than 35 shareholders), but have a different methodology each year they are conducted (making comparisons across time difficult). Race information is taken from Social Security records, resulting in a large problem in counting Latino-owned businesses, since Hispanics were not identified as such in Social Security records until 1981. This means that Latinos are always undercounted in the SMOBE because of the number of owners who received Social Security accounts before 1981. The Latino undercount can be greatly alleviated by using Census of the Population data on the self-employed. This last approach identifies all those who claim to be self-employed in their major occupation or who report self-employment income. Usually, only the count of self-employment by major occupation is used because the count of those with self-employment income includes many part-time self-employed people.

Where public agencies have established MWBE programs, the emphasis of such programs is often on helping MWBEs participate in contracts as subcontractors. Most MWBEs are small firms and are often unable to handle large contracts. This means that programs often award contracts to white male prime contractors but ask that they seek MWBE subcontractors.

Los Angeles County

In Los Angeles County, self-employment has grown for women and minorities, but rates remain well behind those for men and whites. Black and Latino men remain about half as likely as white men to be self-employed.[45]

The county of Los Angeles annually awards about $1 billion in contracts to private firms. Construction contracting is a major share of total contracts (about 24 percent). In 1991, the county adopted an MWBE program and commissioned a disparity study. For calculating utilization, all contracts and purchases for fiscal years 1989–90, 1990–91, and 1991–92 were examined. MWBE status was determined partly through a phone survey of contractors and partly through the use of various MWBE lists used by public agencies. The market for construction was determined to be a five-county area including and surrounding Los Angeles County. Availability estimates were based on the 1987 SMOBE and SWOBE surveys and were updated for 1990 using trend forecasts.

The disparity analysis for the construction industry in Los Angeles County indicated that among prime contractors (Table A-1) there were virtually no disparities for black- or women-owned firms, but there were disparities for Latino- and Asian American–owned firms. The county is the only public agency found in this study that had no disparity for black-owned firms in prime construction contracts prior to instituting a set-aside program. Among subcontractors (Table A-2) there was a disparity for black-owned firms that was statistically significant. There were no statistically significant disparities for other groups among construction subcontractors.

In public hearings, minority and women contractors complained of county practices that acted to exclude MWBEs from contracting with the county. Bonding requirements were viewed as excessive, the county was seen as "unresponsive" to requests from MWBEs for information about contracting practices, and programs that relied on "good-faith" efforts by contractors to use MWBE subcontractors were seen as weak.

Table A-1: County of Los Angeles Construction Industry Disparities: MWBE Prime Contractor Contract Shares (1989–90 Through 1991–92)

Ethnicity/Gender	Availability (%)	Utilization (%)	Disparity
Asian American	6.4	1.7	-4.7
Black	2.6	4.9	2.3
Latino	17.0	8.5	-8.5
Minorities (total)	26.0	15.1	-10.9
Women	6.1	6.9	0.8

Source: Author's calculations based on the "Report on the Results of the Los Angeles County MBE/WBE Utilization and Availability Study" (Los Angeles: County of Los Angeles, Office of Affirmative Action Compliance, 1992).

Table A-2: County of Los Angeles Construction Industry Disparities: MWBE Subcontractor Contract Shares (1989–90 Through 1991–92)

Ethnicity/Gender	Availability (%)	Utilization (%)	Disparity
Asian American	6.4	6.0	-0.4
Black	2.6	0.7	-1.9
Latino	17.0	18.2	1.2
Minorities (total)	26.0	24.9	-1.1
Women	6.1	20.8	14.7

Source: Author's calculations based on the "Los Angeles County MBE/WBE Utilization and Availability Study."

San Francisco

By 1990, San Francisco had become another large city with a majority minority population: Minorities constituted more than 53 percent of the population. Although minority and majority self-employment rates are quite high in the San Francisco metropolitan area, whites are far more likely than Asian Americans or Latinos, and especially blacks, to be self-employed. (The white rate is 15 percent; Asian American and Latino rates are both 8.5 percent, while the black rate is 5.3 percent.)

BPA Economics, Inc. conducted a disparity study for the City and County of San Francisco shortly after the *Croson* decision was announced.[46] For the construction industry, SMOBE and SWOBE counts were used to estimate MWBE availability. For prime contractors, the market area was defined as San Francisco County, and only contracts let in San Francisco were examined. Utilization therefore refers only to San Francisco–based firms.

The San Francisco study (Table A-3), using data for fiscal year 1987–88, showed a substantial disparity between the availability and utilization of minority prime contractors in construction: almost 36 percentage points. For black-owned firms, the utilization rate was only 26 percent

Table A-3: San Francisco City and County Construction Industry Disparities: MWBE Prime Contractor Dollar Shares (1987–1988)

Ethnicity/Gender	Availability (%)	Utilization Dollars (%)*	Disparity
Asian American**	27.7	5.4	-23.4
Black	8.5	2.2	-6.3
Latino	10.7	3.4	-7.3
Minorities (total)	46.9	11.1	-35.8
Women	29.3	1.2	-28.1

*Percentage of contract dollars awarded.

**This category includes Filipinos, in this and all the following tables.

Source: Author's calculations based on BPA Economics, Inc., "Statistical Support for San Francisco's MBE/WBE/LBE Ordinance" (San Francisco, 1989).

of the availability rate. For women-owned firms, the disparity was quite large: Only 1.2 percent of the contracts were for women-owned firms, but more than 29 percent of the available firms were owned by women, leaving a disparity gap of 28.1 percentage points, or only 4 percent of parity. There was no finding of underutilization among subcontractors in construction (or any other industry). San Francisco subsequently legislated a preference program only for prime contractors.

Oakland

Oakland also has a majority minority population, with blacks being the largest population group (43.2 percent). Whites are now a minority in Oakland (28.5 percent). Even in this heavily majority minority city, there are still charges of adverse impacts due to traditional forms of discrimination.

Oakland has had an MWBE program since 1979, when the city council passed Resolution 57926 C.M.S., which established the Minority Business Enterprise Program. Initially, the program was for MBEs; when it was revised in 1982, WBEs were included. A set-aside goal of 30 percent was established for MBEs, with an additional goal of 50 percent of these for small businesses. The goal for WBEs was a 5 percent set-aside, and 50 percent of these were also to be small businesses. The city's policy was to award contracts to the "lowest responsible bidder" who had achieved or made a good-faith effort to achieve the program's goals. The program was focused more on subcontractor opportunities than on prime contractors, and required MWBE certification.

Mason Tillman Associates determined availability by using lists of MWBEs in the local market[47] (again, using lists is a very conservative approach to estimating availability, but was probably necessary given the small market defined).

The local market was defined as the city of Oakland, even though a majority of contracts (57.4 percent) were awarded to firms outside the city. However, it has been city policy to encourage awards to local firms. Contract data were collected from city records for the fiscal years 1991–92, 1992–93, and 1993–94 (Tables A-4 through A-6). Out of 1,135 construction contracts, 418 went to white male–owned firms.

Table A-4: City of Oakland Construction Industry Disparities: MWBE Contract Shares (1987–1988)

Ethnicity/Gender	Availability (%)	Utilization (%)	Disparity
Asian American	11.0	10.1	-0.9
Black	40.9	24.9	-16.0
Latino	8.4	14.6	6.2
Minorities (total)	60.3	49.6	-10.7
Women	11.3	20.4	9.1

Source: Author's calculations based on Mason Tillman Associates, "Disparity Study: Oakland, California" (Oakland: City and Redevelopment Agency, 1996).

Table A-5: City of Oakland Construction Industry Disparities: MWBE Contract Shares (1991–1992)

Ethnicity/Gender	Availability (%)	Utilization (%)	Disparity
Asian American	11.0	7.6	-3.4
Black	40.9	16.6	-24.3
Latino	8.4	20.0	11.6
Minorities (total)	60.3	44.5	-15.8
Women	11.3	18.1	6.8

Source: Author's calculations based on Mason Tillman Associates, "Disparity Study: Oakland."

Table A-6: City of Oakland Construction Industry Disparities: MWBE Contract Shares (1993–1994)

Ethnicity/Gender	Availability (%)	Utilization (%)	Disparity
Asian American	11.0	10.3	-0.7
Black	40.9	28.2	-12.7
Latino	8.4	12.2	3.8
Native American	0.5	1.9	1.4
Minorities (total)	60.8	52.6	-8.2
Women	11.3	17.1	5.8

Source: Author's calculations based on Mason Tillman Associates, "Disparity Study: Oakland."

Oakland has continued its MWBE program since 1989 (post-*Croson*) and has increased the share of contracts awarded to MWBEs in the 1990s. In a comparison of the figures for 1991–92 to those for 1993–94, the minority disparity was reduced from -15.8 to -8.2. In neither period was there a disparity for WBEs. There were disparities in 1991–92 for Asian Americans and blacks in the construction industry, but not for Latinos. While MBE usage increased in 1993–94, this period showed a sizable disparity for black-owned firms.

Richmond

The city of Richmond, California, commissioned a disparity study in 1993 by Mason Tillman Associates and Leong Data Research and Diversity Planners.[48] Richmond had a program, the City Affirmative Action Plan (CAAP), prior to the study and to the *Croson* decision. The city wanted to ensure that the program satisfied the *Croson* guidelines. The CAAP had been adopted in 1984 and was directed at employment as well as at business practices. Despite the CAAP, there were significant disparities in Richmond's contracting, as can be seen in the table below. In a city where more than 40 percent of the population was black and only 31 percent was white, the vast majority of construction contracts went to whites (over 85 percent in 1990–92). Substantial disparities were found for black- and women-owned firms in construction contracting (Table A-7). Smaller, but statistically significant disparities were found for business owned by Asian Americans, Latinos, and Native Americans.

Members of minorities have been officeholders in Richmond since at least the 1960s, and the city has had black mayors. However, the black business community in Richmond has remained small. In 1987, there were only 50 black-owned businesses in Richmond. Richmond's history

Table A-7: City of Richmond Construction Industry Disparities: MWBE Contract Shares (1990–1992)

Ethnicity/Gender	Availability (%)	Utilization (%)	Disparity
Asian American	4.7	3.4	-1.3
Black	23.8	4.4	-19.4
Latino	11.1	6.0	-5.1
Native American	1.2	0.1	-1.1
Minorities (total)	40.8	13.9	-26.9
Women	15.2	2.6	-12.6

Source: Author's calculations based on Mason Tillman Associates and Leong Data Research and Diversity Planners, "City of Richmond Disparity Study" (Richmond, CA: City and Redevelopment Agency, 1994).

reveals standard practices of segregation and discrimination that intensified after World War II and continue to this day. The disparity study noted that intense housing discrimination was the cause of a low black home-ownership rate in Richmond, and that blacks have experienced inferior education in Richmond schools for many years.

For the disparity study, the Richmond market area was determined to be Alameda and Contra Costa counties (where more than 70 percent of all construction contracts were awarded). Availability was estimated using bidder lists and lists of MWBEs from various agencies. For estimating utilization, contract data on prime contractors and subcontractors were collected from all city departments. The method used to estimate availability is very conservative, since it tends to exclude firms that have not tried to get contracts from Richmond. The disparities would likely be much larger if SMOBE/SWOBE data or self-employment estimates were used (these data are available for Alameda and Contra Costa counties).

Sacramento

Sacramento commissioned a disparity study that covered four agencies: the city, the county, the local transit district, and the redevelopment agency. The study was conducted in 1991–92 by MGT Consultants.[49] All contracts that were available were included in the contract database. Market areas were determined by expenditure by county. Utilization was estimated on the basis of contract dollars, while availability was based on number of contractors as determined by using the 1982 and 1987 SMOBE/SWOBE counts. For years other than 1982 and 1987, growth rates were estimated in order to adjust the local firm counts.

The Sacramento study revealed large disparities for all minorities and some disparities for women (Tables A-8 through A-11). In construction, more than 90 percent of all prime and subcontracts went to white male–owned firms in every year that was studied. In no year did black-owned firms receive a single construction contract. Even though the availability of minority-owned firms grew from 1982 through 1990, there was little change in the value of contracts going to minority-owned firms. There was also little change in the value of contracts going to women-owned firms, and almost all of the women-owned firms receiving contracts were owned by whites. Very few subcontracts went to minority-owned firms. The data reported in the tables are only for the city of Sacramento, but each agency had similar numbers. While only construction is reported in the tables, each industry studied yielded similar findings.

The great disparities in Sacramento are found in tandem with a very weak program. For example, the disparity study reported a number of practices that contributed to the low utilization of minority-owned firms.

Table A-8: City of Sacramento Construction Industry Disparities: MWBE Prime Contractor Dollar Shares (1982–1983)

Ethnicity/Gender	Availability (%)	Utilization Dollars (%)	Disparity
Asian American	2.7	0	-2.7
Black	1.0	0	-1.0
Latino	2.1	0	-2.1
Minorities (total)	5.8	0	-5.8
White Women	9.1	9.8	0.7

Source: Author's calculations based on MGT Consultants, "Study of the Utilization of Minority/Women Business Enterprises (M/WBEs), Executive Summary" (Sacramento: Sacramento Housing and Redevelopment Agency, Sacramento Regional Transit District, 1992).

Table A-9: City of Sacramento Construction Industry Disparities: MWBE Prime Contractor Dollar Shares (1990–1991)

Ethnicity/Gender	Availability (%)	Utilization Dollars (%)	Disparity
Asian American	4.3	0.1	-4.2
Black	2.4	0	-2.4
Latino	8.5	2.4	-6.1
Minorities (total)	15.2	2.5	-12.7
White Women	9.6	3.2	-6.4

Source: Author's calculations based on MGT Consultants, "Study of the Utilization of Minority/Women Business Enterprises."

Table A-10: City of Sacramento Construction Industry Disparities: MWBE Prime Contractor and Subcontractor Dollar Shares (1982–1983*)

Ethnicity/Gender	Availability (%)	Utilization Dollars (%)	Disparity
Asian American	2.7	0	-2.7
Black	1.0	0	-1.0
Latino	2.1	0	-2.1
Minorities (total)	5.8	0	-5.8
White Women	9.1	9.8	0.7

*Combining data on prime contractors and subcontractors shows that there were neither minority prime contractors nor minority subcontractors at the time.

Source: Author's calculations based on MGT Consultants, "Study of the Utilization of Minority/Women Business Enterprises."

Table A-11: City of Sacramento Construction Industry Disparities: MWBE Prime Contractor and Subcontractor Dollar Shares (1990–1991)

Ethnicity/Gender	Availability (%)	Utilization Dollars (%)	Disparity
Asian American	4.3	0.4	-3.9
Black	2.4	0.0	-2.4
Latino	8.5	5.6	-2.9
Minorities (total)	15.2	6.0	-9.2
White Women	9.6	3.8	-5.8

Source: Author's calculations based on MGT Consultants, "Study of the Utilization of Minority/Women Business Enterprises."

Bidding processes were informal and not advertised, restricting access to the "usual" firms. Often, verbal price quotations were used, resulting in a tendency to call the same firms over and over and not include minority firms in contacts. The report regarded the certification process for MWBE status as cumbersome. There was a general tendency to conduct business as usual and not examine good-faith efforts by prime contractors to use MWBE subcontractors.

Each of the four agencies studied had in place race- and gender-neutral policies during the years studied. The study recommended augmenting the race- and gender-neutral policies by adding race and gender programs in order to effectively raise MWBE participation rates. The study concluded with a set of race and gender goals for each agency and outlined programs to help achieve these goals. The Sacramento study shows that MWBE usage did not just naturally grow in the 1980s in the public sector. Where no programs are used or programs are weak, we can observe large disparities for MWBEs in the public sector.

San Jose

San Jose is the third-largest city in California, with a 1990 population of 782,225. It also has a majority minority population. In 1970, the city council passed Resolution 37160 to encourage prime contractors to hire workers and subcontractors in a nondiscriminatory manner with regard to race. In 1973, the resolution was broadened to include gender. In 1977, the city council took further steps, feeling that previous resolutions had not been successful in promoting equality in the use of minority contractors. A new resolution (56342) was passed in 1983. Again, the city council believed a stronger program was needed and passed another resolution in 1987. The 1987 resolution required MWBEs to be certified and made prime contractors subject to greater scrutiny in their efforts to attract MWBE subcontractors. Financial penalties for false information or failure to follow the program were added. In addition to the program to promote MWBEs in contracting, San Jose also had a race-neutral program in place throughout the 1980s to promote small-business development.

Shortly after the *Croson* decision, the city commissioned a disparity study, which was completed in 1990.[50] This study compared utilization and availability in two distinct periods, 1981–82 and 1987–88. The early period precedes the era of a strong MWBE preference program, while the later period follows implementation of the stronger program. The data permit not only a disparity analysis but also an evaluation of the effectiveness of the new program.

All contract awards that were not federally funded were part of the database for estimating utilization. Availability estimates were made for a seven-county area using a combination of contract-bidder lists and the San Jose MWBE directory. As discussed above, this is a very conservative way to estimate availability and has likely overlooked many firms that could bid for contracts in San Jose.

Tables A-12 through A-15 report statistics for prime contractors and subcontractors in the construction industry by race and gender. It might be argued that more MWBEs were used in 1987–88 because of greater availability, but the disparity analysis indicates that availability did not improve for all minorities, even as disparities were reduced. Once again, the presence of a strong MWBE program, even one without quotas or goals, is associated with much greater usage of MWBEs.

Table A-12: City of San Jose Construction Industry Disparities: MWBE Prime Contractor Contract Shares (1981–1982)

Ethnicity/Gender	Availability (%)	Utilization (%)	Disparity
Asian American	3.8	2.7	-1.1
Black	9.7	2.7	-7.0
Latino	27.6	2.7	-24.9
Minorities (total)	41.0	8.1	-32.9
Women	6.1	0	-6.1

Source: Author's calculations based on BPA Economics, Mason Tillman Associates, and Boasberg and Norton, "MBE/WBE Disparity Study for the City of San Jose" (San Jose, 1990).

Table A-13: San Jose Construction Industry Disparities: MWBE Prime-Contractor
Contract Shares (1987–1988)

Ethnicity/Gender	Availability (%)	Utilization (%)	Disparity
Asian American	3.8	0	B3.8
Black	9.7	0	B9.7
Latino	27.6	17.7	B9.9
Minorities (total)	41.1	17.7	B23.4
Women	6.1	1.3	B4.8

Source: Author's calculations based on BPA Economics et al., "MBE/WBE Disparity Study for
the City of San Jose."

Table A-14: City of San Jose Construction Industry Disparities: MWBE
Subcontractor Contract Shares (1981–1982)

Ethnicity/Gender	Availability (%)	Utilization (%)	Disparity
Asian American	3.8	0	-3.8
Black	9.7	0	-9.7
Latino	27.6	17.7	-9.9
Minorities (total)	41.1	17.7	-23.4
Women	6.1	1.3	-4.8

Source: Author's calculations based on BPA Economics, et al., "MBE/WBE Disparity Study
for the City of San Jose.

Table A-15: City of San Jose Construction Industry Disparities: MWBE
Subcontractor Contract Shares (1987–1988)

Ethnicity/Gender	Availability (%)	Utilization (%)	Disparity
Asian American	5.8	7.8	2.0
Black	4.9	1.5	-3.4
Latino	18.0	22.9	4.9
Minorities (total)	28.7	32.2	3.5
Women	10.7	12.2	1.5

Source: Author's calculations based on BPA Economics, et al., "MBE/WBE Disparity Study
for the City of San Jose."

Appendix B

Estimating Potential Availability of the Self-Employed Among Minorities And Women

The calculations for Table 3 (page 147) are based on Census of the Population data that are used to measure the availability of MWBEs in terms of self-employment. The measure of self-employment is based on individuals self-reporting their employment status. Individuals may be self-employed, employed for someone else, unemployed, or not in the labor force. For individuals who are both self-employed and work for someone else, only one response is allowed.

The procedure used by Larson, Ochoa, and Levine[51] was to estimate self-employment rates that would exist if everyone was treated as if they were either white or male. First, logit estimations of a model of the determinants of self-employment were performed. The logit—or logistic probability—model is a variety of probability model which assumes that the probability distribution of a qualitative dependent variable has a logistic rather than a linear form (hence when estimating this model by regression techniques, we perform logistic rather than linear regressions). The logit model is widely used for estimating qualitative-dependent-variable models because of its superior statistical properties.[52]

The Table 3 estimates do not adjust for all discrimination, since they ignore the causes of unequal levels of education, assets, and so forth. Instead, estimates are based on what we should expect if women and minorities were currently treated the same as similarly situated whites or males. The methodology is as follows. First, estimate the influence of a number of factors on the probability of self-employment for a population that is generally "preferred" (whites or men). This estimation yields a set of coefficients that measure the strength of the influence of each variable (such as education or assets) on the probability of self-employment when there is no discrimination. Second, use these nondiscriminatory coefficients and calculate the probability of self-employment for minority groups. Assuming that education has a positive effect on self-employment, and given that whites on average have higher levels of education than African Americans, one would expect that whites would have higher levels of self-employment (which they do). The estimation sums the products of the means (X) and the coefficients (B) via the following formula:

$$P(\text{self-employment}) = 1/(1 + e^{-z})$$

where $z = B + BX$. This procedure indicates whether, after taking into account differences in education, assets, and other factors that affect self-employment, the predicted rate of black self-employment is higher than the observed rate. If the observed rate is lower than the predicted rate, the unexplained difference is assumed to be due to discrimination. The technique is thus able to disentangle the combined effect of discrimination and differences in other characteristics that influence self-employment and measure their relative contribution to observed disparities in self-employment among groups.

In all applied econometric work that uses existing data sets, the researcher faces the problem of having to use as predictors variables that may not be direct determinants of the dependent variable values. In the extreme—especially when dealing with small data sets—this can lead to spurious relationships being established because of randomly occurring correlations among variables, or to other systematic extraneous patterns, especially in time series. This is clearly not the case for the data used here. With an enormous data set of 217,550 cross-sectional observations (i.e., not time series), these potential sources of error are not a factor.

The fact that the variables used as predictors are not direct causes of self-employment is not an obstacle to statistical analysis. All we are looking for is evidence that there is significant correlation between values of these predictor variables and the probability of self-employment, as well as an estimation of the coefficients that relate values of the former to the latter. This may be done through direct influence, or through correlation to a third variable that is the true cause (in this case, the variable used acts as a proxy variable).

Logit Variables: The Determinants of Self-Employment

Variable	Definition
Age	Age in years
Age squared	Age times age
Married	Equals 1 if married, zero otherwise
High school	Equals 1 if a high school graduate (only)
Some college	Equals 1 if has some college
B.A. degree	Equals 1 if person has a B.A. degree (as their highest degree)
M.A. degree	Equals 1 if person has an M.A. or M.S. degree
Ph.D. degree	Equals 1 if person has a Ph.D. degree
Foreign-born	Equals 1 if foreign-born
Disabled	Equals 1 if disabled
Dividend income	A measure of assets, in dollars
Home ownership	Equals 1 if a homeowner
English	Equals 1 if command of English is poor

Notes

1. "Set-aside" commonly refers to programs that either create preferences for MWBEs or establish affirmative action programs for them. However, especially since the 1989 *Croson* decision, such programs are best described simply as affirmative action programs since it is generally not the case that any contracts are truly set aside for MWBEs, but rather that a target number of contracts, or goals, for MWBEs is set. In this paper, affirmative action is a preferred use for post-1989 programs, and set-aside is not intended to mean actual set-asides—unless such is specified.

2. "Utilization rate" ("utilization") refers to the proportion of contracts, in terms of either the number or the dollar value, awarded to MBEs or WBEs by a government agency.

3. Timothy Bates, *Banking on Black Enterprise: The Potential of Emerging Firms for Revitalizing Urban Economies* (Washington, DC: Joint Center for Political and Economic Studies, 1993).

4. Ibid.

5. Tom Larson, "Availability of Minority- and Women-Owned Businesses in Southern California" (California State University, Los Angeles, Center for Minority Youth Employment Studies, 1996).

6. Bates, *Banking on Black Enterprise*; Mitchell F. Rice, "State and Local Government Set-Aside Programs, Disparity Studies, and Minority Business Development in the Post-*Croson* Era," *Journal of Urban Affairs* 15 (6): 529–553 (1993).

7. Bates, *Banking on Black Enterprise,* p. 22.

8. Little Hoover Commission, "California's $4 Billion Bottom Line: Getting Best Value out of the Procurement Process" (Sacramento: Commission on California State Government Organization and Economy, 1993).

9. Not all economists feel that discrimination is simply inefficient. Marxists argue that discrimination may serve to help business owners earn higher profits. A complete review of labor market discrimination views is available in Robert Cherry, *Discrimination* (Lexington, MA: Lexington Books, 1989).

10. Ivan Light and Carolyn Rosenstein, *Race, Ethnicity and Entrepreneurship in Urban America* (New York: Aldine de Gruyter, 1995).

11. Robert Glover, *Minority Enterprise in Construction* (New York: Praeger Press, 1977).

12. Pyong Gap Min, "Ethnic Business Enterprise: Korean Small Business in Atlanta" (Center for Migration Studies, New York, 1984).

13. Light and Rosenstein, *Race, Ethnicity and Entrepreneurship in Urban America.*

14. Robert Boyd, "Black and Asian Self-employment in Large Metropolitan Areas: A Comparative Analysis," *Social Problems* 37: 258–273 (1990).

15. George Borjas and Stephen Bronars, "Consumer Discrimination and Self-Employment," *Journal of Political Economy* 97 (3): 581–605 (1989).

16. Robert E. Suggs, *Minorities and Privatization: Economic Mobility at Risk* (Lanham, MD: Joint Center for Political Studies/University Press of America, 1989).

17. Timothy Bates, "Government Promotion of Minority Group Entrepreneurship: Trends and Consequences" (University of Wisconsin, Madison, Institute for Research on Poverty, Discussion Paper No. 197-74, 1974).

18. William Tabb, "What Happened to Black Economic Development?" *The Review of Black Political Economy* 17 (2): 65–88 (1988).

19. Steven Kelman, "Procurement and Public Management: The Fear of Discretion and the Quality of Government Performance" (Washington, DC: American Enterprise Institute, 1990).

20. Bates, *Banking on Black Enterprise.*

21. Rice, "State and Local Government Set-Aside Programs."

22. Suggs, *Minorities and Privatization.*

23. Anne Krueger, "The Economics of Discrimination," *Journal of Political Economy* 71: 481–486 (1963). In Krueger's model, the white community exports capital to the black community and imports black labor. Discrimination acts as a barrier on trade similar to a tariff. Just as there is a possibility of an "optimal" tariff in international trade, there is also a possibility that discrimination may produce trade gains for the white community. Generally, economists believe that a large economy such as that of the United States cannot benefit from any "optimal" tariff, and the same would be true for discrimination. Discrimination would simply reduce the gains to be made from trade and is opposed because it produces an inefficient result.

24. Suggs, *Minorities and Privatization.*

25. Bates, *Banking on Black Enterprise*; Rice, "State and Local Government Set-Aside Programs."

26. Bates, *Banking on Black Enterprise.*

27. 488 U.S. 469 (1989).

28. Availability can be roughly defined as the number of firms in a position to be considered candidates for contracts in a given market or industry.

29. Rice, "State and Local Government Set-Aside Programs."

30. This chapter reviews disparity studies or data for the following six California cities: Los Angeles, Oakland, Richmond, San Jose, San Francisco, and Sacramento. A disparity study for Los Angeles County is also reviewed.

31. Tom Larson, Eduardo Ochoa, and Ned Levine, "MWBE Contracting with the City of Los Angeles" (Unpublished manuscript, California State University, Los Angeles, 1996).

32. One caveat in interpreting these data is that MWBE counts may be biased. MWBE status was based on self-identification and not on verifiable certification. Therefore, utilization counts of MWBEs may be overestimated because of the presence of "fronts," firms that reported being an MWBE but were owned and/or controlled by white men. Nonetheless, it is unlikely that all contracts went to fronts, and although it is impossible to determine precisely how much of the increased contracting went to legitimate MWBEs, there is little question that the program had a positive effect.

33. Larson, Ochoa, and Levine, "MWBE Contracting."

34. Appendix B explains how potential availability was estimated.

35. MGT of America, Inc. "Final Report: City of Tallahassee MBE Disparity Fact-Finding Disparity Study" (Tallahassee, FL: 1990).

36. Maria E. Enchautegui, Michael Fix, Pamela Loprest, Sarah C. von der Lippe, and Douglas Wissocker, "Do Minority-Owned Businesses Get a Fair Share of Government Contracts?" (The Urban Institute, Washington, DC: 1998). The full report is available at the Urban Institute web site: *www.urban.org.* The Urban Institute

study looks at contract values rather than at contract numbers. There is a close, but not exact correlation between share of contracts by value and by count.

37. BPA Economics, Mason Tillman Associates, and Boasberg and Norton, "MBE/WBE Disparity Study for the City of San Jose" (San Jose: 1990).

38. Virginia Ellis and John Hurst, "Women, Minorities Still Lag in Government Contracting, Jobs: Affirmative Action Programs Have Been Largely Ineffective, Records Show," *Los Angeles Times* (September 11, 1995), p. A1.

39. MGT Consultants, "Study of the Utilization of Minority/Women Business Enterprises (M/WBEs), Executive Summary" (Sacramento: City of Sacramento, County of Sacramento, Sacramento Housing and Redevelopment Agency, Sacramento Regional Transit District, 1992).

40. Rice, "State and Local Government Set-Aside Programs."

41. Mason Tillman Associates, "Disparity Study: Oakland, California" (Oakland: City and Redevelopment Agency, 1996).

42. Larson, "Availability of Minority and Women-Owned Businesses."

43. Rice, "State and Local Government Set-Aside Programs."

44. Patricia A. Meagher, "Minority and Women Contracting Programs: As California Goes, So Goes the Nation?" *The Procurement Lawyer* 33 (4) (summer 1998).

45. Larson, "Availability of Minority and Women-Owned Businesses in Southern California."

46. BPA Economics, Inc., "Statistical Support for San Francisco's MBE/WBE/LBE Ordinance" (San Francisco, 1989).

47. Mason Tillman Associates, "Disparity Study: Oakland, California" (Oakland: City and Redevelopment Agency, 1996).

48. Mason Tillman Associates and Leong Data Research and Diversity Planners, "City of Richmond Disparity Study" (Richmond, CA: City and Redevelopment Agency, 1994).

49. MGT Consultants, "Study of the Utilization of Minority/Women Business Enterprises."

50. BPA Economics, Inc., "MBE/WBE Disparity Study for the City of San Jose."

51. Larson, Ochoa, and Levine, "MWBE Contracting with the City of Los Angeles."

52. J. Kmenta, *Elements of Econometrics,* 2nd edition (New York: Macmillan, 1986), pp. 548–553.

Chapter 8

Affirmative Action and Admission to the University of California

Cecilia A. Conrad

Introduction

Along with programs designed to increase minority contracting and employment, affirmative action programs have been developed to address racial disparities in higher education. The evidence shows extensive underrepresentation of minorities in California's postsecondary institutions. African Americans represent 7.4 percent of the state's high school graduates in 1990 and 6.6 percent of the state's postsecondary enrollment. Hispanics represent 23.3 percent of the state's high school graduates and 12.9 percent of the postsecondary enrollment.[1] Moreover, African American and Hispanic enrollment in postsecondary institutions is concentrated in two-year colleges and vocational programs. African Americans represent less than 6 percent of enrollment in four-year colleges and universities; Hispanics, less than 11 percent.

The reasons for these small numbers are complex.[2] One important factor is racial disparity in elementary and secondary education. Compared with whites, a smaller percentage of African Americans and Hispanics graduate from high school, enroll in academic or college preparatory programs, take the college entrance examination, and file applications to postsecondary institutions.[3] Those who do take the college entrance examinations have, on average, lower scores than their white and Asian American counterparts. Less than 1 percent of black and less than 3 percent of Hispanic 1992 college-bound high school graduates met all of the requirements for admission to a selective four-year college or university,[4] while nearly 9 percent of Asian Americans and 7 percent of whites met these requirements.[5] For Hispanics, differences in aspirations also contribute to their underrepresentation in postsecondary institutions. In 1988, only 55 percent of eighth-grade Hispanics expected to obtain a bachelor's or higher degree, compared with 72 percent of Asians and Pacific Islanders, 64 percent of blacks, and 68 percent of whites.[6] Finally, experts cite the cost of higher education as critical to racial differences in participation because a disproportionately large number of African American and Hispanic students have fewer resources to finance the ever-increasing cost of schooling.[7]

Whatever the causes, the relative scarcity of college-educated African Americans and Hispanics has contributed to racial inequality in the past, and it is likely to become a more significant factor in the future. Differences in educational attainment explain a large portion of the earnings gap between Hispanic and white men and between black and white men.[8] Differences in educational attainment have become even more important as technological changes and the globalization of the economy have increased the demand for college graduates. As a consequence of these changes, the monetary returns to those with higher education have increased, while the returns to those with less education have decreased, a shift that has widened the gap between the earnings of minority and white men.

To counteract these economic trends, proponents of affirmative action in college and university admissions argue that increasing minority enrollment is necessary. Active outreach and recruitment and special consideration are necessary to reduce group disparities in educational attainment and encourage the development of individual talent. Affirmative action programs can help identify students who have the ability and potential to succeed in college despite a less than stellar performance on standardized tests. In doing so, colleges and universities give a signal to underrepresented minorities (URMs) that they are welcome in postsecondary institutions, resulting in increased aspirations and application rates. The potential benefits of affirmative action are not limited to minority students. Proponents assert that racial and ethnic diversity in the student body improves the quality of education received by all students. "In the world of ideas, the greatest source of intellectual growth comes from the challenge to one's assumptions, perspectives and ways of thinking. Exposure to peers with varying backgrounds is an important source of this kind of challenge."[9]

Affirmative action also provides a method to enforce nondiscrimination in the admissions process. "Even when invidious discriminatory standards are abandoned there remain subtle and tenacious forms of discrimination and structural factors which limit the application of new norms of equality."[10] The university admissions process is affected both directly and indirectly by the subjective judgments of individuals—

directly through the evaluations of secondary school teachers and indirectly through the assignment of students to college preparatory courses.[11] Since the admissions process involves subjective judgments, it would be difficult to evaluate whether the process discriminates against a particular group without reference to specific outcomes.

Finally, support for affirmative action programs can be rationalized as a form of reparations for historical discrimination. Persistent residential segregation coupled with labor-market discrimination has limited the quality of elementary and secondary education for certain groups. Jim Crow laws restricted access to higher education for an older generation, and this, in turn, has had an impact on the probability of success for their children.[12] The impact is not just limited to the adversely affected populations. When parental resources constrain children's decision-making about education, the resulting distribution of educational resources will be inefficient for the whole economy.[13]

Critics of affirmative action, on the other hand, offer a different interpretation of its effects. They argue that affirmative action converts a race-neutral decision-making process into one that discriminates against whites and Asian Americans. Some African American and Hispanic students are admitted with lower grade-point averages and lower scores on standardized tests than those of whites and Asian Americans denied admission. Affirmative action, according to its critics, diverts resources from students likely to excel in college to those likely to fail. Moreover, the critics argue, the policy hurts the minority groups it is intended to help by reducing incentives for academic achievement and creating a mismatch of students with institutions. Coates and Loury set forth the theoretical argument that lower requirements for some groups of students reduce their incentive to work hard in school and thus perform less well on entrance examinations.[14] Datcher-Loury and Garman describe the problem of academic mismatch, arguing that affirmative action programs divert minority students to more competitive institutions where they have lower levels of academic achievement.[15] This can have ramifications for the students if the earnings premium associated with attending a selective college is offset by a low grade-point average and a low probability of completion.

Furthermore, the potential ramifications are not solely monetary. Several prominent African Americans have argued that affirmative action stigmatizes its beneficiaries. Carol M. Swain, an associate professor of politics and public affairs at the Woodrow Wilson School at Princeton University, writes: "Besides encouraging many to play the victim, affirmative action policy telegraphs an equally harmful subliminal message to its beneficiaries. It says in effect that you, as a woman or minority, are less capable than a white male and will need special preference in order to compete successfully in a world dominated by white males. . . . Affirmative action sends a message to whites that minorities and women need this help, contributing to white denigration of minorities and women."[16]

Finally, critics fear that affirmative action will reduce the quality of education for all students by watering down the curriculum. "When poor preparation and weak motivation are coupled with government policies to promote—indeed, almost force—educational participation, even if more students were formally enrolled, the quality of learning might deteriorate."[17]

The University of California (UC) has been at the center of the controversy over affirmative action in college and university admissions. After years of efforts to increase minority enrollment through special admissions, the University of California has recently reversed course. Resolution SP-1 of the Board of Regents of the University of California mandated that effective January 1, 1997, the University of California shall not use race, religion, sex, color, ethnicity, or national origin as criteria for admission to the university system or any program of study. The subsequent passage of the California Civil Rights Initiative, Proposition 209, reinforced this mandate. These changes pose a crucial question: What will California lose by ending race-based affirmative action in the UC system? To answer this question, the rest of this chapter examines UC admissions policies before the Board of Regents' resolution and Proposition 209 to assess the potential benefits and costs of these policies.

Undergraduate Admissions

The California Master Plan for Higher Education limits admission to the University of California to the top 12.5 percent of graduating high school seniors in the state. Eligibility is determined by scores on standardized tests and by high school grade-point average (GPA).[18] The lower the GPA, the higher the Scholastic Aptitude Examination (SAT) score required for admission.[19] Asian Americans have the highest eligibility rates, illustrated in Figure 1. Nearly 40 percent of Asian American graduates of California public high schools are UC-eligible, compared with less than 10 percent of African American graduates. A little more than 20 percent of white California public high school graduates are UC-eligible.

In principle, there is space available for all UC-eligible students within the UC system. However, as Figure 2 illustrates, some campuses are more popular than others. UC Berkeley, UC Los Angeles (UCLA) and, to a lesser extent, UC San Diego (UCSD) have many more eligible applicants than spaces for the entering class. Because of the stiff competition, these campuses must apply criteria beyond the UC-eligibility standards to select

Figure 1: Rates of UC Eligibility by Race/Ethnicity (1990)

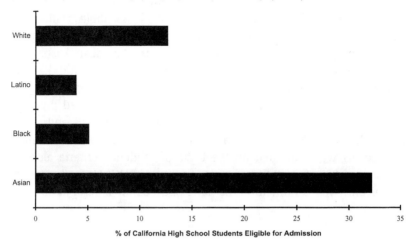

Source: California Postsecondary Education Commission, "Eligibility of California's 1996 High School Graduates for Admission to the State's Public Universities" (December 1996).

Figure 2: Admitted Students as Proportion of All Applicants by Campus (Fall 1995)

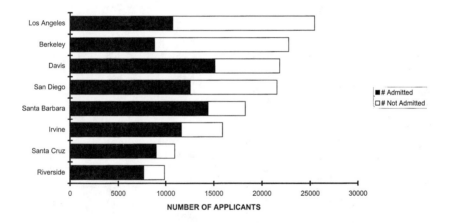

Source: Unpublished tables, University of California Office of the President.

their entering class. At the heart of the debate over affirmative action is a debate over what these criteria should be.

Prior to SP-1, all campuses did not apply the same criteria, but there were some common elements. In general, the first 50–60 percent of the spaces were allocated purely on academic merit—high school GPA, SAT scores, achievement test scores, and the number of honors or advanced placement courses taken in high school. The remaining applicants competed on the basis of a broader range of criteria—athletic skills, artistic talent, leadership ability, socioeconomic disadvantage, or membership in an underrepresented minority group, among others. As Table 1 illustrates, acceptance rates were higher for non-Asian minorities at every campus.[20] With academic credentials held constant, an African American, Hispanic, or Native American had a better chance of admission to UC than did a white or Asian American. At the most competitive campuses, the percentages of African Americans, Hispanics, and Native Americans admitted purely on academic merit were smaller than those for Asian Americans and whites. For example, in UCLA's entering class of 1994, 77 of 663 African Americans (11.6 percent) were admitted on the basis of academic criteria alone. In comparison, 6,801 of the 9,862 students admitted in UCLA's freshman class (68.9 percent) were admitted on the basis of academic criteria alone.[21]

Table 1: Admissions Rates and Yield Rates by Race/Ethnicity (Fall 1995)

	# of Applicants	# Admitted	Acceptance Rate	# Enrolled	Yield Rate
All Campuses, Unduplicated Counts					
Black	2,432	1,436	0.59	793	0.55
Native American	495	384	0.78	243	0.63
Asian American	13,183	10,382	0.79	8,531	0.82
Chicano	5,533	4,014	0.73	2,238	0.56
Filipino	2,309	1,743	0.75	1,108	0.64
Latino	2,149	1,553	0.72	896	0.58
Unknown	2,092	1,739	0.83	883	0.51
White/Other	23,545	18,913	0.80	9,554	0.51
Total	51,738	40,164	0.78	22,226	0.55
UC Berkeley					
Black	1,204	530	0.44	178	0.34
Native American	197	130	0.66	60	0.46
Asian American	7,580	2,611	0.34	1,154	0.44
Chicano	1,906	1,116	0.59	385	0.34
Filipino	917	157	0.17	59	0.38
Latino	861	332	0.39	112	0.34
Unknown	1,075	450	0.42	165	0.37
White/Other	9,166	3,403	0.37	1,179	0.35
Total	22,908	8,729	0.38	3,292	0.38
UC Davis					
Black	659	366	0.56	77	0.21
Native American	181	142	0.78	42	0.30
Asian American	4,966	3,252	0.65	877	0.27
Chicano	1,354	1,017	0.75	224	0.22
Filipino	754	376	0.50	112	0.30
Latino	608	485	0.80	123	0.25
Unknown	721	543	0.75	102	0.19
White/Other	8,469	5,987	0.71	1,487	0.25
Total	17,712	12,148	0.69	3,044	0.25

Table 1 continued on next page

Table 1 continued from previous page

	# of Applicants	# Admitted	Acceptance Rate	# Enrolled	Yield Rate
UC Irvine					
Black	634	267	0.42	50	0.19
Native American	101	65	0.64	14	0.22
Asian American	6,403	4,589	0.72	1,389	0.30
Chicano	1,783	1,024	0.57	214	0.21
Filipino	996	729	0.73	263	0.36
Latino	618	386	0.62	94	0.24
Unknown	478	376	0.79	76	0.20
White/Other	4,899	3,730	0.76	734	0.20
Total	15,912	11,166	0.70	2,834	0.25
UC Los Angeles					
Black	1,444	668	0.46	249	0.37
Native American	166	111	0.67	44	0.40
Asian American	8,389	3,244	0.39	1,055	0.33
Chicano	2,709	1,474	0.54	538	0.36
Filipino	1,181	491	0.42	259	0.53
Latino	1,137	649	0.57	247	0.38
Unknown	1,031	460	0.45	120	0.26
White/Other	9,401	3,626	0.39	1,087	0.30
Total	25,458	10,623	0.42	3,599	0.34
UC Riverside					
Black	539	241	0.45	64	0.27
Native American	59	39	0.66	8	0.21
Asian American	3,696	2,687	0.73	446	0.17
Chicano	1,422	820	0.58	212	0.26
Filipino	577	463	0.80	110	0.24
Latino	400	235	0.59	51	0.22
Unknown	257	200	0.78	34	0.17
White/Other	2,917	2,346	0.80	488	0.21
Total	9,867	7,031	0.71	1,413	0.20
UC San Diego					
Black	681	291	0.43	41	0.14
Native American	183	131	0.72	22	0.17
Asian American	6,268	3,788	0.60	963	0.25
Chicano	1,813	1,081	0.60	212	0.20
Filipino	990	467	0.47	145	0.31
Latino	733	300	0.41	62	0.21
Unknown	998	677	0.68	152	0.22
White/Other	9,917	5,791	0.58	1,450	0.25
Total	21,583	12,526	0.58	3,047	0.24
UC Santa Barbara					
Black	583	336	0.58	57	0.17
Native American	190	144	0.76	26	0.18
Asian American	3,733	2,829	0.76	454	0.16
Chicano	1,919	1,294	0.67	248	0.19
Filipino	622	497	0.80	105	0.21
Latino	816	587	0.72	114	0.19
Unknown	709	595	0.84	111	0.19
White/Other	9,719	8,121	0.84	2,043	0.25
Total	18,291	14,403	0.79	3,158	0.22

Table 1 continued on next page

Table 1 continued from previous page

	# of Applicants	# Admitted	Acceptance Rate	# Enrolled	Yield Rate
UC Santa Cruz					
Black	412	249	0.60	35	0.14
Native American	146	106	0.73	23	0.22
Asian American	2,041	1,464	0.72	154	0.11
Chicano	1,369	975	0.71	135	0.14
Filipino	352	289	0.82	51	0.18
Latino	558	426	0.76	71	0.17
Unknown	550	464	0.84	95	0.20
White/Other	5,978	5,032	0.84	1,046	0.21
Total	11,404	9,005	0.79	1,610	0.18

Source: Unpublished tables, University of California, Office of the President.

Despite the higher acceptance rates for African American, Hispanic, and Native American students, they continue to be underrepresented in freshman classes. This reflects not only their underrepresentation in the pool of eligible high school graduates but also differences in yield rates (those ultimately enrolled as a percent of those admitted). At the most competitive campuses, yield rates were lower for African American and Hispanic students than for white and Asian American students. Furthermore, yield rates appear to be particularly low for the most academically talented African American students. In 1994, 17 percent of all admitted students with the highest academic rank chose to attend UCLA. For African American students in this category, the yield was only 10 percent.[22] This disparity in yield rates has important implications for comparisons of the academic credentials of admitted students. Even if acceptance rates were identical for students with identical academic credentials, the URMs enrolled in the freshman class would tend to have lower high school GPAs and SAT scores than would non-URMs.[23]

Simulations of the effects of a change in admissions policy indicate that affirmative action had a noticeable impact on the racial composition of UC's undergraduate population. In 1995, the Office of the President conducted an analysis of the potential impact of a change in admissions criteria on enrollments for three UC campuses—Berkeley, San Diego, and Santa Cruz.[24] The simulation was based on the characteristics of the 1994 applicant pool. It assumed the new criteria increased the weight given to socioeconomically disadvantaged applicants (defined by parental income and education). The analysis assumed no change in applicant pool and no change in yield rates as a result of this change in policy. The results, summarized in Table 2, show that without race-based affirmative action the numbers of African American, Hispanic, and Native American students would decline, particularly at the most competitive campuses. The number of Asian American students would increase, and the number of white students would also increase but only slightly.

One weakness of the Office of the President's simulation is the questionable assumption that application and yield rates will not change in response to a change in admissions policy. As noted in the study's appendix, the policy change could affect the pattern of applications. Admissions officers voiced the concern that the publicity surrounding SP-1 and CCRI discouraged URMs from applying to UC campuses. The change in policy is also likely to change yield rates. Non-URMs, particularly Asian American students, cite the perceived unfairness of admissions policies toward Asian American students as one reason they chose not to attend the University of California.[25] In a survey of nonmatriculating students conducted in 1990, 22.4 percent of Asian American students, 35.4 percent of Filipino students, and 18.6 percent of white students cited not being admitted to their preferred UC campus as a factor in their decision not to attend any UC school. In comparison, only 10 percent of Mexican American students and 3.4 percent of black students cited this as a factor.[26] As acceptance and yield rates increase for Asian Americans, Filipinos, and whites at UCLA and Berkeley, the yield rates at less popular campuses would decrease. In contrast, as fewer blacks and Mexican Americans are accepted at UC Berkeley, more would accept offers of admission at the less competitive campuses. Yield rates are likely to increase for these groups at San Diego, Davis, Irvine, Santa Barbara, Santa Cruz, and Riverside. The complex interaction between acceptance and yield rates would therefore minimize the net impact of eliminating race-conscious affirmative action for the whole UC system, but there would be a redistribution of URMs from the more competitive campuses to the other campuses.

One strong inference coming out of the simulation and the modifications suggested by the author is that race-based affirmative action increased the number of African American, Hispanic, and Native American students admitted—particularly at the most competitive campuses. It reduced the number of Asian American and white students on individual campuses, but had only a small impact on their numbers in the UC system. Hence, the primary effect of race-based affirmative action was to redistribute students among UC campuses so as to increase diversity at UC Berkeley and UCLA.

Benefits of Undergraduate Affirmative Action

This section examines the private costs and benefits of race-based affirmative action in undergraduate admissions at the University of California.[27] To estimate the costs and benefits, it assumes that neither the size of the entering classes at each campus nor the number of UC campuses will change.

Table 2: Impact on UC Undergraduate Enrollment of Substituting Socioeconomic Status for Race in Simulation Studies

(1) UNIVERSITY OF CALIFORNIA, OFFICE OF THE PRESIDENT SIMULATION

	Actual Enrollment	Simulated Enrollment	Change	Change in %	Actual %	Simulated %
Universitywide						
Black	309	178	-131	-42.4%	3.9%	2.2%
Native American	89	51	-39	-43.3%	1.1%	0.6%
Asian American	2289	2740	451	19.7%	28.7%	33.3%
Chicano/Latino	1146	999	-148	-12.9%	14.4%	12.1%
Filipino	261	272	11	4.0%	3.3%	3.3%
White/Other	3876	3991	115	3.0%	48.6%	48.5%
Total	7970	8229				
Berkeley						
Black	203	98	-106	-52.0%	6.1%	2.8%
Native American	37	14	-24	-63.5%	1.1%	0.4%
Asian American	1257	1627	370	29.4%	37.5%	46.6%
Chicano/Latino	498	376	-122	-24.5%	14.9%	10.8%
Filipino	56	70	14	25.0%	1.7%	2.0%
White/Other	1297	1305	8	0.6%	38.7%	37.4%
Total	3348	3489				
San Diego						
Black	67	49	-18	-26.9%	2.3%	1.7%
Native American	34	22	-13	-36.8%	1.2%	0.8%
Asian American	839	883	44	5.2%	29.4%	30.2%
Chicano/Latino	347	335	-12	-3.5%	12.1%	11.5%
Filipino	149	141	-8	-5.4%	5.2%	4.8%
White/Other	1421	1495	74	5.2%	49.7%	51.1%
Total	2857	2924				
Santa Cruz						
Black	39	32	-8	-19.2%	2.2%	1.8%
Native American	18	16	-3	-13.9%	1.0%	0.9%
Asian American	193	230	37	19.2%	10.9%	12.7%
Chicano/Latino	301	288	-14	-4.5%	17.1%	15.8%
Filipino	56	61	5	8.0%	3.2%	3.4%
White/Other	1158	1191	33	2.8%	65.6%	65.5%
Total	1765	1818				

Table 2 continued on next page

With the size of each entering class fixed, an admissions policy that leads to the acceptance of one applicant is likely to lead to the rejection of another. In other words, the gains to minority applicants who benefit from race-based affirmative action must be weighed against the costs imposed on other applicants. The critical issue is who gains the most from attending the most selective UC campuses. With equal weight given to each applicant, no spillover effects, equal marginal cost of schooling, and equal marginal ben-

Table 2 continued from previous page

(2) UNIVERSITY OF CALIFORNIA SAN DIEGO SIMULATION:

	Actual Enrollment	Simulated Enrollment	Change	Change in %	Actual %	Simulated %
Black	298	217	-81	-27.2%	2.4%	1.7%
Native American	130	83	-47	-36.2%	1.0%	0.7%
Asian American	3835	3917	82	2.1%	30.3%	30.8%
Chicano/Latino	1410	1202	-208	-14.8%	11.1%	9.5%
Filipino	469	564	95	20.3%	3.7%	4.4%
White/Other	6523	6714	191	2.9%	51.5%	52.9%
Total	12,665	12,697				

* The universitywide effects are based on results from Berkeley, San Diego, and Santa Cruz simulations.

Sources: Office of the President, University of California, May 1995, and University of California, San Diego, 1996.

efit of attendance, there would be no efficiency consequences of race-based affirmative action. On the other hand, if the marginal benefits are not equal, race-based affirmative action may make society better off or worse off depending on the relative rewards of a UC education.

The marginal benefit of enrollment for an applicant is the difference between his valuation of attending a UC campus and his next best alternative. An applicant rejected from a UC campus has three alternatives: (1) to attend a four-year college or university other than that UC campus, including another UC campus; (2) to attend a postsecondary institution other than a four-year college or university (a vocational program or a two-year community college); and (3) not to attend a postsecondary educational institution. Unfortunately, the information available to predict the most likely scenario is limited. Colleges and universities devote resources to analyzing what happens to students who were admitted but chose not to attend. These institutions have shown little interest in what happens to students who were rejected.

The most probable scenario is that a student rejected from the most competitive UC campuses would attend another four-year institution. For starters, the applicant in question is UC-eligible, thus he or she is likely to be accepted at a less competitive UC campus, at a California State University campus, or at an equally or less selective private institution. Additional information on the probabilities of the alternative scenarios is available from the High School and Beyond survey conducted by the National Center for Education Statistics, a longitudinal study of students who were seniors in 1980. Table 3 reports degree attainment of these students by acceptance status. The recorded differences in educational attainment are trivial. In fact, students not accepted at their first-choice institution were slightly more likely to have completed their bachelor's degree. Hence, to calculate the cost and benefits to individuals of a change in policy, we assume that the next best alternative for a student denied admission at one UC campus would be to attend a less selective college or university.

Most of the research from both sociology and economics suggests that college selectivity affects posteducational outcomes, including earnings.[28] According to one estimate, controlling for other factors, college quality explains on average between 1 and 1.5 percent of differences in individual earnings.[29] The selectivity of a college enhances educational attainment, which, in turn, affects earnings. College selectivity also affects the chances of attending a prestigious graduate school. For identical undergraduate grade-point averages, UC medical schools give more weight to the one from a more competitive school than to the one from a less competitive school. GPAs are adjusted to reflect differences in average MCAT scores across colleges. UC law schools make similar adjustments.

Minority students are likely to receive a higher earnings premium from attending a selective college than are white students for two reasons. First, employers generally have imperfect information about the productivity of individual job applicants. Because it is costly or sometimes impossible to measure productivity pre-employment, employers are likely to judge workers based on attributes. The selectivity of the college that the applicant attended can be a signal of his or her quality. If employers have less information about minority workers than about other workers, attending a selective college could have a bigger impact on the probability of employment or on the salary of a minority worker. Second, college is an important source of contacts and information about jobs. Students from communities where job networks are weak get a bigger boost from access to this information than do students already plugged into a job network.

Datcher-Loury and Garman control for differences in individual characteristics, family background, and grade-point average in their analysis of the effect of college selectivity on earnings.[30] They find that the magnitude of the effect of selectivity on earnings depends on the academic aptitude of the individual student. For an African American male college graduate with a composite SAT score greater than 850, attending a college with a median SAT score of 1,000 points rather than 900 points increases his yearly earnings by $769.[31] This translates into an increase in the present discounted value of lifetime earnings of $18,652. For an African American male with an SAT score of less than 850 but greater than 700, the increase in yearly earnings is only $72. College selectivity has a positive effect on earnings even for those who fail to complete the degree. For an African American male college drop-out with a composite SAT score greater than 850, attending a college with a median SAT score of 1,000 points rather than 900 points increases his yearly earnings by $591 a year, or the pre-

Table 3: Degree Attained by Race/Ethnicity for 1980 High School Seniors

	Certificate	Associate Degree	Bachelors Degree	Advanced Degree
*Accepted by First-Choice Institution**				
Hispanic	12.1%	11.2%	15.0%	0.3%
Native American	12.0%	19.3%	20.1%	0.0%
Asian**	9.9%	10.2%	30.3%	1.4%
Black	11.4%	8.0%	16.5%	0.3%
White	8.1%	9.6%	32.6%	1.5%
Not Accepted by First-Choice Institution				
Hispanic	18.4%	5.1%	16.6%	0.0%
Native American	Low n	Low n	Low n	Low n
Asian**	4.2%	13.7%	44.7%	7.0%
Black	15.9%	7.3%	13.1%	0.0%
White	10.0%	3.0%	40.6%	0.4%

*Table includes only students who applied to a postsecondary institution.
**Asian includes Asian and Pacific Islanders.
"Low n" indicates a insignificant sample size.

Source: National Center for Educational Statistics (NCES), "High School and Beyond" (data extracted over the Internet using NCES Data Analysis System, June 7, 1996).

sent discounted value of lifetime earnings by $3,682. In contrast, for a high-achieving white male, attending a college with a median SAT score of 1,000 points rather than 900 points increases earnings by $253–$298 if he graduates and by $283 if he drops out.

For the most talented minority students, the gains associated with attending a selective college or university persist despite the potential for academic mismatch. Datcher-Loury and Garman find that for an African American male with a composite SAT score greater than 850, the difference in graduation rates associated with attendance at a more selective college is 25 percent.[32] However, the increase in earnings associated with attending a more selective college outweighs the earnings reduction associated with a lower probability of graduation. Since most UC-eligible students would have scores higher than 850, the problem of academic mismatch is not likely to significantly reduce the gains from selectivity.

One of the potential costs of affirmative action is the creation of negative stereotypes that stigmatize the perceived beneficiaries.[33] However, if the costs associated with this stigma exceed the perceived benefits of attending a UC campus, then a URM would either not apply to the UC system or would reject an offer of admission. Herbert Nickens and Jordan Cohen address the problem of affirmative action and the stigmatization of minority achievement as follows:

Accounts of early minority pioneers . . . make it clear that they suffered from the hostility of some of their classmates and teachers, and all too often suffered alone. We think that most of those pioneers, and their contemporary counterparts, would regard questions about their legitimacy to be there as a small price to pay for increasing opportunities available to minority students, and for increasing the number of young Americans who are educated on campuses that are racially and ethnically diverse.[34]

Furthermore, a change in admissions policies would not eliminate racial prejudice that exists independent of affirmative action programs. Indeed, if there are few African Americans and Hispanics on college campuses, there will be little opportunity to undermine the racial stereotypes students bring with them from home.

Race-based affirmative action can also generate benefits and costs for students whose admissions decision is not directly affected by the policy. Affirmative action increases racial and ethnic diversity in classrooms, which many educators strongly believe improves the quality of education received by all students. According to Neil Rudenstine, president of Harvard University, a diverse educational environment challenges students "to see issues from various sides, to rethink their own premises, to achieve the kind of understanding that comes only from testing their own hypotheses against those of other people with other views."[35] James McLeod, vice-chancellor for students at Washington University, says that "understanding different kinds of people is a mark of an educated person."[36] A study of student opinions at the Berkeley campus found that students support the concept of racial and ethnic diversity on UC campuses, although the concept had different meanings for different groups of students.[37]

Unfortunately, the hypothesis that diversity improves educational outcomes has not been subjected to much empirical scrutiny. Deppe investigates the relationship between social concern and the racial diversity (nonwhite students as percent of all students) of the student body.[38] "Social concern" is defined as the importance students placed on influencing political structure, influencing social values, helping others who are in difficulty, developing a meaningful philosophy of life, participating in community action, and helping to promote racial understanding. Deppe finds that racial diversity did not contribute either positively or negatively to student value development.[39] Deppe, citing other studies, concludes that the racial integration of campuses has improved neither intergroup contact nor racial attitudes.[40] On the other hand, Astin reports that socializing with students from different racial/ethnic groups has strong positive effects on cultural awareness and commitment to promoting racial understanding.[41] It has a negative effect on beliefs that racial discrimination is no longer a problem in America and that the individual can do little to change society.

In summary, the gains to minority students who are beneficiaries of affirmative action probably outweigh the losses imposed on students whose probability of admission is reduced. It is more difficult to quantify the impact of the policy on the educational environment. If, as its proponents argue, racial diversity of the student body enhances the educational experience of all students, then it seems likely that the net impact of race-based affirmative action has been positive.

Law and Medical School Admissions

The excess demand for slots in the UC law and medical schools is even greater than for the undergraduate programs at UC Berkeley and UCLA. In 1994, there were 13,458 applicants for 754 spaces in UC schools of law and 26,416 applicants for 592 spaces in UC schools of medicine.[42] There are no strict eligibility requirements for admission to professional schools. Admission is based on a variety of criteria with emphasis placed on academic merit. Since there are differences in the admissions procedures between law and medicine, they are discussed separately.

To select a first-year class, UC law schools rely on a two-step procedure. All applications are initially ranked primarily on the basis of their academic credentials: LSAT score, undergraduate GPA (UGPA), and letters of recommendation. UCLA admits up to 60 percent of its entering class almost entirely on the basis of academic criteria; Boalt Hall, up to 50 percent.[43] The remainder of the class is filled on the basis of academic criteria combined with other factors, including institutional diversity. For example, at UC Davis, consideration is given to growth and maturity, economic disadvantage, physical handicap, and, pre-SP-1, racial or ethnic minority status.

Prior to SP-1, all three law schools considered race and ethnicity in the admissions process. Boalt Hall had specific numerical goals for racial and ethnic minorities. The other campuses did not. At UCLA, the dean of admissions reviewed all files not admitted automatically on the basis of academic credentials for possible admission under a diversity program. The majority of students admitted under this category were members of racial or ethnic minorities.[44]

Figure 3 summarizes the results of this admissions process for the three UC law schools based on the cumulative number of applicants and admits for 1992–1995. Acceptance rates were not consistently higher for underrepresented minorities than for whites: 19.5 percent of African American applicants and 19.2 percent of white applicants were accepted

Figure 3: Ratio of Matriculants to Admitted Students, UC Law Schools (1992–1995)

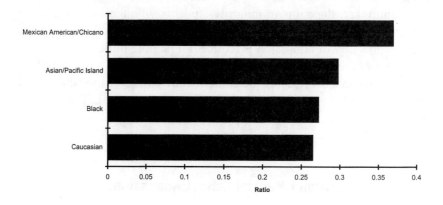

Source: Unpublished tables, University of California Office of the President.

for admission. Acceptance rates were lower for Asian Americans and Hispanics.[45] There are, however, consistent racial differences in yield rates, as depicted in Figure 4. For the 1992–1995 period, yield rates are consistently lower for African Americans than for other groups.

Table 4 provides a more detailed picture of the admissions process at UC Berkeley. Most Asian American and white applicants were admitted from Group I, where LSAT scores and undergraduate GPA are heavily weighted. Most African Americans and Hispanics were admitted from the second category, after a review of non-numerical indicators. A similar pattern held at UCLA. Most white and Asian American applicants were admitted in the first 60 percent of the class. For this top group, the admission decision is based primarily on LSAT scores and UGPA. Most African Americans, Hispanics, and Native Americans were admitted in the 40 percent group.[46]

Given the small numbers of African Americans and Hispanics admitted on the basis of academic criteria alone, a change in admissions policies to give greater weight to UGPA and LSAT scores could have a dramatic effect on the number of non-Asian minorities studying law at Boalt Hall.

Admission to medical school is even more competitive than law school. Approximately 5,000 students apply to each UC medical school each year. Each campus selects only 100 for admission. All campuses use a generic medical school application from the American Medical College Application Service (AMCAS) and all screen applicants with a labor-intensive multistage process. Applications are initially sorted on the basis of grades and MCAT scores. Applicants who survive this initial screening are asked to submit a secondary application. On the basis of information in the AMCAS and in the

Table 4: Minority Admissions, UC Berkeley School of Law (1994)

	Applicants	Admitted	Acceptance Rate	Enrolled	Yield
Highest Academic Rank					
Asian American	234	93	40%	31	33%
Black	13	13	100%	3	23%
Chicano/Latino	47	34	72%	6	18%
Native American	8	5	63%	1	20%
Nonminority	1432	520	36%	154	38%
Other					
Asian American	547	10	2%	6	60%
Black	426	72	17%	28	39%
Chicano/Latino	485	50	10%	29	58%
Native American	60	9	15%	3	33%
Nonminority	1924	17	1%	8	47%

Source: University of California, Berkeley, School of Law, Admissions Report 1994.

secondary application, some candidates will be invited for an interview. Approximately 18,000 hours per school year are devoted to this effort.[47]

Although there are variations across campuses in admissions procedures, all of the medical schools stress that students with high grades and scores could be rejected in favor of students with lower grades and scores based on other criteria, including patient orientation and clinical experience. Prior to SP-1, admissions committees also considered the race and ethnicity of the candidate. For example, UCSD used a different numerical cutoff to determine which applicants made it to the next step in the process, but has discontinued this practice.[48] At UCSF, students who self-identified as either a member of an underrepresented racial and ethnic group or as financially disadvantaged were given additional points for their disadvantage. UC Irvine divided applicants into three pools: traditional, members of underrepresented racial or ethnic groups, or financially disadvantaged. Applicants were evaluated according to the national performance of their pool. Applicants meeting the minimum academic requirement for their respective pool were sent a secondary application.

Table 5 describes the outcome of this admissions process over the four-year period from 1992–1995. Acceptance rates were higher for African Americans, Native Americans, and Hispanics than for Asian Americans and whites. University officials acknowledge that average MCAT scores and undergraduate GPAs were lower for the African Americans, Native Americans, and Hispanics admitted to UC medical schools than for Asian Americans and whites; however, they stress the importance of other qualities such as commitment to service, honesty, integrity, and perseverance that cannot be assessed by quantitative measures such as

Table 5: Applicants, Admits, and Matriculants, University of California Medical Schools, by Race/Ethnicity (1992–1995)

	Applicants	Admitted	Acceptance Rate	Enrolled	Yield
Native American/ Alaskan Native	961	29	15	3.0%	51.7%
Black	6,649	444	169	6.7%	38.1%
Chicano	6,832	583	238	8.5%	40.8%
Puerto Rica	562	21	10	3.7%	47.6%
Asian/Pacific Islander	45,089	1,408	733	3.1%	52.0%
Other Hispanic	3,669	163	98	4.4%	60.1%
Other	4,286	102	58	2.4%	56.8%
Caucasian	60,297	1,913	1,032	3.2%	53.9%
Total	128,345	4,664	2,353	3.6%	50.5%

Source: Unpublished tables, Office of the President, University of California.

UGPA or MCAT scores.[49] In testimony to the UC Board of Regents, Dr. Michael Drake argued: "Medical school admission is not a prize. Rather we work to select a class that will produce doctors who serve the needs of society. Applicants tend to look at the act of admission as an end itself, we focus more on the product, the doctor the student will become."[50] Admissions officers believe that these other factors could be as important in predicting success as the MCAT.[51]

Benefits of Affirmative Action in Professional School

In the case of professional school admissions, more so than at the undergraduate level, rejection could lead to a student's failure to complete the degree. There is greater excess demand for slots in law and medicine than at the undergraduate level. There are fewer options for a rejected student. The admissions process is more subjective, leading to greater variability in possible outcomes.

The returns to being a doctor or lawyer do not appear to differ systematically by race. However, a strict comparison of the monetary returns associated with being a doctor or lawyer is problematic for two reasons. One, not all medical school and law school graduates go on to practice medicine and law. Graduates must pass certification exams before they are admitted to the profession. Racial differences in passing rates could lead to differences in the marginal benefit of schooling even if there are no racial differences in salaries. Two, there is likely to be an inverse relationship between earnings and psychic income. A student who practices medicine in an underserved community could have a high private return, but low earnings. The spillover benefits of a medical education, described below, are also likely to be negatively correlated with earnings.

Differences in rates of passing board-certification exams and bar exams have been a focal point for critics of the pre–SP-1 admissions policies.[52] A smaller percentage of African American, Mexican American, Puerto Rican, and American Indian students pass step one of the National Boards on their first try.[53] However, data presented by Dr. Michael Drake of UCSF show that the percentages passing on either the first or second try are quite similar. [54] For the purpose of calculating the private return to medical education, passing on the second try is equivalent to passing on the first.

Completion rates for UC law school students are quite high. The overall completion rate for classes entering between 1986 and 1990 exceeded 90 percent.[55] However, completion rates tend to be lower for minority students. For the 1990 entering class, 89.4 percent of minorities and 95.9 percent of whites completed the program.[56] For the first-year cohorts of 1986, 1987, 1988, 1989, and 1990, the average completion rate for minority students was 90.5 percent, and 94.3 percent for white students. A smaller percentage of minority students pass the California State Bar examination on the first try. In 1994, 97.5 percent of white and 83.0 percent of minority UC law school graduates who were first-time takers passed the bar exam. For any UC graduating class, 90 percent of minorities and 100 percent of nonminorities taking the bar exam pass within nine months of graduation (either on the first or second attempt).[57] These differences in completion rates suggest racial differences in the marginal benefits of admission to law school. However, there are benefits and costs of a change in policy beyond the impact on individuals.

Educators in law and medicine are especially adamant about the educational value of a diverse campus. Medical educators stress the importance of understanding differences in culture and social practice for the effective delivery of health-care services and credit minority students with improving the "cultural competence" of their nonminority classmates.[58] Michael Drake, associate dean of medicine at the UC San Francisco Medical school, testified to the UC Board of Regents:

> Educational diversity is important to all physicians regardless of the predominant practice mix. This is because medicine is practiced on a diverse population in our society. Students learn from books, from professors, from patients and from each other. We learn invaluable lessons about working on people different from ourselves by working with people different from ourselves. Lessons about communicating, lessons about rejecting stereotypes, are

often best taught by our peers . . . a diverse medical school class serves to make all of its members better doctors. I know that I'm better at caring for elderly Chinese women, because I trained with Asian women who helped teach me a better approach."[59]

Justice William Powell's decision in *Bakke*, 438 U.S. 314, affirmed the importance of diversity to the education of lawyers:

The law school, the proving ground for legal learning and practice, cannot be effective in isolation from the individuals and institutions with which the law interacts. Few students and no one who has practiced law would choose to study in an academic vacuum, removed from the interplay of ideas and the exchange of views with which the law is concerned.

Legal educators also cite the role of minority students in improving the cultural competence of their nonminority classmates.[60] Legal educators argue that diversity of intellectual tradition and background helps students identify areas where the law is "inconsistent, inappropriate, or unresponsive to the needs of society."[61]

Furthermore, educators stress the importance of the presence of a critical mass of underrepresented minority students. The report of the Admissions Policy Task Force at Boalt Hall argues that a critical mass of minority students is essential to maintaining an active exchange of ideas.[62] According to the report, when minority students are enrolled in small numbers, they often experience feelings of alienation and isolation that make them less likely to participate in class discussions. Tokenism, according to the report, can "silence the very voices that are crucial to building a diverse and intellectually stimulating law school."[63]

The impact of affirmative action goes beyond what happens in the professional schools. Proponents of affirmative action in law and medicine typically cite not the private benefits to individuals but the spillover benefits for society as a whole derived from increasing the supply of minorities in these professions. The size of this spillover depends on the link between the underrepresentation of African Americans and Hispanics in law and medicine and the racial disparities in the utilization of these services.

There is an especially rich body of literature documenting a link between the training of minority doctors and the delivery of health-care services to minority communities.[64] All physicians tend to care for patients of their own race and ethnicity, but this is especially true for black and Hispanic physicians.[65] On average, black physicians care for nearly six times as many black patients and Hispanic physicians care for nearly three times as many Hispanic patients as other physicians.[66] Black, Asian, and Hispanic physicians are more likely to serve patients who are Medicaid recipients.[67] According to the Association of American Medical Colleges (AAMC), nearly 40 percent of underrepresented minority physicians practice in deprived areas, while less than 10 percent of non-URMs do. The AAMC also reported that URM students were more likely to participate in public-health screening clinics, deliver medical services to underserved populations outside clinical rotations, and volunteer to educate high school and college students about science and medicine.[68] Doctors admitted under a special admissions program at UC San Diego saw more patients per day and were more likely to have a poor clientele than were their classmates.[69]

Reducing the number of African American and Hispanic medical school graduates could have negative consequences for the delivery of health-care services to these communities. However, there is a flip side to this argument. Will an increase in the number of white and Asian American graduates increase the delivery of health-care services to their communities? The answer is probably yes, but the marginal effect is likely to be smaller for two reasons. First, as noted above, African Americans and Hispanics have a greater tendency to care for patients of their own race and ethnicity than for other racial groups. Second, there is a greater shortage of health-care providers in black and Hispanic communities. Communities with high proportions of black and Hispanic residents were four times as likely as others to have a shortage of physicians, regardless of community income.[70] These two factors lead to a conclusion that a decline in the number of African American and Hispanic medical school students will have detrimental effects on health-care delivery in minority communities. These effects are likely to outweigh any benefits from an increase in the delivery of health-care services to white and Asian communities.

Legal scholars argue that increasing the diversity of the legal profession is essential to the preservation of trust in the American legal system,[71] that black lawyers have a better understanding of the legal problems faced by a fellow black,[72] and that black clients feel more comfortable with lawyers from the same racial background.[73] However, there is no body of empirical research, comparable to that in medicine, that documents the social benefits of educating minority lawyers.

The Impact of Proposition 209: A Preliminary Appraisal

The admissions data for the pre-1997 period show that affirmative action in UC admissions increased the number of African American and Hispanic students at the most competitive UC campuses and in law and medical schools. Such an increase in the racial diversity of the student body has several positive implications for the economy and society. One, African American, Hispanic, and Native American graduates enjoy the earnings premium associated with attending a selective college or university. Since the admission of any one student to the selective campus implies the rejection of another, the appropriate question is not whether any one student enjoys a premium but whether the premium is greater for that student than for someone else. The available evidence suggests that black students enjoy a higher premium than whites. Hence, as measured by the size of the total pie, society is better off. Two, the increase in racial diversity on campuses probably improves the educational environment for all students. Despite the lack of quantitative indicators of improvement, there is a strong consensus among educational leaders—who are in the best position to judge the impacts—that this is the case. Racial diversity improves the cultural competence of all students. And three, the increase in the diversity of holders of professional degrees generates benefits for minority communities. A rich body of research documents the link between the training of minority doctors and the delivery of health-care services to minority communities.

Eliminating race as a criterion in undergraduate and professional admissions is likely to significantly reduce these benefits. As UC simulations have demonstrated, alternative admissions criteria, such as an increased emphasis on socioeconomic disadvantage, are unlikely to replicate the racial diversity achieved with affirmative action.

Notes

1. This chapter focuses on the major racial/ethnic populations: whites, Hispanics, African Americans, and Asian Americans. The term "Hispanics" includes all persons of Mexican, Puerto Rican, Dominican, Central and South American, and Cuban origin. Native Americans are also underrepresented in postsecondary insitutions, but it is beyond the scope of this chapter to cover them systematically.

2. See Reginald Wilson, *The State of Black America 1989* (Washington, DC: National Urban League, Inc., 1989) and Gerald Jaynes, ed., *A Common Destiny: Blacks and American Society* (Washington, DC: National Academy Press, 1989) for a discussion of factors contributing to the decline in African American enrollments in postsecondary institutions. For a discussion of factors influencing college attendance among Hispanics, see Richard Santos, "Hispanic High School Graduates: Making Choices," in Michael A. Olivas, ed., *Latino College Students* (New York: Teachers College Press, 1986); also see Alexander Astin, *Minorities in Higher Education* (San Francisco: Jossey-Bass, Inc., 1982).

3. United States Department of Education, National Center for Education Statistics, "1988–1994, Descriptive Summary Report" (NCES No. 96-175, 1996). Also available on the Internet: *www.ed.gov/NCES/pubs/96175.html*; United States

Department of Education, National Center for Education Statistics, "Dropout Rates in the United States, 1994" (NCES No. 96-845): *www.ed.gov/NCES/pubs/r94*; Jaynes, *A Common Destiny*; Wilson, *The State of Black America*; Santos, "Hispanic High School Graduates"; Astin, *Minorities in Higher Education*.

4. The five criteria specified as important in the admissions decision were: (1) high school grade-point average of 3.5 of higher; (2) SAT equivalent score of 1,100 or higher; (3) four accumulated credits in English, three in math, three in science, three in social studies, and two in foreign language; (4) positive teacher evaluations; and (5) participation in two or more extracurricular activities.

5. Jeffrey Owings, Marilyn McMillen, and John Burkett, "Statistical Brief: Making the Cut: Who Meets Highly Selective Entrance Criteria?" (National Center for Educational Statistics, NCES No. 95-732, April 1995).

6. U.S. Department of Education, "Dropout Rates in the United States, 1994."

7. Wilson, *The State of Black America*; Jaynes, *A Common Destiny*; Manuel Justiz, "Demographic Trends and the Challenges to American Higher Education," in Manuel Justiz, Reginald Wilson, and Lars G. Bjork, eds., *Minorities in Higher Education* (Phoenix, AZ: The American Council on Education, 1994).

8. Cordelia Reimers, "A Comparative Analysis of the Wages of Hispanics, Blacks, and Non-Hispanic Whites," in George Borjas and M. Tienda, *Hispanics in the U.S. Economy* (New York: Academic Press, 1985); June O'Neill, "The Role of Human Capital in Earnings Differences Between Black and White Men," *The Journal of Economic Perspectives* 4 (4): 25–46 (Fall 1990).

9. University of California, Office of the President, "The Use of Socio-Economic Status in Place of Ethnicity in Undergraduate Admissions: A Report on the Results of an Exploratory Computer Simulation," Occasional Paper 5, May 1995.

10. Marc Galanter, "The Structure and Operation of an Affirmative Action Programme: An Outline of Choices and Problems," in *Affirmative Action in a New South Africa: The Apartheid Legacy and Comparative International Experiences and Mechanisms of Enforcement* (Cape Town, South Africa: The Centre for Development Studies, University of Western Cape, May 1992).

11. See pages 356–357 of James, *A Common Destiny*, for a concise discussion of the role that teacher expectations and tracking can play in later achievement.

12. James C. Hearn, "Academic and Nonacademic Influences on the College Destinations of 1980 High School Graduates," *Sociology of Education* 64: 158–171 (July 1991). Among fall 1994 applicants to the UC system, 83.1 percent of white students had fathers with a B.A. degree or higher. Only 36.2 percent of African American students and 25 percent of Chicano/Latino applicants had fathers with similar educational attainment. Mike Aldaco, "University of California Testimony on Undergraduate Admissions" (testimony before the Assembly Judiciary Committee, California State Legislature, May 4, 1995). The average parental income of white applicants was $85,592; of African American applicants, $45,715; of Chicano/Latino applicants, $42,411.

13. Glenn Loury, "A Dynamic Theory of Racial Income Differences," in Phyllis A. Wallace, ed., *Women, Minorities and Employment Discrimination* (Lexington, MA: Lexington Books, 1977).

14. Stephen Coates and Glenn Loury, "Will Affirmative-Action Policies Eliminate Negative Stereotypes?" *American Economic Review* 83 (4): 1220–1240 (1993). Dean

P. Foster and Rakesh V. Vohra ("An Economic Argument for Affirmative Action," *Rationality and Society* 4 [2]: 176–188 [1992]) show that Coates and Loury's conclusion is not robust. A change in assumptions about the joint distribution of true abilities and test scores reverses their findings. In addition, the Coates/Loury model implicitly assumes that there is space for all eligible candidates. In fact, the admissions process at the most competitive UC campuses is better modeled as a winner-take-all game. Each participant has an incentive to work as hard as possible because even within the minority group category only those with the highest scores will win.

15. Linda Datcher-Loury and David Garman, "College Selectivity and Earnings," *Journal of Labor Economics* 13 (2): 289–308 (1995).

16. Carol M. Swain, "A Cost Too High to Bear," *The New Democrat* 7 (3): 19 (1995).

17. William H. Pickens, "California Perspectives: Three Viewpoints, Higher Education and Society's Needs," *Change* (September/October 1989), pp. 43–51.

18. UC campuses can admit a limited number of students (up to 5 percent of the entering class) who do not meet these criteria.

19. Students outside of this eligibility range have the option of attending a California State University (CSU) campus if they fall within the top third of California graduating seniors, attending a community college, or attending one of the private degree granting institutions.

20. Universitywide, the acceptance rates are higher for Asians and whites than for African Americans and Hispanics.

21. University of California, Los Angeles, "Affirmative Action and Freshman Admission to the College of Letters and Science" (n.d.).

22. UCLA, "Affirmation Action." Data also based on author's calculations.

23. This is due to the fact that URMs comprise a much smaller percent of those with the highest academic scores relative to the URM share of those with relatively lower academic scores. With equal yield rates, URMs would comprise a much smaller percent of enrollees with the highest academic scores relative the URM share of those with relatively lower academic scores. The result is that the academic scores of all enrolled URMs would be on the average lower than the academic scores of all enrolled non-URMs.

24. University of California, Office of the President, "The Use of Socio-Economic Status in Place of Ethnicity in Undergraduate Admissions."

25. University of California, Office of the President, "Universitywide Survey of Fall 1990 Non-Matriculants" (April 1991).

26. Ibid.

27. Private costs and benefits are those accrued by individuals. This section does not cover social or group costs and benefits, although it does cover some of the externalities generated by a more diverse student body.

28. Terence Wales, "The Effect of College Quality on Earnings: Results from the NBER-THORNDIKE Data," *Journal of Human Resources* 8 (3): 306–317 (1972); Hearn, "Academic and Nonacademic Influences on the College Destinations of 1980 High School Gradudates"; Datcher-Loury and Garman, "College Selectivity and Earnings"; Estelle James, et al., "College Quality and Future Earnings: Where Should You Send Your Child to College?" *American Economic Review* (May): 247–252 (1989).

29. Ernest T. Pascarella and Patrick T. Terenzini, *How College Affects Students: Findings and Insights from Twenty Years of Research* (San Francisco: Jossey-Bass Inc., 1991).

30. Datcher-Loury and Garman, "College Selectivity and Earnings."

31. Datcher-Loury and Garman do not estimate the effect of college selectivity on earnings for Hispanics, Asians, or women.

32. Datcher-Loury and Garman, "College Selectivity and Earnings."

33. Madeline E. Heilman, Caryn Block, and Jonathan Lucas, "Presumed Incompetent? Stigmatization and Affirmative Action Efforts," *The Journal of Applied Psychology* 77: 536–544 (1992); Luis T. Garcia, Nancy Erskine, Kathy Hawn, and Susanne R. Casmay, "The Effect of Affirmative Action on Attributions About Minority Group Members," *Journal of Personality* 49 (December): 427–437 (1981).

34. Hebert W. Nickens and J. Cohen Jordan, "Policy Perspectives: On Affirmative Action," *JAMA* 275 (7): 572–574 (February 21, 1996).

35. As cited in Jane Schoenfeld, "Learning to Live in a Diverse World," *St. Louis Post-Dispatch*, June 18, 1996.

36. As cited in Schoenfeld, "Learning to Live in a Diverse World."

37. University of California, Berkeley, Institute for the Study of Social Change, "The Diversity Project: Final Report" (Berkeley: University of California, November 1991).

38. Marilyn J. Deppe, "The Impact of Racial Diversity and Involvement on College Students' Social Concern Values" (Paper presented at the Annual Meeting of the Association for the Study of Higher Education, Atlanta, GA, Nov. 2–5, 1989).

39. Ibid.

40. Ibid.

41. Alexander W. Astin, *What Matters in College? Four Critical Years Revisited* (San Francisco: Jossey-Bass, Inc., 1993).

42. University of California, Office of the President, "Affirmative Action and Graduate and Professional School Admissions" (September 1995).

43. At Boalt, the director of admissions admits the first 50 percent of applicants. In this initial screening, the director considers both quantitative and nonquantitative factors.

44. University of California, Office of the President, "Affirmative Action and Graduate and Professional School Admissions."

45. For the purposes of law school admissions, Asians are an underrepresented minority.

46. University of California, Office of the President, "The Use of Socio-Economic Status in Place of Ethnicity in Undergraduate Admissions."

47. University of California, "Pertinent Questions and Answers Regarding UC Medical Admissions" (November 15, 1994).

48. University of California, San Diego, School of Medicine, "Entering Class" (Unpublished tables dated August 22, 1996).

49. Garry Morrison, letter to Regent Clair W. Burgener (July 12, 1994); Michael Drake, "Remarks to the Board of Regents" (Presentation to the University of California Board of Regents, November 17, 1994); Nickens and Cohen, "Policy Perspectives."

50. Drake, "Remarks to the Board of Regents."

51. Nickens and Cohen report finding only one study that examined the correlation between numerical indicators (MCATs and UGPA) and outcomes and its findings were inconclusive (Nickens and Cohen, "Policy Perspectives").

52. Ellen Cook, "Race and UC Medical School Admissions: A Study of Applicants and Admission in the UC Medical Schools" (Testimony to Assembly Judiciary Committee, California State Legislature, May 4, 1995).

53. Ellen Cook, "Affirmative Action FACTS" (*http:/pwaa.acusd.edu/ ~ e_cook/*) (updated September 2, 1996).

54. Drake, "Remarks to the Board of Regents."

55. University of California, Office of the President, "Affirmative Action and Graduate and Professional School Admissions."

56. Ibid.

57. Ibid.

58. Herbert W. Nickens, telephone interview with Rhonda Sharpe, Mechanicsville, Virginia (July 23, 1996).

59. Drake, "Remarks to the Board of Regents."

60. Okechukwu Oko, "Laboring in the Vineyards of Equality: Promoting Diversity in Legal Education Through Affirmative Action," *Southern University Law Review* 23 (Winter 1996).

61. Herma Hill Kay, "Presentation to Regents on Law School Admissions" (Presentation to the University of California Board of Regents, May 18, 1995).

62. University of California, Berkeley, School of Law, "Admissions Policy Statement and Task Force Report" (August 31, 1993).

63. Ibid, p. 5.

64. For additional references, see Nickens and Cohen, "Policy Perspectives"; and Dr. Miriam Komaromy et al., "The Role of Black and Hispanic Physicians in Providing Health Care for Underserved Populations," *The New England Journal of Medicine* 334 (20): 1305–1310 (1996).

65. Komaromy, "The Role of Black and Hispanic Physicians."

66. Ibid.

67. Komaromy, "The Role of Black and Hispanic Physicians"; Association of American Medical Colleges, "Minority Students in Medical Education: Facts and Figures IX" (Washington, DC: Association of American Medical Colleges, 1995).

68. Association of American Medical Colleges, "Minorities Underrepresented in Medicine Are Consistently More Likely to Work in Underserved Areas" (AAMC Press Release, Washington, DC, May 22, 1996).

69. Nolan Penn et al., "Affirmative Action at Work: A Survey of Graduates of the University of California, San Diego, Medical School" *American Journal of Public Health* 76 (9): 1144–1146 (1996).

70. Komaromy, "The Role of Black and Hispanic Physicians."

71. Kay, "Presentation to Regents on Law School Admissions."

72. Oko, "Laboring in the Vineyards of Equality."

73. Additional citations can be found in Oko, "Laboring in the Vineyards of Equality."

Chapter 9

Proposition 209 and Its Implications

Paul Ong

In 1996, California was at the epicenter of a political tremor that has shaken the foundation of this nation's policy on how to redress the difficult, complex, and persistent problem of racial and gender inequality. As discussed in Chapter 1, affirmative action has been challenged with some success in the courts, and neoconservative administrations have weakened the enforcement of affirmative action (and equal opportunity) programs. Actors within California were party to these earlier attacks. In 1978, Allan Bakke won his case against the University of California before the U.S. Supreme Court, claiming that he was illegally denied admission to the medical school on the UC Davis campus because of preferential treatment given to minority applicants. Support for civil rights programs within the executive branch began to wane in the 1980s. As documented in Chapter 3, funding for enforcement of antidiscrimination laws declined noticeably during this period. Another indication of the antipathy toward affirmative action was a failure to conduct an analysis of California's set-aside program. Given the strict scrutiny standard set by the U.S. Supreme Court, the state had to undertake such an analysis if it wanted to continue such a program. Inaction was tantamount to letting the program wither. In 1995, Governor Pete Wilson and his appointees to the Board of Regents of the University of California pushed through two resolutions, SP-1 and SP-2, which directed the university to end the use of race, religion, sex, color, ethnicity, or national origin in its admission process, contracting, and employment.

The third front in the attack on affirmative action in California was a direct appeal to the voting public through the initiative process. In 1996, 54 percent of the voters in the Golden State passed Proposition 209, which requires the state and its local jurisdictions to "not discriminate against, or grant preferential treatment to, any individual or group on the basis of race, sex, color, ethnicity, or national origin in the operation of public employment, public education, or public contracting." Although the proposition was titled the California Civil Rights Initiative, the purpose behind it was to end the use of the more aggressive affirmative action programs.

The election result sent a shock wave throughout the nation, triggering similar campaigns in other locations, with the backers of Proposition 209 aggressively exporting their expertise. One year later, in 1997, voters in the city of Houston voted on Proposition A, which posed the question, "Shall the Charter of the City of Houston be amended to end the use of affirmative action?" Unlike California, the vote went against the initiative, by a majority of 55 percent. In the following year, Initiative 200 was placed on the Washington State ballot. It stated, "The state shall not discriminate against, or grant preferential treatment to, any individual or group on the basis of race, sex, color, ethnicity, or national origin in the operation of public employment, public education, or public contracting." The initiative passed by a majority of 58 percent. Similar initiatives and legislative efforts are being pursued in other states, including Colorado, Florida, Ohio, Michigan, Missouri, New Jersey, and Texas.[1]

The impact at the national level is a little more difficult to discern. The success of the California and Washington initiatives has encouraged some conservative members of Congress to discuss the enactment of legislation designed to have a similar impact nationally.[2] The impact on the Clinton administration appears to be one of intimidation, forcing it to lower its profile. The mend-not-end strategy already represented a middle-of-the-road approach, which is consistent with the administration's prevailing moderate political philosophy. What is intriguing, and perhaps telling, is the report from the Advisory Board to the President's Initiative on Race, in which the discussion on affirmative action is largely descriptive and noncommittal.[3]

These events raise several questions: Why did the use of direct appeal to the voting public start in California? Why are there differences in voting results on different ballots? What should be done in the wake of 209?

The California Origins

The third front in the attack on affirmative action—the initiative approach—originated in California because of an unusual set of political, social, and economic conditions. There are two defining political characteristics that provided a foundation for this Proposition 209. The first is that the 1996 campaign traveled the well-beaten path of using ballot initiatives as a form of populist politics—a path that has become increasingly dominated by special-interest groups and big money. The state's initiative process was established in 1911 as a part of the progressive movement to counter potentially corrupt and unresponsive elected officials. The relationship between race and this process is not new to California. In 1964, 55 percent of the voters passed Proposition 14, which was written to negate the 1963 Rumford Act outlawing discrimination against home buyers and apartment renters.[4] Proposition 14 did not overtly support the right to discriminate but instead couched its arguments in the rhetoric of individual rights and antigovernment. The initiative stated: "Neither the State nor any subdivision or agency thereof shall deny, limit or abridge, directly or indirectly, the right of any person, who is willing or desires to sell, lease or rent any part or all of his real property, to decline to sell, lease or rent such property to such person or persons as he, in his absolute discretion, chooses." Despite its passage, the proposition had limited impact. Decisive action by the federal government to cut housing funds to California dampened the willingness of other states to place such an initiative before their voters, and within months, California's Supreme Court ruled that the proposition violated the Fourteenth Amendment.

The potency of the initiative process as populist politics became more apparent with the 1979 Proposition 13, which was at the forefront of the "tax rebellion."[5] The passage of this proposition, which withstood court challenges, accelerated the use of initiatives in California and other states. Since that time, turning to initiatives has become a common practice, one supported by the establishment of organizations that exist to facilitate the process. While those using the initiatives still claim this avenue provides for direct democracy, much of the process has been taken over by special interest and big money.[6] Initiatives have been used by groups on both sides of the political spectrum to push narrow agendas. Success in collecting the required signatures to place an initiative on the ballot frequently depends heavily on paid petition workers, while the expense of supporting and opposing propositions often costs more than campaigns for major elected offices.

The initiative process provides any well-financed disgruntled group an avenue to seek a political solution not addressed by their elected officials. Two individuals, Glynn Custer and Thomas Wood, took advantage of the process to place 209 on the ballot.[7] Both were highly educated white males who disliked the social changes associated with minority demands. One, an anthropology professor, had become increasing disturbed by the multicultural transformation of the curriculum and faculty on his college campus, and the other felt that affirmative action denied him an academic position because of preferential treatment given to a black woman. Although the two ran an independent, populist-type operation to get the initiative process started, they eventually had to rely on funds, support, and organizational help from neoconservatives.

While the initiative process provided an opening to attack affirmative action, a second aspect of California politics—Governor Wilson's reliance on wedge issues—was a necessary ingredient. In the 1994 gubernatorial race, Wilson rebuilt his popularity and won reelection in part by using divisive issues founded on the fears of the majority of the voters, such as immigration and crime. He continued to pursue these and other hot-button issues, including efforts to weaken unions and civil rights programs. These tactics were motivated by his political ambitions to seek the presidency. His failed effort to become the GOP candidate was built in part on his claim to represent conservative interests. Attacking affirmative action was very much a wedge issue, one that the Governor supported actively.

Social changes well before Proposition 209 created a climate that was conducive to the initiative. California's demographic recomposition created a backlash from an increasing number of whites who felt uneasy and displaced by the changes. The demographic transformation was rooted in the liberalization of national immigration laws in the mid-1960s, which ended racially motivated quotas. The renewal of large-scale immigration in the 1960s transformed the nation, increasing the foreign-born population from 9.6 million in 1970 to 25.8 million in 1997, and from 4.7 to 9.6 percent of the total population.[8] The dramatic growth in the immigrant population was accompanied by an ethnic and racial shift as Asian and Latin American countries replaced European countries as the primary source of immigration. By 1997, those of European ancestry accounted for only one-sixth of the immigrants, while Asians accounted for more than one-quarter and Latinos accounted for nearly one-half. Nowhere has the resulting demographic transformation been more dramatic than in California. About one-third of this nation's foreign-born population resides in California, and approximately one-quarter of the state's population is foreign-born.

This demographic change produced nativist reactions, first in the form of cities trying to stem the tide of cultural changes brought in by Asians and Latinos,[9] and later in the form of a statewide proposition. While the state's population has become ethnically diverse, non-Hispanic whites still dominate at the election polls. In 1994, non-Hispanic whites comprised 52 percent of the population[10] but an estimated 81 percent of the voters in the November 1994 election.[11] That year, the majority of the voters passed Proposition 187, an initiative designed to prevent undocumented aliens from receiving public social services, public health-care services, and public education at elementary, secondary, and postsecondary levels.[12] The proponents argued that the people of California "have suffered and are suffering economic hardship caused by the presence of illegal aliens," and "have suffered and are suffering personal injury and damage caused by the criminal conduct of illegal aliens." Although the proposition was formally aimed at undocumented aliens, there was a strong anti-immigrant undercurrent. Four years later, anti-immigrant sentiments resurfaced with the passage of Proposition 227, the English Language in Public Schools Initiative. In an effort to reassert the cultural dominance of the majority population, the initiative stated that the "English language is the national public language of the United States of America and of the State of California." Clearly, there are many backers of both Proposition 187 and Proposition 227 who are neither racist nor against legal immigrants, yet it is difficult to deny the fact that both initiatives are propelled in part by nativist sentiments.

Economic conditions also played a role by creating uncertainty and anxiety over employment and educational opportunities, particularly among white males. Starting in 1991, the state experienced a much deeper and longer recession than the rest of the nation. By mid-1993, the state's unemployment rate was over 9 percent, compared to about 7 percent for the nation. In the four months preceding the November 1996 elections—when Proposition 209 was on the ballot—the unemployment rate averaged over 7.7 percent, compared to 5.3 percent for the United States. Moreover, there was continued distress over the permanent loss of high-paying jobs, particularly in aerospace, due to cuts in the defense industry after the end of the Cold War.[13] These lost jobs were not being replaced with new high-wage jobs that could reabsorb most of the displaced workers, the majority of whom were white males. These economic problems interacted with a widely held perception that whites were losing out to less qualified minorities.[14] The dominant view, then, was one of a zero-sum game, and the gains made by some under affirmative action were perceived to have come at the expense of others. These concerns were amplified in California. Bad economic times turned the concerns over a zero-sum game into a fight to preserve shares of a shrinking pie.

The political, social, and economic factors combined into a potent force that produced a majority supporting Proposition 209. Not surprisingly, support was strongest among conservatives (77 percent for), Republicans (80 percent for), whites (63 percent for), and males (61 percent for).[15] While the specific conditions in California explain why California took the lead in opening the third front in the attack on affirmative action, subsequent events show that this form of populist politics has wider appeal. Just as in a physical earthquake, a political tremor is the product of a deep underlying tension—the confrontation of powerful and opposing ideological forces.

The Semantics of Affirmative Action

Affirmative action has created a conundrum over how this nation ought to come to terms with intergroup inequality. This strategy, which evolved out of the political history of the latter half of the 20th century, is at the heart of a debate that deeply divides this nation and the state of California. In the heat of the debate, which is often dominated by polemics rather than thoughtful discussion, it is convenient to focus narrowly on the particular strategy and forget the larger context: persistent inequality along racial and gender lines. Numerous studies, including those in this book, show that women and people of color still have far fewer employment and business opportunities than do white men. The disparities are the result of conscious and unconscious biases in hiring and business decisions, of unequal access to training and education, and of institutionalized practices, many of which are not explicitly racist or sexist. Unless these patterns and practices are altered, women and minorities will continue to be denied equal employment and business opportunities.

A consensus on what should be done eludes us. As a society, we value personal initiative and believe in an economic system that rewards people for merit and performance; therefore, it is not surprising that a majority supports eliminating overt discrimination in the workplace and the business world. Moreover, most accept the fact that discrimination has not been eliminated. For example, three-quarters of the nation agree with the statement, "Black people still face discrimination," including employment and housing discrimination.[16] In California, six out of seven believe that "discrimination is still common," and even among white males, four out of five agree with this statement.[17] These attitudes are the basis for the strong public support for antidiscriminatory policies.

For many, prohibiting discriminatory behavior is necessary but not sufficient. For them, eliminating inequality cannot be achieved simply by a promise to treat everyone the same, but rather requires attacking the systemic roots of inequality. Affirmative action has been devised as a way to counter the historical legacies of racism and sexism and to dismantle contemporary institutional barriers. Under affirmative action, concrete steps are taken to produce outcomes in employment and business that could be expected if social inequality were absent. Its very nature and logic have led to the creation of programs that target and assist minorities and women.

For a growing number in our society, on the other hand, affirmative action goes too far. They argue that white men are bearing an unfair burden of remedying a societal problem not of their making. These opponents charge that affirmative action is merely preferential treatment that violates the goal of treating people fairly as individuals. They charge that affirmative action is based on practices that are equivalent to using quotas.

Although affirmative action programs have been refined over the years to adhere to the laws forbidding the use of quotas, the critics nevertheless raise the legitimate point that society should be cautious in using such broad measures, even to eliminate the historical legacies of discrimination.

Caution, however, is not equivalent to accepting the argument that all forms of affirmative action are unacceptable. Most Americans find the disparities produced by discrimination and prejudice unacceptable, but public support for alternative solutions varies greatly. There is great resistance to giving preferential treatment, and this creates the duality of supporting antidiscrimination policies but opposing affirmative action.[18] The dichotomy, however, is not as simple as it appears. There are different opinions on the various forms of affirmative action. A large majority of the public support "increase[d] recruitment" and a "sincere effort to hire" fully qualified blacks in order to reach parity.[19] There is then a nuance in the support and opposition to affirmative action, and this can be seen in a survey of Houston voters prior to the 1997 election.[20] Sixty-nine percent of the respondents, including a majority of blacks, said they would support a proposition stating: "The city of Houston shall not discriminate against, or grant preferential treatment to, any individual or group on the basis of race, sex, ethnicity, or national origin in the operation of public employment and public contracting." However, support fell to 47 percent for a proposition stating: "Shall the Charter of the City of Houston be amended to end the use of Affirmative Action for women and minorities in the operation of City of Houston employment and contracting, including ending the current program and any similar programs in the future?" In the end, a majority of the voters opposed Proposition A, which stated: "Shall the Charter of the City of Houston be amended to end the use of affirmative action?" If Houston's Proposition A had been worded like those in California and Washington, it is likely that the outcome would have been different.

Given the evidence, it is clear that the appeal to direct plebiscites relies on a simplistic and undesirable reduction of the underlying concerns. This insight has not been lost on either proponents or opponents of affirmative action. Each side would like to frame the wording so as to appeal to only one of two fundamental values, the need to address inequality and the aversion to preferential treatment. The initiative process is ill suited to formulating a policy based on an acceptable compromise and pragmatic trade-off of two conflicting principles, but this type of politics cannot be avoided. As the old saying goes, "The genie is out of the bottle." With such high stakes, the bitter political contest now revolves around semantics.

Acknowledging political reality, however, is not the same as accepting it. If the early civil rights movement hinged on winning public support, then very little progress would have been made, even over color-blind policies. Despite the trend of reductionist politics, we should elevate the debate to address as fully as possible these value-laden questions: What is the nation's obligation to correct historical wrongs? What price are we, as a nation, willing to pay for our actions or inactions? When should we adopt color- and gender-blind policies? And how strongly are we committed to racial and gender equality as an outcome?

The Effectiveness of Affirmative Action

Finding a balance rests in part on understanding what affirmative action has accomplished in order to shed light on what would be lost if the policy were eliminated. As stated in Chapter 1, the book's contributors undertook this project with the hope of elevating the current debate through an assessment of the affirmative action programs prior to Proposition 209. As social scientists dedicated to improving this understanding, we are guided by the principle that research into the effects of government policies and programs on hiring and contracting should coincide with the geography of political discourse. While the discussion over the future of affirmative action is a national one, it is also being conducted at the state level, with California leading the way. Unfortunately, we know very little about how these programs have operated in California or any other state. The existing literature is dominated by analyses using national data. State and regional variations are at best secondary considerations, and analyses often have included only crude control variables for those variations. What is clear is that it is not possible to simply extrapolate the experience at the national level to that of the states. Each state has a different historical and demographic context that influences the nature and extent of socioeconomic inequality. Each state also has a different legislative history with regard to affirmative action, as well as a different experience in implementing programs. More information is needed on the particular impacts of affirmative action across states in order to raise our understanding of what approaches have or have not been successful and why.

The studies presented in this book help fill the gap in California-specific data by analyzing the historical impact of affirmative action programs on employment and business opportunities for minorities and women. While this book provides new insights, it is far from comprehensive. It does not cover such important topics as set-aside contracting at the state level, the impact of federal regulation on the public sector, or the costs and benefits of implementing affirmative action. Even with the limited number of outcomes under study, it is difficult to isolate the effects of affirmative action programs from all the other factors that affect employer hiring practices and the viability of women- and minority-owned small businesses.

Despite these limitations, the analyses do identify the direction and the rough magnitude of changes attributable to affirmative action. Progress was made during the 1960s, 1970s, and 1980s in redressing racial and gender disparities in employment and business opportunities. State and local governments did a better job than the private sector in providing opportunities to minorities and women, and private firms covered by affirmative action programs provided more opportunities than those that were not. Yet despite the changes brought about by affirmative action programs and policies and concomitant laws combating discrimination in employment, there remains a sizable gap in economic status due to race and gender.

The findings in these studies provide glimpses into the potential consequences of eliminating affirmative action programs. As Badgett points out in Chapter 4, eliminating results-oriented requirements for public employers could reduce public-sector demand for women and minorities. Under this scenario, the number of female and minority workers who would have been employed in the public sector and could instead be readily absorbed into the private sector will depend on the strength of the labor market in the private sector. However, a shift in demand away from minority and female workers, a likely outcome of Proposition 209, may result in lower wages for these populations, given the existing wage gaps between sectors. Badgett also suggests that there could be underemployment for some female and minority employees in managerial and professional positions.

There may be similar effects on minority- and women-owned businesses that contract with the state, depending on the transitional issues they would face. Information from a recent survey of public agencies shows that Proposition 209 has already hurt minority and women contracting.[21] This is, however, only a part of the impact. As Williams notes in Chapter 6, even if these firms were to experience a significant reduction in revenue from state/local government sources, the impact of the policy change on any firm will depend on its ability to enter alternative markets and on whether there will be demand for the firm's output. Without an existing alternative market, the cost of switching to production for the private sector will determine Proposition 209's impact. In many cases, Williams suggests, it may be possible to replace sales to California state/local governments by supplying federal agencies, or by supplying state and local governments other than those in California.

The one place where the impact has been immediate and highly visible is admission to the University of California. Compared with the previous year, new registration by underrepresented minorities for the entering 1998 freshmen class fell by 30 percent at UCLA and 52 percent at UC Berkeley, the two most competitive campuses in the system.[22] As predicted by Conrad (in Chapter 8), this was offset by an increase at the other campuses, so that the total decrease was only 10 percent. Minority enrollment in law schools also decreased, and this was particularly noticeable at Boalt Law School at UC Berkeley. None of the 14 blacks admitted to Boalt Hall registered, partly as a protest and partly because other prestigious law schools proved to be more welcoming and attractive. The impact at the medical schools, however, appears to be nonexistent, with the number of new registrants and their distribution across campuses holding fairly constant over the last three years.[23] This may be due to the modifications made by the medical schools since the landmark 1978 *Bakke* decision. The ultimate impact on minority enrollment in higher education will depend on the ability of the UC system to find alternative ways to maintain its diversity.

Intriguing as the effects hypothesized by the authors might be, one must be cautious about projecting future outcomes based on the past effects of local and state affirmative action programs. Real-world outcomes will be influenced by many other societal transformations that have taken place over the last two to three decades. Changes in public attitudes, economic transformations, and demographic shifts all share in determining who gets hired and for what jobs. There are specific federal hiring requirements that will continue to apply to state and private employers. Social conditions are also far different than they were 20 or 30 years ago. Today, there are networks for recruitment of minorities and women, and referrals that did not previously exist and will continue to function. Finally, many firms will continue to make a conscious effort to diversify their workforce to better serve an increasingly diverse consumer base. Given these complexities, statements about the effects of curtailing or eliminating affirmative action efforts remain highly speculative.

The Pursuit of Social Justice

Even the passage of Proposition 209 in November 1996 does not tell us what is permitted and what is prohibited. A federal appellate court has upheld the initiative's constitutionality, deciding that the state may limit its own authority to remedy the effects of discrimination even if it would otherwise be constitutional for it to act. The full reach of Proposition 209 still remains to be tested because eliminating "preferential treatment," as the language of the initiative states, need not be equivalent to banning all affirmative action. Programs that merely provide technical assistance to women and minorities without guaranteeing any special treatment might still be permitted. In any event, race- and gender-neutral programs aimed at assisting socially or economically disadvantaged people would still be available.

Clearly, Proposition 209 should not be turned into an excuse for denying the reality of discrimination in society or ignoring the fact that women and minorities do not currently enjoy equal access to employment and business opportunities. Affirmative action programs may be curtailed or eliminated, but there remains a national and state commitment to prohibiting racial and gender discrimination in public and private hiring. As Thomas and Garrett point out in Chapter 2, federal law imposes liabilities for employment practices having a discriminatory effect even where there is no intent to discriminate. Significantly, in a post-election editorial (*Los Angeles Times*, April 9, 1997), Ward Connerly, one of the chief proponents of Proposition 209, reiterated the importance of guaranteeing minorities and women opportunities in hiring and contracting. Connerly stressed the need to reassure those potentially affected by eliminating preferences that they will not face discrimination or loss of job opportunities.

Although Proposition 209 does not represent a wholesale reversal of the movement to promote equal opportunity for minorities and women, guaranteeing equal opportunity is now a greater challenge. One way to meet this challenge is for state policy makers to support strong enforcement of the state's own antidiscrimination laws. Inadequate state funding for investigations of complaints, as noted in Chapter 3, is a disturbing trend and ought to be reversed. State and local officials, educators, and the public at large need to dedicate themselves to a greater effort to make quality education and training available to all individuals regardless of race or gender and to provide assistance to economically disadvantaged people and communities, possibly through new lending and technical assistance programs. If we as a society are to continue to make progress in eliminating racial and gender disparities, this nation—and this state—must pursue the goal of ensuring equality of access to obtaining the skills and resources that people need to compete effectively in the marketplace. By addressing the various causes of social inequality more sensitively, we can improve on our efforts at achieving a just society.

This book has documented the increased opportunity, primarily in the public sphere, made possible by affirmative action policies and programs. As legislative and judicial decisions modify public policy intended to address racial and gender discrimination, the impacts of these changes on employment and business opportunities for women and minorities should be closely monitored and evaluated. This may be best done by a joint effort involving researchers and state agencies. The public and their representatives need to know what works and what does not; otherwise the continuing debate over affirmative action will simply be reduced to exchanging polemics. A better understanding of the unfolding dynamics of these processes can point to better ways to ensure social fairness.

Notes

1. American Civil Rights Coalition: *www.acrcl.org/pr100997.html*.

2. See, for example, the proposed Civil Rights Act of 1997, American Civil Rights Coalition: *www.acrcl.org/pr061797.html*.

3. The President's Initiative on Race Advisory Board, "One America in the 21st Century: The President's Initiative on Race" (Washington, DC: U.S. Government Printing Office, 1998), pp. 99–102.

4. Thomas W. Casstevens, "Politics, Housing, and Race Relations: California's Rumford Act and Proposition 14" (Berkeley: Institute of Governmental Studies, University of California, 1967).

5. David O. Sears and Jack Citrin, *Tax Revolt: Something for Nothing in California* (Cambridge, MA: Harvard University Press, 1985); Clarence Y. H. Lo, *Small Property versus Big Government: Social Origins of the Property Tax Revolt* (Berkeley: University of California Press, 1990).

6. California Commission on Campaign Financing, *Democracy by Initiative: Shaping California's Fourth Branch of Government* (Los Angeles: Center for Responsive Government, 1992); Jim Shultz, *The Initiative Cookbook: Recipes and Stories from California's Ballot Wars* (San Francisco: Democracy Center, 1996).

7. The discussion on the development of Proposition 209 is based on Lydia Chavez, *The Color Bind: California's Battle to End Affirmative Action* (Berkeley: University of California Press, 1998).

8. U.S. Immigration and Naturalization Services, "Total and Foreign-born U.S. Population: 1900–90" (*www.ins.usdoj.gov/stats/308.html*); U.S. Bureau of the Census, "Foreign-born Population Reaches 25.8 Million, According to Census Bureau" (*www.census.gov/Press-Release/cb98-57.html*).

9. Leland T. Saito, *Race and Politics: Asian Americans, Latinos, and Whites in a Los Angeles Suburb* (Urbana: University of Illinois Press, 1998).

10. U.S. Bureau of the Census, "Estimates of the Population of States by Race and Hispanic Origin: July 1, 1994" (*www.census.gov/population/estimates/state/srh/shrus94.txt*).

11. *Los Angeles Times*, November 10, 1994, p. B4.

12. The proposition passed on the strength of the white vote, with 63 percent supporting 187. On the other hand, a majority of nonwhites voted against the proposition.

13. Paul Ong and Janet Lawrence, "Race and Employment Dislocation in California's Aerospace Industry," *Review of Black Political Economy* 23 (3): 91–101 (Winter 1995).

14. Tom Smith, "Intergroup Relations in Contemporary America: An Overview of Survey Research," in Wayne Winborne and Renae Cohen, eds., *Intergroup Relations in the United States: Research Perspectives* (Bloomsburg, PA: Hadden Craftsmen, Inc. for the National Conference for Community and Justice, 1998), p. 151.

15. *Los Angeles Times*, November 7, 1996, p. A29. Although a large majority of all minority groups opposed the proposition, they comprised only a quarter of the voters.

16. Smith, "Intergroup Relations in Contemporary America," pp. 113–115.

17. Tabulation by Michela Zonta of the Field Institute's California Poll, October 1–October 9, 1996.

18. Laurence Bobo and Ryan Smith, "Anti-Poverty Policy, Affirmative Action, and Racial Attitudes," in S. Danzinger, G. Sandefur, and D. Weinberg, eds., *Confronting Poverty: Prescriptions for Change* (New York: Russell Sage Foundation, and Cambridge, MA: Harvard University Press, 1994), pp. 365–395; Dan Morain, "The Times Poll: 60 Percent of State's Voters Say They Back Prop. 209," *Los Angeles Times*, September 19, 1996, p. A1.

19. Smith, "Intergroup Relations in Contemporary America," p. 144.

20. University of Houston Center for Public Policy and Rice University's Baker Institute for Public Policy, cited in Julie Mason, *Houston Chronicle*, October 2, 1997.

21. Chinese for Affirmative Action and Equal Rights Advocates, "Opportunities Lost: The State of Public Sector Affirmative Action in Post–Proposition 209 California" (San Francisco: Chinese for Affirmative Action and Equal Rights Advocates, 1998).

22. Based on statements of intent to register as reported by the University of California, Office of the President (*www.ucop.edu/ucophome/commserv/admissions/sirtable2.html*).

23. *www.ucop.edu/ucophome/commserv/medenroll/98enroll.html*.

About the Contributors

M. V. Lee Badgett is an assistant professor of economics at the University of Massachusetts, Amherst. She received a doctorate in economics from the University of California, Berkeley, and she has also taught at Yale University and the University of Maryland. She serves as the acting executive director of the Institute for Gay and Lesbian Strategic Studies, a national think tank. Her research focuses primarily on race, gender, and sexual orientation in labor markets, and she is writing a book on the economic lives of lesbians and gay men. She has published articles on affirmative action and sexual orientation discrimination in *Feminist Economics and Feminist Studies, Industrial and Labor Relations Review, Industrial Relations,* and the *Review of Black Political Economy.*

Cecilia A. Conrad is an associate professor of economics at Pomona College and an adjunct scholar with the Joint Center for Political and Economic Studies in Washington, D.C. She received a doctorate in economics from Stanford University. Conrad has recently published in the *Review of Black Political Economy,* and the edited volumes *Fathers Under Fire: The Revolution in Child Support Enforcement* (Russell Sage Foundation, 1998) and *A Different Vision: Asian American Economic Thought, Volume One* (Routledge, 1997). She is a member of the board of economists of *Black Enterprise* magazine and of the American Economic Association's Committee on Economic Education.

Mark Garrett is a Los Angeles attorney specializing in land use planning and environmental issues. He received a J.D. and an M.A. in urban planning from UCLA. He is the co-author of *Transportation Planning on Trial: The Clean Air Act and Travel Forecasting* (Sage, 1996). As a practicing lawyer he has advised local governments on zoning, subdivision and redevelopment law, inverse condemnation, and growth management. He is currently a Ph.D. candidate at UCLA, and his dissertation research examines the impact of civil rights law on public transit. Mr. Garrett was named an Eno Transportation Foundation Fellow for 1998.

Tom Larson is a professor in the Department of Economics and Statistics at California State University, Los Angeles, and is director of the Minority Youth Employment Studies Center. He received a doctorate in economics from the University of California, Berkeley, and has specialized in labor and urban development issues. He has conducted research on black youth employment, black migration, contingent employment, and the economy of South Central Los Angeles. Currently Larson is focusing on inner-city economies. His has published in *Review of Black Political Economy, Journal of Economic Issues, Applied Economics, California Politics and Policy,* and *Cities: The International Journal of Urban Planning.*

PAUL ONG is a professor in the School of Public Policy and Social Research at the University of California, Los Angeles, where he is the director of the Lewis Center for Regional Policy Studies. He received a doctorate in economics from the University of California, Berkeley. His research focuses on disadvantaged populations and policies addressing socioeconomic inequality. Ong has conducted studies on environmental impacts on minority communities, Asian and Latino immigration, displaced workers, transportation access, home ownership and residential patterns, and welfare reform. His works have appeared in *Journal of Policy Analysis & Management, Urban Studies, Review of Black Political Economy, Industrial and Labor Relations Review, Industrial Relations,* and *International Migration Review.* He currently serves on the Race and Ethnic Advisory Committee for the U.S. Bureau of the Census.

WILLIAM M. RODGERS III is the Francis L. and Edwin L. Cummings Associate Professor of Economics at The College of William and Mary, and an adjunct-associate of the Humphrey Institute, University of Minnesota. He received a doctorate in economics from Harvard University. His primary research is in labor economics; however, he has written in public finance and development. Rodgers has published articles in *The American Economic Review Papers and Proceedings, Urban Studies, Review of Black Political Economy,* and *Industrial and Labor Relations Review.* His policy work includes testifying before the Joint Economic Committee, U.S. Congress on raising the federal minimum wage and the Virginia Joint Subcommittee Studying the Status and Needs of Virginia's African American Males, and working as a consultant to Labor Secretary Reich's chief economist.

WARD THOMAS has extensive experience studying economic development, policy and labor-market issues. Thomas recently completed his Ph.D. in urban planning at the University of California, Los Angeles. His dissertation examines labor markets and minority hiring practices through a case study of the electronics industry in Los Angeles. Thomas currently works as a research associate at the Lewis Center for Regional Policy Studies at the University of California, Los Angeles.

DARRELL L. WILLIAMS is a visiting professor of economics at UCLA. He received a doctorate in economics from Washington University. His primary area of research is industrial organization and regulation, and he has written on minority-owned businesses. Williams has published articles in the *American Economic Review Papers and Proceedings, Journal of Urban Affairs,* and *Social Science Quarterly.* He has been a visiting research associate at the Center for Economic Studies at the U.S. Bureau of the Census, and has worked for the U.S. Securities and Exchange Commission and the President's Council of Economic Advisers.

Index